Charlotte Brooke

Reliques of Irish poetry

Consisting of Heroic Poems, Odes, Elegies, and Songs, Translated into English Verse

Charlotte Brooke

Reliques of Irish poetry

Consisting of Heroic Poems, Odes, Elegies, and Songs, Translated into English Verse

ISBN/EAN: 9783744740623

Printed in Europe, USA, Canada, Australia, Japan

Cover: Foto ©Thomas Meinert / pixelio.de

More available books at **www.hansebooks.com**

RELIQUES
OF
IRISH POETRY:

CONSISTING OF

HEROIC POEMS, ODES, ELEGIES, AND SONGS,

TRANSLATED INTO

ENGLISH VERSE:

WITH

NOTES EXPLANATORY AND HISTORICAL;

AND THE

ORIGINALS IN THE IRISH CHARACTER.

TO WHICH IS SUBJOINED

AN IRISH TALE.

BY MISS BROOKE.

A Oisin, as bjñ ljñ vo ⸱geata.
          Cat Zabjia.

GEORGE BONHAM, PRINTER,
SOUTH GREAT GEORGE'S-STREET, DUBLIN.

M.DCC.LXXXIX.

PREFACE.

IN a preface to a tranflation of ancient Irifh poetry, the reader will naturally expect to fee the fubject elucidated and enlarged upon, with the pen of learning and antiquity. I lament that the limited circle of my knowledge does not include the power of anfwering fo juft an expectation; but my regret at this circumftance is confiderably leffened, when I reflect, that had I been poffeffed of all the learning requifite for fuch an undertaking, it would only have qualified me for an unneceffary foil to the names of O'CONOR, O'HALLORAN and VALLANCEY.

MY comparatively feeble hand afpires only (like the ladies of ancient Rome) to ftrew flowers in the paths of thefe laureled champions of my country. The flowers of earth, the *terreftrial* offspring of Phœbus, were fcattered before the fteps of victorious WAR; but, for triumphant GENIUS are referved the *cœleftial* children of his beams, the unfading flowers of the Mufe. To pluck, and thus to beftow them, is mine, and I hold myfelf honoured in the tafk.

"THE esteem (says Mr. O'HALLORAN) which mankind conceive of nations in general, is always in proportion to the figure they have made in arts and in arms. It is on this account that all civilized countries are eager to display their heroes, legislators, poets and philosophers—and with justice, since every individual participates in the glory of his illustrious countrymen."—But where, alas, is this thirst for national glory? when a subject of such importance is permitted to a pen like mine! Why does not some *son of Anak* in genius step forward, and boldly throw his gauntlet to Prejudice, the avowed and approved champion of his country's lovely muse?

IT is impossible for imagination to conceive too highly of the pitch of excellence to which a science must have soared which was cherished with such enthusiastic regard and cultivation as that of poetry, in this country. It was absolutely, for ages, the vital soul of the nation*; and shall we then have no curiosity respecting the productions of genius once so celebrated, and so prized?

TRUE it is, indeed, and much to be lamented, that few of the compositions of those ages that were famed, in Irish annals, for the *light of song*, are now to be obtained by the most diligent research. The greater number of the poetical remains of our Bards, yet extant, were written during the middle ages; periods when the genius of Ireland was in its wane,

---

* See the elegant and faithful O'CONOR upon this subject; *(Dissertations on the History of Ireland,* p. 66.) and he is supported by the testimonies of the most authentic of antient and modern historians.

" —— Yet

"———— Yet ſtill, not loſt
" All its original brightneſs————."
On the contrary, many of the productions of thoſe times breathe the true ſpirit of poetry, beſides the merit they poſſeſs with the Hiſtorian and Antiquary, as ſo many faithful delineations of the manners and ideas of the periods in which they were compoſed.

WITH a view to throw ſome light on the antiquities of this country, to vindicate, in part, its hiſtory, and prove its claim to ſcientific as well as to military fame, I have been induced to undertake the following work. Beſides the four different ſpecies of compoſition which it contains, (the HEROIC POEM, the ODE, the ELEGY, and the SONG) others yet remain unattempted by tranſlation :—the ROMANCE, in particular, which unites the fire of Homer with the enchanting wildneſs of Arioſto. But the limits of my preſent plan have neceſſarily excluded many beautiful productions of genius, as little more can be done, within the compaſs of a ſingle volume, than merely to give a few ſpecimens, in the hope of awakening a juſt and uſeful curioſity, on the ſubject of our poetical compoſitions.

UNACQUAINTED with the rules of tranſlation, I know not how far thoſe rules may cenſure, or acquit me. I do not profeſs to give a merely literal verſion of my originals, for that I ſhould have found an impoſſible undertaking.—Beſides the ſpirit which they breathe, and which lifts the imagination far above the tameneſs, let me ſay, the *injuſtice*, of ſuch a taſk,—there are many complex words that could not be tranſlated literally, with-
out

out great injury to the original,—without being " falſe to its " ſenſe, and falſer to its fame."

I AM aware that in the following poems there will ſometimes be found a ſameneſs, and repetition of thought, appearing but too plainly in the Engliſh verſion, though ſcarcely perceivable in the original Iriſh, ſo great is the variety as well as beauty peculiar to that language. The number of ſynonima * in which it abounds, enables it, perhaps beyond any other, to repeat the ſame thought, without tiring the fancy or the ear.

IT is really aſtoniſhing of what various and comprehenſive powers this neglected language is poſſeſſed. In the pathetic, it breathes the moſt beautiful and affecting ſimplicity; and in the bolder ſpecies of compoſition, it is diſtinguiſhed by a force of expreſſion, a ſublime dignity, and rapid energy, which it is ſcarcely poſſible for any tranſlation fully to convey; as it ſometimes fills the mind with ideas altogether new, and which, perhaps, no modern language is entirely prepared to expreſs. One compound epithet muſt often be tranſlated by two lines of Engliſh verſe, and, on ſuch occaſions, much of the beauty is neceſſarily loſt; the force and effect of the thought being weakened by too ſlow an introduction on the mind; juſt as that light which dazzles, when flaſhing ſwiftly on the eye, will be gazed at with indifference, if let in by degrees.

BUT, though I am conſcious of having, in many inſtances, failed in my attempts to do all the juſtice I wiſhed to my origi-

* There are upwards of forty names to expreſs a *Ship* in the Iriſh language, and nearly an equal number for a *Horſe*, &c.

nals,

nals, yet ſtill, ſome of their beauties are, I hope, preſerved; and I truſt I am doing an acceptable ſervice to my country, while I endeavour to reſcue from oblivion a few of the invaluable reliques of her ancient genius; and while I put it in the power of the public to form ſome idea of them, by clothing the thoughts of our Iriſh muſe in a language with which they are familiar, at the ſame time that I give the originals, as vouchers for the fidelity of my tranſlation, as far as two idioms ſo widely different would allow.

However deficient in the powers requiſite to ſo important a taſk, I may yet be permitted to point out ſome of the good conſequences which might reſult from it, if it were but performed to my wiſhes. The productions of our Iriſh Bards exhibit a glow of cultivated genius,—a ſpirit of elevated heroiſm,—ſentiments of pure honor,—inſtances of diſintereſted patriotiſm,—and manners of a degree of refinement, totally aſtoniſhing, at a period when the reſt of Europe was nearly funk in barbariſm: And is not all this very honorable to our countrymen? Will they not be benefited,—will they not be gratified, at the luſtre reflected on them by anceſtors ſo very different from what modern prejudice has been ſtudious to repreſent them? But this is not all.——

As yet, we are too little known to our noble neighbour of Britain; were we better acquainted, we ſhould be better friends. The Britiſh muſe is not yet informed that ſhe has an elder ſiſter in this iſle; let us then introduce them to each other! together let them walk abroad from their bowers, ſweet ambaſſadreſſes of cordial union between two countries that ſeem formed by nature

(viii)

to be joined by every bond of intereſt, and of amity. Let them entreat of Britain to cultivate a nearer acquaintance with her neighbouring iſle. Let them conciliate for us her eſteem, and her affection will follow of courſe. Let them tell her, that the portion of her blood which flows in our veins is rather ennobled than diſgraced by the mingling tides that deſcended from our heroic anceſtors. Let them come—but will they anſwer to a voice like mine? Will they not rather depute ſome favoured pen, to chide me back to the ſhade whence I have been allured, and where, perhaps, I ought to have remained, in reſpect to the memory, and ſuperior genius of a Father—it avails not to ſay how dear!— But my feeble efforts preſume not to emulate,—and they cannot injure his fame.

To guard againſt criticiſm I am no way prepared, nor do I ſuppoſe I ſhall eſcape it; nay, indeed, I do not wiſh to eſcape the pen of the *candid* critic: And I would willingly believe that an individual capable of no offence, and pretending to no pre-eminence, cannot poſſibly meet with any ſeverity of criticiſm, but what the miſtakes, or the deficiencies of this performance, may be juſtly deemed to merit; and what, indeed, could ſcarcely be avoided by one unſkilled in compoſition, and now, with extreme diffidence, preſenting, for the firſt time, her literary face to the world.

It yet remains to ſay a few words relative to the Tale which is annexed to this volume: for that I had no original; the ſtory, however, is not my own; it is taken from a revolution in the hiſtory of ancient Ireland, Anno Mundi 3649. And no where

will

(ix)

will the Mufe be furnifhed with nobler fubjects than that neglected hiftory affords. The whole reign of CEALLACHAIN is one continued feries of heroifm, and high-wrought honor, that rifes fuperior to all the flight of Romance, and defies Poet c fable to furpafs it. Alfo, the reign of BRIAN BOIROIMH, and the famous retreat of the glorious tribe of DALGAIS; befides many other inftances too numerous for detail; amongft which I felected the ftory of MAON, as a fubject more fuited to my limited powers, than thofe which demand a " Mufe of fire," to record them.

I CANNOT conclude this preface without the gratification of acknowledging the favours with which I have been honored, fince the commencement of my work.

FROM the judgment and tafte of DOMINICK TRANT, Efq; (a gentleman too well known to need my panegyric) I have received much information and affiftance.

TO the Right Honorable the Countefs of MOIRA I am indebted for fome valuable communications; as alfo to the learned WILLIAM BEAUFORD, Efq; of Athy; to RALPH OUSLEY, Efq; of Limerick; and to THEOPHILUS O'FLANAGAN, Efq; of Trinity College, Dublin.

TO the learning and public fpirit of SYLVESTER O'HALLORAN, Efq; I owe innumerable obligations; and JOSEPH C. WALKER, Efq; has afforded every affiftance which zeal, judgment, and extenfive knowledge, could give.

b BESIDES

BESIDES the literary favours of my friends, there are others which I cannot omit to acknowledge as they equally tend to evince their wishes for the succefs of this undertaking.

THE accomplished family of CASTLE-BROWNE, in the county of Kildare, have exerted all the influence of taste, and character, to extend the subfcription to this work. The learned author of the HISTORICAL MEMOIRS OF THE IRISH BARDS, and his brother, SAMUEL WALKER, Efq; late of Trinity College Dublin, have alfo been equally zealous and fuccefsful; and to thefe two families I am indebted for the greater number of my fubfcribers, in this kingdom. For the reft, I am obliged to the influence of the Honorable Juftice HELLEN; DOMINICK TRANT, Efq; RICHARD GRIFFITH, Efq; the Reverend EDWARD RYAN, D. D. the Reverend T. B. MEARES, and feveral other friends.

AMONGST thofe of our fifter country who have exerted themfelves to promote the fuccefs of this work, the liberal fpirit of WILLIAM HAYLEY, Efq; has been moft particularly active. From the height of his own pre-eminence in literary fame, he is ever ready to reach, unafked, the voluntary hand to thofe who come to pay their vows at the fhrine of his favourite Mufe. I have alfo the fame obligations to the Reverend Doctor WARNER, the fon of him whofe hiftorical juftice, fuperior to modern prejudices, fo generoufly afferted the dignity and character of Ireland, in a work which muft ever reflect the higheft honor on the candour, and philanthropy, as well as the abilities of its author.

[The

[*The Publication of this Work has been delayed some Time, for the purpose of being enabled to give the following List complete;—still there are several Subscribers whose Names are not yet come to hand, and the List is therefore necessarily, though reluctantly, printed without them.*]

SUBSCRIBERS NAMES.

A.

RIGHT Honorable Lord Viscount Allen.
Lady Viscountess Allen.
Sir Fitzgerald Aylmer, Bart. M. P.
Michael Aylmer, Esq; *(Grange.)*
Robert Alexander, Esq;
Reverend William Adair, A. M. T. C. D.
James Arbuckle, Esq;
Mrs. Armstrong.
Reverend Mervyn Archdall, M. R. I. A.

B.

Right Honorable Countess of Bective.
Cardinal Boncompagni, *(Rome.)*
Honorable Mrs. Beresford.
Wogan Browne, Esq; M. R. I. A. *(Castle-Browne,)* six Copies.
Mrs. Browne, six Copies.
Miss Browne, three Copies.
Miss Eliza Browne, three Copies.

Reverend John Buck, B. D. and M. R. I. A.
Mrs. Birch.
Arthur Burdett, Efq; *(Bella-villa.)*
John Blachford, Efq;
Charles Bufhe, Efq;
Allan Bellingham, Efq;
O'Brien Bellingham, Efq;
William Bellew, Efq;
Benjamin Ball, Efq;
Mrs. Blake.
Mrs. Bendge.
John Braine, Efq;
Reverend Matthew Blacker.
James Braddifh, Efq;
Reverend John Bradfhaw, A. M.
Packenham Beaty, Efq;
Captain Burrowes, *(London.)*
Alexander Burrowes, Efq; *(Fernfborough.)*
Thomas Burrowes, Efq; *(Fernfborough.)*
John Burrowes, Efq;
J. O'Brien, Efq;
Reverend D. A. Beaufort, L. L. D. and M. R. I. A.
John Birmingham, Efq;
Reverend William Brooke.
Henry Brooke, Efq; fix Copies.
Thomas Brooke, Efq; fix Copies.
Mifs Brooke, *(Great George's-ftreet, Rutland-fquare,)* ten Copies.
Mr. Henry Brooke.

Alexander Boswell, Esq;
Mr. Patrick Byrne, Bookseller, six Copies.
Mr. George Bonham, Printer.

C.

His Grace the Lord Archbishop of Cashel, M. R. I. A.
Right Honorable Lord Viscount Conyngham.
Right Honorable William Conyngham, M. P. and M. R. I. A.
Right Honorable Lord Chief Justice Carleton. M. R. I. A.
Mrs. Carleton.
- John Philpot Curran, Esq; M. P. and M. R. I. A.
Daniel Corneille, Esq;
Charles O'Conor, Esq; M. R. I. A. *(Belanagar.)*
Reverend Charles O'Conor, D. D. *(Rome.)*
Signior Abbate Melchior Cesarotti, *(Padova.)*
Turner Camac, Esq;
Austin Cooper, Esq;
John Cooke, Esq;
Thomas Cobbe, Esq; *(Newbridge.)*
Mrs. Crowe, *(Kells.)*
Miss Carey, *(Portarlington.)*
John Corry, Esq;
Edward Croker, Esq;
Nathaniel Cairnes, Esq;
Walter Kavanagh, Esq;
John Clarke, Esq;
Miss Cuthbert.

D. Right

D.

Right Honorable Lord Donoghmore, M. R. I. A.
Right Honorable Lord Doneraile.
Right Reverend Lord Bishop of Dromore, F. R. S. and M. R. I. A. two Copies.
Right Honorable Lord Viscount Delvin, M. R. I. A.
Anthony Dopping, Esq; *(Low-town.)*
Major Doyle, M. P.
Reverend Dive Downes, D. D.
Arthur Dawson, Esq; M. P.
Mrs. Daniel.
Malachy Donnelan, Esq;
Hugh Dickson, Esq;
Robert Douglas, Esq; two Copies.
Charles Duflin, Esq;
Mr. Sylvester Dempsey, *(Kells.)*
Matthew Donnelan, Esq;
John De Courcy, Esq;
Counsellor Disney, *(Bray.)*

E.

Right Honorable Lord Earlsfort, M. R. I. A.
Lady Earlsfort.
Mrs. Esmond.
Mrs. Eccles.
Daniel Eccles, Esq; *(Eccles-ville.)*

Ifaac Eccles, Efq;
Gafper Erck, Efq;
Richard Eaton, Efq;
Reverend George Evans.

F.

Lady Fingal.
John Bourke O'Flaherty, Efq; M. P. and L. L. D.
Major Fitzgerald.
Mrs. Fitzgerald, *(Killbegs.)*
Major Ffolliott.
Theophilus O'Flanagan, Efq; A. B. T. C. D.
Mrs. Fox.
Anthony Fergufon, Efq;
Mifs Ferrar, *(Limerick.)*
Mrs. Frazier, *(Waterford.)*
Charles Faucett, Efq;
Mr. James Forbes.
Mrs. Anne Forbes.
Mrs. Sarah Forbes.

G.

Richard Griffith, Efq; M. P. and M. R. I. A. *(Millicent.)*
Mrs. Griffith.
Mrs. Griffith, fen.
Mrs. Gordon, *(Clonmel.)*
Reverend P. Gouldfbury.

Richard

Richard Gough, Esq; V. P. Antiq. Soc. *London.*
Mrs. Guy.
Mrs. St. George, two Copies.
John Geale, Esq;
Mr. Thomas B. Gaugh.

H.

Honorable Justice Hellen, M. R. I. A.
Mrs. Hellen.
William Hayley, Esq; *(Eartham, Suffex.)*
Sylvester O'Halloran, Esq; M. R. I. A. *(Limerick.)*
Thomas Hacket, Esq; two Copies.
Miss Hacket.
Edward Hill, Esq; M. D.
Mrs. Hamilton, *(Killilea Castle.)*
Mrs. Holloway.
Mrs. F. Hamilton.
Richard Hornedge, Esq;
James Hussey, Esq;
Mrs. Hamilton, *(Anne-brook.)*
Edward Hodson, Esq;
Leonard Hodson, Esq;
Richard Hickes, Esq; *(London.)*
Henry Hugh Hoare, Esq;
Mrs. Hugh Hoare.
Charles Hoare, Esq;
Mrs. Hughes.

Mrs. G. Hamilton.
James Edward Hamilton, Efq; *(London.)*

I.

Right Honorable Theophilus Jones, M. P.
William Todd Jones, Efq; M. P.
Francis Ifdall, Efq;
Eyles Irwin, Efq; *(Belleview, County Fermanagh.)*
Mrs. Irwin.
Reverend Mr. Johnfon, *(Shrewfbury.)*
Mrs. Irwin, *(Kentfield, County Galway.)*
Reverend Thomas Jamefon.
Jofeph Jamefon, Efq;

K.

Lord Killeen.
Countefs Kollowrath, *(Prague.)*
Reverend Walter Blake Kirwan.
Right Honorable Juftice Kelly.
Mark Kerr, Efq;
Brien Paul Lynch De Killy-kelly, *(Bilboa.)*
John Kelly, Efq;
Mr. James King, two Copies.

L. Right

L.

Right Honorable Lord Loftus.
Right Honorable Lord Longford, two Copies.
Lady Longford, two Copies.
Right Reverend Lord Bifhop of Landaff.
Reverend Edward Ledwich, L. L. D. and F. S A.
Mrs. Langley, *(London.)*
John Leefon, Efq;
P. Lattin, Efq; *(Morriftown)* three Copies.
Mrs. Peter La Touche, two Copies.
William Lloyd, Efq;
Mrs. S. Lynam.
Mrs. L'Eftrange.
Mifs Lennox.
Mrs. John La Touche.
Mrs. Litton.
Mifs Letablere.
Mrs. Leigh.
John Leech, Efq;
William Long, Efq;
Michael Lewis, Efq;

M.

General Maffey.
Signior Giovanni Marfigli, P. P. di Botanica, *(Padova.)*

Mrs.

Mrs. Mauvillon, *(London.)*
Alexander Marsden, Esq; M. R. I. A.
Miss Marsden.
William Marsden, Esq; L. L. D. F. R. S. and M. R. I. A. two Copies.
George Maunsel, Esq; *(Limerick.)*
Mrs. Maunsell, *(Corville.)*
John Thomas Munsell, Esq;
Samuel Malcolm, Esq; *(London.)*
Mrs. Macquay.
J. Macartney, Esq;
Reverend Thomas Burrowes Meares, *(Ballycorkey.*
Cornet Whitney Mackean.
Mr. James Moore, Bookseller, six Copies.

N.

Sir William G. Newcomen, Bart.
Lady Newcomen.
Count Frederick Nostitz, *(Prague.)*
Miss Anne M'Neven, *(Prague.)*
Miss Biddy M'Neven, *(Prague.)*
William James M'Neven, Esq; M. D. *(Dublin.)*
Richard Neville, Esq; M. P.
Christopher Nangle, Esq;
John Nesbitt, Esq; *(London.)*
Arnold Nesbitt, Esq; *(London.)*
Mr. Thomas Neil.

O.

Ralph Oufeley, Efq; M. R. I. A. *(Limerick.)*
Cornet William Oufeley.
James Ormſby, Efq;
Archibald Ormſton, Efq;

P.

Mrs. Pollock.
Miſs Hannah Pettigrew.

R.

Right Honorable Earl of Roſs.
Honorable Mrs. Roper.
George Romney, Efq; *(London.)*
James O'Reilly, Efq;
Reverend Edward Ryan, D. D.
Mrs. Ryan.
Mrs. O'Rielly.
Mrs. Rawlins.
Brien Rielly, Efq;
Thomas Roberts, Efq;
Robert Roberts, Efq;
Mr. Samuel Ruſſell.
J. Ritſon, Efq; *(Gray's-Inn, London.)*

Stephen Edward Rice, Esq;
―――― Reynolds, Esq;

S.

Right Honorable Lord Viscount Sackville.
Cardinal G. Salviati, *(Rome.)*
Bowen Southwell, Esq;
John Scanlan, Esq;
Nathaniel Nesbit Smith, Esq;
Miss Seward, *(Litchfield.)*
Miss Sisson.
Mrs. Stannard.
Reverend William Sandford.
Samuel Stock, Esq;
Whitley Stokes, Esq; F. T. C. D. and M. R. I. A.
William Stokes, Esq;
Reverend Gabriel Stokes.
John Stewart, Esq;
Mrs. Charlotte Smith, *(Middlesex.)*
John Sargent, Esq;
Edward Smith, Esq;
John Smith, Esq;
Mr. John Strangman.
Mrs. Mary C. Strangman.
Mr. William Sleater.

T.

Lady Tuite, *(Sonna,)* six Copies.
Lady Tynte.
Dominick Trant, Esq; M. R. I. A. six Copies.
Mrs. Trant, six Copies.
Grenville Temple, Esq;
Mrs. Trotter.
Mrs. Cassandra Travers.
Daniel Tracey, Esq;
Richard Turner, Esq; *(Castle-Caulfield.)*
Mrs. Tuke.
George Tandy, Esq;
Charles Thesiger, Esq; *(London.)*
John Thompson, Esq;
Marmaduke Taylor, Esq;
Miss Taylor, *(Lewes, Sussex.)*
Miss Tennison.

V.

Colonel Charles Vallancey, F. R. S. and M. R. I. A.
Il Proposto Curzio di Marchesi Venuti, *(Cortona.)*

W.

Solicitor General Wolfe, M. P. and M. R. I. A.
Right Reverend Lord Bishop of Waterford, M. R. I. A.
Nicholas Westby, Esq; M. P.

Mrs. Wade.
Robert Watson Wade, Esq; M. R. I. A.
Joseph C. Walker, Esq; M. R. I. A.
Samuel Walker, Esq; A. B.
Peter Walsh, Esq;
Charles Wilde, Esq;
John Wetherall, Esq;
Rogers Wetherall, Esq;
John Wolfe, Esq; M. P. and M. R. I. A.
Reverend Mr. Walsh.
Mr. James Richard Walsh, *(Irish College, Rome.)*
Thomas Walker, Esq;
Matthew Weld, Esq;
Mrs. Mary West.
Reverend John Warner, D. D.
Samuel Whyte, Esq;
Mr. William Wilson.

Y.

Right Honorable Lord Chief Baron Yelverton.
Mrs. Yelverton.
John Young, Esq;
Reverend Matthew Young, D. D. F. T. C. D. and M. R. I. A.

CONTENTS.

HEROIC POEMS.

	Page
An Introductory Discourse to the Poem of Conloch. By Sylvester O'Halloran, Esq; M. R. I. A.	3
I. *Conloch*	9
— *Original of ditto*	265
The Lamentation of Cucullen over the Body of his Son Conloch	24
— *Original of ditto*	269
II. *Magnus the Great*	37
— *Original of ditto*	271
III. *The Chase*	73
— *Original of ditto*	278
IV. *Moira Borb*	121
— *Original of ditto*	288

ODES.

ODES.

	Page
An Introductory Discourse to the War Ode	137
I. War Ode to Ofgur, the Son of Oifin, in the front of the Battle of Gabhra	151
— Original of ditto	296
II. Ode to Gaul, the Son of Morni	165
— Original of ditto	298
III. Ode, by Fitzgerald, written on his setting out on a Voyage to Spain	181
— Original of ditto	300

ELEGIES.

I. Elegy to the Daughter of Owen	191
— Original of ditto	304
II. Elegy	200
— Original of ditto	306
III. Elegy	208
— Original of ditto	307
IV. Elegy on the Death of John Burke Carrentryle, Esq;	217
— Original of ditto	309
V. Elegy on the Death of Carolan	225
— Original of ditto	311

SONGS.

(xxvi)

SONGS.

	Page
Thoughts on Irish Song - - - -	229
I. *Song, for Gracey Nugent. By Carolan* - - -	246
— *Original of ditto* - - - - -	315
II. *Song, for Mable Kelly. By Carolan* - - -	250
— *Original of ditto* - - - - -	316
III. *Song. By Patrick Linden* - - -	255
— *Original of ditto* - - - - -	318
IV. *The Maid of the Valley* - - - -	259
— *Original of ditto* - - - - -	319

IRISH TALE.

Introduction - - - - - -	325
Máon: An Irish Tale - - - - -	331

HEROIC POEMS.

I.

CONLOCH:

A
POEM.

ADVERTISEMENT.

I HAVE not been able to difcover the Author of the Poem of CONLOCH, *nor can I afcertain the exact time in which it was written; but it is impoffible to avoid afcribing it to a very early period, as the language is fo much older than that of any of my Originals,* (the War Odes *excepted,) and quite different from the ftyle of thofe Pieces which are known to be the compofitions of the middle ages.*

With equal pride and pleafure, I prefix to it the following Introduction, *and regard it as an ornament and an honor to my work. For many other valuable communications, I am alfo indebted to* Mr. O'Halloran; *and am happy in this opportunity of returning my public acknowledgments for the kind zeal with which he has affifted me in the courfe of my undertaking; befides the information which (in common with his other admiring readers) I have received from his ineftimable* Introduction to the Hiftory and Antiquities of Ireland; *a work fraught with learning, rich with the treafures of ages, and animated by the very foul of Patriotifm, and genuine Honor!*

AN

INTRODUCTORY DISCOURSE

TO THE

POEM OF *CONLOCH.*

By SYLVESTER O'HALLORAN, Esq; *M. R. I. A.*

HAD the ancient history and language of Ireland been regarded in the very important light which both most assuredly merit, our accounts of the Laws, Customs, Legislation and Manners of the early Celtæ would not now be so imperfect and confused; nor would modern writers presume so flatly to contradict the facts recorded of them by the ancient Greek and Roman historians. But this is not the place to expatiate on so interesting a subject: As an introduction to the following Poem, I shall only say a few words relative to the antiquity of Chivalry in Europe.

It is a fact unanimously subscribed to, that the custom of creating Knights in Europe originated not from the Romans, but amongst the Celtæ themselves. The Romans, wherever they carried their arms, waged war against arts and sciences, as well as against mankind; and hence it partly proceeds that our accounts of the greatest nations of antiquity are now so meagre and mutilated. The ancient Celtæ were amongst the number of those states that experienced this sad truth; for though the early Greeks confess how much they were indebted to them for Letters and Philosophy, though Pausanias bears testimony to their Knights, and though Cæsar—an eye witness—confesses that these Knights were the second order amongst the Gauls; yet, because the succeeding Romans were so industrious in the destruction of their records, that scarce a trace remains behind, our writers of the present, and of the two last centuries, agree that the first institution of chivalry in Europe was about the time of the croisades. But though all the other nations in Europe were overrun, and of course their annals destroyed, yet Ireland still remained free and independent, receiving into her fostering arms the distressed, and the proscribed of Britain and of the Continent. *Here* did those Arts and Sciences flourish, which *there* were annihilated by war and rapine; and *here* it is that Pezron, Menage, Bochart, Aldrite, &c. should have appealed for a satisfactory explanation of the feodal laws and customs; the want of which has led them to represent their early ancestors as a rude and illiterate people, (notwithstanding the fullest Greek and Roman testimonies to the contrary,) and that the feodal system and military tenures were

instituted,

inſtituted, *for the firſt time*, after the expulſion of the Romans from Gaul; whereas *theſe*, as well as chivalry, flouriſhed among the Celtæ in thoſe days of politeneſs and erudition, which long preceded the conqueſts in Gaul, and were always in force in Ireland.

With us chivalry flouriſhed from the remoteſt antiquity: there were five orders of it; four for the provinces, and one confined to the blood-royal; and ſo highly was this profeſſion reſpected among us, that a Prince could not become a candidate for the monarchy, who had not the Gradh-Gaoisge, or order of Knighthood, conferred upon him. At a very tender age, the intended cavalier had a golden chain hung round his neck, and a ſword and ſpear put into his hands. At ſeven years old he was taken from the care of the women, and deeply inſtructed in Philoſophy, Hiſtory, Poetry and Genealogy. The uſing his Weapons with judgment, elegance and addreſs, was alſo carefully attended to; principles of Morality were ſeduluouſly inculcated, and a reverence and tender reſpect for the Fair, completed the education of the young hero. By his vows he was obliged to protect and redreſs the injured and the oppreſſed. He was not to reveal his name or his country to any uncourteous Knight, who ſeemed to demand it as a right. He was not to go out of his road for any menace. He could not decline the combat with any knight, how intrepid ſoever. And ſtill further to ſhew to what a pitch of elevation they carried their ideas of military glory; even in death, they were to face this deſtroyer of mankind,

kind, *armed*, and ready to oppose force to force. This is so true, that on Cuchullin's being mortally wounded at the battle of Muirthievne, he had his back placed against a rock, with his sword and spear in his hands, &c. And Eogain-more, after the battle of Lena, was laid out completely armed, as our history has recorded. See also how these accounts illustrate later periods: De Saint Palaye, in his MEMOIRS OF ANCIENT CHIVALRY, tells us, that always, on the decease of a Knight, he was laid out in complete armour. And Hume mentions an English Knight, who, dying, ordered himself to be armed, with his lance and sword by him, as if ready to encounter death! The Chevalier Bayard, one of the bravest and most accomplished Knights of France, during the reign of Francis the first, finding himself mortally wounded in battle, ordered his attendants to place his back against a tree, with his sword in his hand, and died thus facing his conquering, though commiserating, enemies.

THE history of the following Poem is briefly this:—In the reign of Conor Mac-Nessa, King of Ulster, (about the year of the world 3950) Ireland abounded in heroes of the most shining intrepidity; insomuch that they were all over Europe, by way of eminence, called the HEROES OF THE WESTERN ISLE. Amongst these were Cuchullin, the son of Sualthach; Conal-cearach, and the three sons of Uisneach, Naoise, Ainle, and Ardan, all cousins-german. Cuchullin, in one of his continental expeditions, returning home by way of Albany, or modern Scotland, fell in love, at Dun-Sgathach, with the beautiful Aife, daughter to Airdgenny.

genny. The affairs of his country calling him home, he left the lady pregnant; but, on taking leave, he directed, in cafe his child fhould be a fon, to have him carefully brought up to arms, at the academy of Dun-Sgathach: He gave her a chain of gold to be put round his neck, and defired that he fhould be fent to Ulfter, as foon as his military ftudies were completed, and that he fhould there recognize him by means of the golden chain. He alfo left the following injunctions for his conduct: That he fhould never reveal his name to a foe; that he fhould not give the way to any man, who feemed to demand it as a right; and that he fhould never decline the fingle combat with any Knight under the fun.

The youth (his education completed,) came to Ireland to feek his father; but it appears that he arrived in armour; a manifeft proof, according to the etiquette of thofe days, that he came with an hoftile intention, and to look for occafions to fignalize his valour. On his approaching Emania, the royal refidence of the Ulfter Kings, and of the Croabh-ruadh, or Ulfter Knights, Conor fent a herald to know who he was? A direct anfwer, and he armed, would have been improper; it would have been an acknowledgment of timidity: In fhort, the queftion was only a challenge; and his being afked to pay an eric, or tribute, implied no more than that he fhould confefs the fuperiority of the Ulfter Knights. On his refufal to anfwer the queftion, Cuchullin appeared: they engaged, and the latter, hard preffed, threw a fpear, with fuch direction at the young hero, as to wound him mortally.

mortally. The dying youth then acknowledged himself his son, and that he fell in obedience to the injunctions of his mother. It appears, however, from the poem, that when Cuchullin left her those injunctions, he was far from expecting that his son should have put them in force upon his arrival in Ireland. On the contrary, it appears the effect of jealousy in the lady, and of revenge, hoping that Cuchullin (now advanced in years) might himself fall in the conflict; for, though a gallant and most intrepid knight, yet our history proves that he was by no means constant in his attachments to the fair.

As to the numbers of knights engaged and vanquished by Conloch, previous to his conflict with Cuchullin, it is all poetic fiction, to raise the characters of the two heroes. Even Conall-Cearnach, Master of the Ulster Knights, is made to submit to Conloch, who then falls the greater victim to the glory of his own father.

CONLOCH:

A POEM[a].

CONLOCH, haughty, bold, and brave,
Rides upon Ierne's wave!—
Flush'd with loud-applauding fame,
From Dunfcaik's walls he came;
Came to visit Erin's coast;
Came to prove her mighty Host!

Welcome,

---

[a] It is feared the measure chosen for the translation of this Poem, may appear greatly out of rule: but, in truth, I tried several others, and could succeed in none but this. I am conscious that the measure of an irregular Ode is not strictly suited to an Heroick Poem; the reader, however, as he advances, will perhaps find reason to acquit me; as he will perceive that the variety in the subject, required a variety in the measure; it is much too animated for the languid flow of Elegy, and too much broken by passion for the stately march of Heroicks:—at least it exceeded my limited powers to transfuse into either the spirit of my original.

Welcome, O youth of the intrepid mien,
  In glittering armour drest!
Yet, *thus* to see thee come, I ween,
  Speaks a stray'd course, illustrious Guest[b]!
  But now, that safe the Eastern gale
    Has given thee to our view;
Recount thy travels, give the high detail
Of those exploits from whence thy glory grew.

Do not, like others of Albania's land,
    Reject our fair demand;
Nor from its sheath the sword of conquest call,
    To cause thy youth, like theirs, to fall:
Should'st thou, like them, with fruitless pride, delay
The usual tribute of the bridge to pay.

" If such, (the youth replied) ere while,
" Has been the practice of your worthless Isle[c];
" Yet never more a Chief shall it disgrace,
" For this right arm shall your proud Law efface."

                                    Thus

[b] It is here evident that the Herald only *affects* to mistake the meaning of Conloch's martial appearance, with a view, perhaps, to engage him to change his intention; or, possibly, through politeness to a *Stranger*, he would not seem to think him an enemy, until he had positively declared himself such. But, be this as it may, we cannot avoid perceiving the extreme elegance and delicacy with which the Herald addresses him, and makes his demand.

[c] The fierceness of this reply plainly denotes the impression which Conloch had received of Ireland, from the jealousy and resentment of his Mother, and that he came firmly purposed to evince it by all his actions.

Thus, while he spoke, collecting all his might,
Fierce he addrest his conquering arms to fight;
No stop, no stay his furious faulchion found,
Till his dire hand an hundred warriors bound:
Vanquish'd they sunk beneath his dreadful sway,
And low on earth their bleeding glories lay.

Then Conor [d] to his blushing host exclaim'd,
" Of all our Chiefs, for feats of prowess fam'd,
" Is there not one our glory to restore?
" So cold is then become our martial heat,
" That none will dare yon haughty youth to meet,
    " His name and errand to explore,
" The slaughter of his dreadful arm restrain,
" And force his pride its purpose to explain!"

'Twas then the kindling soul of Conall [e] rose,
Victorious name! the terror of his foes!
His threatening arm aloft the hero rais'd,
And in his grasp the deadly faulchion blaz'd!

   Secure of conquest, on he moved,
     The youthful foe to meet;
But there a force, till then unknown, he proved!
   Amazed we saw the strange defeat;

---

[d] Conor Mac-Neila, King of Ulster.

[e] Conall Cearnach, Master of the Ulster Knights, cousin-german and intimate friend to Cucullin.

We saw our Champion bound;
Subdued beneath fierce Conloch's arm he lay;
No more, as erst, to boast unvanquished sway,
A name, till then, for victory still renown'd.

" Quick let a rapid courier fly!
    (Indignant Auliffe cried,)
" Quick with the shameful tidings let him hie,
    " And to our aid the first of heroes call,
        " From fair Dundalgan's [f] lofty wall,
            " Or Dethin's [g] ancient pride!"

" Welcome, Cucullin! [h] mighty chief!
" Though late, O welcome to thy friend's relief!
" Behold the havoc of yon deadly blade!
" Behold our hundred warriors bite the ground!
    " Behold thy friend, thy Conall bound!
" Behold—nor be thy vengeful arm delay'd!"

" No

---

[f] Dundalgan, (now Dundalk,) the residence of Cucullin.

[g] Dun-Dethin, the residence of Dethin, the mother of Cucullin.

[h] This passage exhibits a species of beauty that has been often, and deservedly admired: Here is the poet's true magical chariot, that annihilates space and circumstance in its speed! We scarce know that the messenger of Conor is gone, until we find him returned; and without the tedious intervention of narrative, the bard places his hero at once before our eyes.—Thus, in the inimitable ballad of *Hardyknute*:

> The little Page flew swift as dart,
>   Flung from his Master's arm;
> " Cum down, cum down Lord Hardyknute,
>   " And red your King frae harm!"

" No wonder (he replied,) each foreign knight
  " Should now infult our coaft!
" Loft are the fouls of martial might,
  " The pride of Erin's hoft!
" Oh! fince your deaths, ye fav'rite fons of fame¹!
" Difmay, defeat, diftrefs, and well-earn'd fhame,
" Alike our lofs, and our reproach proclaim!——

                                                " For

---

¹ Cucullin here alludes to the death of his kinfmen, the three fons of Ufnoth, (or Uifneach,) who were cut off fome time before by the perfidy of Conor. As their ftory may perhaps be acceptable to my readers, I will here prefent them with it, in all its fabulous array.

Deirdre, the beautiful daughter of Feidlim Mac-Doill, fecretary to Conor king of Ulfter, had, from her infancy, been fhut up and ftrictly guarded in a fortrefs, to fruftrate the prophecy of a Druid, who had foretold at her birth, that fhe fhould be fatal to the houfe of Ulfter. On a day, as fhe looked abroad from her prifon, fhe perceived a raven feeding on the blood of a calf, that had been killed for her table, and had tinged with crimfon fome new-fallen fnow.—Immediately turning to Leavarcam, (her governefs,) fhe afked, if there was any one in the world fo beautiful as to have hair black as that raven's wing; cheeks of as bright and pure a red as that blood; and a fkin of the fame dazzling fairnefs as that fnow? Leavarcam replied, that there was; and that Naoife, the fon of Ufnoth, more than anfwered the defcription.

Deirdre, curious to behold this wonder, entreated her governefs to contrive fome means by which fhe might procure a fight of him; and Leavarcam, pitying her fituation and confinement, and thinking this a good opportunity to effect her deliverance from it; went directly to the young and gallant Naoife, informed him of the circumftance, extolled her pupil's charms, and promifed to indulge him with an interview, provided he would, on his part, engage to free the fair captive, and make her his wife. Naoife joyfully accepted the invitation:—they met;—mutual aftonifhment and admiration concluded in vows of the moft paffionate love! Naoife, with the aid of his brothers, Ainle and Ardan, ftormed the fortrefs, and carried off his prize; and efcaping thence to Scotland, they were there joined in marriage.

                                                But

"For me, my friends, what now remains,
"When I behold yon mighty Chief in chains?
                                            " With

But the fatal beauty of Deirdre prevented the peaceable enjoyment of her happiness:—a Prince of great power in Albany saw her and was enamoured; and finding that it was vain to sue, he had recourse to arms, to force her from the protection of her husband. But Naoise, with a few faithful followers, cut his way through all opposition, and made good his retreat to one of the adjacent islands; where expecting to be again attacked, he dispatched messengers to Ulster, to entreat the aid of his friends.

The nobility of that province, on being informed of his situation, went in a body to the King, requesting that Naoise might be assisted and recalled; and Conor now trembling for the event of the prophecy, and perceiving that he could not by open force effect the deaths of those whose lives he feared would fulfil it, veiled his treacherous purpose under the masque of generous forgiveness to the rashness of a youthful lover; he affected to engage with pleasure in the cause of the unhappy pair; he granted the desired repealment, and sent a ship to convey them back to Ireland, and a body of troops to wait their arrival on the shore, and escort them to the palace of Emania. But Eogain, the commander of this body, had received private orders from the King to cut off the little band of Naoise on their landing; and particularly not to let Deirdre and the three sons of Usnoth escape. His commands were too successfully obeyed, and in spight of the most gallant resistance, the unhappy brothers were slain. But Deirdre was reserved for still further woe: the murderous Eogain, struck with her beauty, could not lift his arm against her; he therefore brought her back a prisoner to the palace, and requested her from the King, as the reward of his guilty service. The base and inhuman Conor consented to his wishes, on obtaining a promise that she should be kept confined, and strictly watched, to prevent the accomplishment of the prediction. The wretched victim was accordingly placed in the chariot, and by the side of her husband's murderer, who aggravated her anguish by the most brutal raillery; and convinced her that death alone could free her from horrors, yet worse than any she had hitherto endured. Inspired with the sudden resolution of despair, she watched a moment favourable to her purpose, and springing with violence from the chariot, she dashed herself against a rock and expired.

But the cruel Conor drew down on his house the denunciation that he dreaded, by the very means through which he sought to avoid it. The friends of the unhappy lovers,

enraged

" With fuch a hero's conqueror fhould I cope,
" What could my humbler boaſt of prowefs hope [k]?
" How fhould you think *my* arms could e'er prevail,
" Where Conall-Cearnach's fkill and courage fail?"——

" And wilt thou then decline the fight,
 " O arm of Erin's fame!
" Her glorious, her unconquered knight,
 " Her firſt and fav'rite name!
" No, brave Cucullin! mighty chief
 " Of bright victorious ſteel!
" Fly to thy Conall, to thy friend's relief,
" And teach the foe fuperior force to feel!"

" Then,

enraged at his perfidy, affembled all their forces, and took ample vengeance on the tyrant for his cruelty and breach of faith. His whole army was routed; his palace of Emania was feized upon, and given up to the plunder of the foldiery; and his favourite fon, together with the chief officers of his houfehold, and all who were fuppofed to be his friends, fell in the carnage of that day, as fo many victims to the manes of the murdered fons of Ufnoth.

Whatever part Cucullin had taken in revenging the deaths of his young kinfmen, it appears that a kind of fullen reconciliation was afterwards effected between him and the King of Ulſter; fince we here find him (though reluctantly) confenting to fight his battles, and obey his commands. But the feverity of reproach, and the bitternefs of recollection, which is implied in the fpeech before us, plainly demonſtrate that his grief and his injuries were ſtill keenly felt, and warmly refented.

[k] Cucullin had been once a candidate for the Maſterſhip of the Ulſter Knights, but voluntarily refigned his claim to his kinfman Conall, as to one who had exhibited greater proof of foldierfhip than he himfelf had, at that time, been happy enough to have an opportunity of evincing.

Then, with firm ſtep, and dauntleſs air,
Cucullin went, and thus the foe addreſt:
" Let me, O valiant knight, (he cried)
  " Thy courteſy requeſt!
" To me thy purpoſe, and thy name confide,
" And what thy lineage and thy land declare?
  " Do not my friendly hand refuſe,
    " And proffer'd peace decline;——
" Yet, if thou wilt the doubtful combat chuſe,
" The combat then, O fair-hair'd youth! be thine!"

    " Never ſhall aught ſo baſe as fear
      " The hero's boſom ſway!
    " Never, to pleaſe a curious ear,
      " Will I my fame betray!
    " No, gallant chief! I will to none
  " My name, my purpoſe, or my birth reveal;
" Nor even from *thee* the combat will I ſhun,
" Strong though thine arm appear, and tried thy martial
  " ſteel.

    " Yet hear me own, that, did the vow
      " Of chivalry allow,
      " I would not thy requeſt withſtand,
    " But gladly take, in peace, thy proffer'd hand.

                                            " So

" So does that face each hoftile thought controul'!
" So does that noble mien poffefs my foul!"

Reluctant then the chiefs commenc'd the fight,
Till glowing honor rous'd their flumbering might!
Dire was the ftrife each valiant arm maintain'd,
And undecided long their fates remain'd;
For, till that hour, no eye had ever view'd
A field *fo* fought, a conqueft *fo* purfu'd!
At length Cucullin's kindling foul arofe;
Indignant fhame recruited fury lends;
With fatal aim his glittering lance he throws,
And low on earth the dying youth extends.

Flown with the fpear, his rage forfook
  The hero's generous breaft,
And, with foft voice, and pitying look,
He thus his brave unhappy foe addreft.

" Gallant youth! that wound, I fear,
" Is paft the power of art to heal!
" Now then, thy name and lineage let me hear,
 " And whence, and why we fee thee here, reveal!

D   " That

 Deeply, as it is evident, that Conloch had been prepoffeffed againft Cucullin, yet nature here begins to work; and the fight of the paternal face raifes ftrong emotions in his breaft. This is finely introduced by the mafterly poet, to heighten the diftrefs of the cataftrophe.

" That so thy tomb with honor we may raise,
" And give to glory's song thy deathless praise!"

" Approach!"—the wounded youth reply'd [m] :—
" Yet—yet more closely nigh!
" On this dear earth—by that dear side
" O let me die!——
" Thy hand—my Father!—hapless chief!—
" And you, ye warriors of our isle, draw near,
" The anguish of my soul to hear,
" For I must kill a father's heart with grief!

" O first of heroes! hear thy son,
" Thy Conloch's parting breath!
" See Dunscaik's early care [n]!
" See Dundalgan's cherish'd heir!
" See, alas! thy hapless child,
" By female arts beguil'd,
" And by a fatal promise won,
" Falls the sad victim of untimely death!"

" O my

---

[m] From this line, to the end of the poem, my readers will perceive the necessity of an irregular measure in the translation.

[n] Dun-Sgathach (i. e. the fortress of Sgathach) in the Isle of Sky.—It took its name from a celebrated Albanian heroine, who established an academy there, and taught the use of arms.

".O my loſt ſon!—relentleſs fate!—
"By this curſt arm to fall!—
"Come wretched Aifè, from thy childleſs hall,
"And learn the woes that thy pierc'd ſoul await!
"Why wert thou abſent in this fatal hour?—
"A mother's tender power
"Might ſure have ſway'd my Conloch's filial breaſt!
"My ſon, my hero then had ſtood confeſt!

"But it is paſt!—he dies!—ah woe!—
"Come, Aifè, come, and let thy ſorrows flow!
"Bathe his dear wounds!—ſupport his languid head!
"Waſh, with a mother's tears, away the blood a father ſhed!"

"No more (the dying youth exclaim'd,)
"No more on Aifè call!
"Curſt be her art!—the treacherous ſnare ſhe fram'd
"Has wrought thy Conloch's fall!
"Curſe on the tongue that arm'd my hand
"Againſt a father's breaſt!
"That bound me to obey her dire command,
"And with a lying tale my ſoul poſſeſt;
"That made me think my youth no more thy care,
"And bade me of thy cruel arts beware!

"Curſt

" Curſt be the tongue to whoſe deceit
" The anguiſh of my father's heart I owe.
 " While thus, to bathe his ſacred feet,
  " Through this unhappy ſide,
 " He ſees the ſame rich crimſon tide
" That fills his own heroic boſom flow!

 " O yes! too ſurely am I thine!
" No longer I the fatal truth conceal.
 " Never before did any foe
 " The name of Conloch know;
" Nor would I now to thee my birth reveal,
" But ſafety, even from thy dear hand decline,
" Did not my ebbing blood, and ſhort'ning breath,
" Secure thy Conloch's honor—in his death.

 " But, ah Cucullin!—dauntleſs knight!—
 " Ah!—had'ſt thou better mark'd the fight!
" Thy ſkill in arms might ſoon have made thee know
 " That I was only *half* a foe!
" Thou would'ſt have ſeen, for glory though I fought,
  " Defence,—not blood I fought.
 " Thou would'ſt have ſeen, from that dear breaſt,
" Nature and love thy Conloch's arm arreſt!

" Thou

" Thou would'st have seen his spear instinctive stray;
" And, when occasion dar'd its force,
" Still from that form it fondly turn'd away,
" And gave to air its course°."

No answer the unhappy sire return'd,
But wildly thus, in frantic sorrow mourn'd.
" O my lov'd Conloch! beam of glory's light!
" O set not yet in night!
" Live, live my son, to aid thy father's sword!
" O live, to conquest and to fame restor'd!
" Companions of the war, my son, we'll go,
" Mow down the ranks, and chase the routed foe!
" Ourselves an host, sweep o'er the prostrate field,
" And squadrons to my hero's arm shall yield!
" Not mighty Erin's self, from wave to wave,
" Not all her chiefs could our joint prowess brave!

" Gone!—art thou gone?—O wretched eyes!
" See where my child! my murder'd Conloch lies!
" Lo!—in the dust his shield of conquest laid!
" And prostrate, now, his once victorious blade!

" O let

° Here is one of those delicate strokes of nature and sentiment, that pass so directly to the heart, and so powerfully awaken its feelings!—Sympathy bleeds at every line of this passage, and the anguish of the father and the son are at once transfused into our breasts!

" O let me turn from the foul-torturing fight!
" O wretch! deferted and forlorn!
" With age's fharpeft anguifh torn!—
" Stript of each tender tie! each fond delight!

" Cruel father!—cruel ftroke!—
" See the heart of nature broke!—
" Yes, I have murder'd thee, my lovely child!
" Red with thy blood this fatal hand I view!—
" Oh, from the fight diftraction will enfue,
" And grief will turn with tearlefs horror wild!——

" Reafon!—whither art thou fled?—
" Art thou with my Conloch dead?—
" Is this loft wretch no more thy care?
" Not one kind ray to light my foul;
" To free it from the black controul
" Of this deep, deep defpair!——

" As the lone fkiff is tofs'd from wave to wave,
" No pilot's hand to fave!
" Thus, thus my devious foul is borne!
" Wild with my woes, I only live to mourn!

" But all in death will fhortly end,
" And forrow to the grave its victim fend!

" Yes

"Yes, yes, I feel the near approach of peace,
 "And misery soon will cease!
"As the ripe fruit, at shady autumn's call,
"Shakes to each blast, and trembles to its fall;
"I wait the hour that shall afford me rest,
"And lay, O earth! my sorrows in thy breast.

Here ends the Poem of CONLOCH: the subject is indeed continued in the following pages; but it is in a distinct and separate piece, of which I have seen a number of copies, all in some degree differing from each other, and none of them connected with the above, except in this one copy, which I got from Mr. O'HALLORAN. The following poem, however, is possessed of considerable merit; and, besides the pathos that it breathes, it exhibits a species of originality in its way, that is *unique*, and striking to a very great degree.

The above translation is made from Mr. O'HALLORAN's copy, but the original of the poem here subjoined, being rather fuller than the one which was annexed to his, I have for that reason adopted it.

THE LAMENTATION OF CUCULLIN,

OVER THE

BODY OF HIS SON CONLOCH.

Alas, alas for thee,
 O Aife's haplefs fon!
And oh, of fires the moft undone,
My child! my child! woe, tenfold woe to me!
 Alas! that e'er thefe fatal plains
 Thy valiant fteps receiv'd!
And oh, for Cualnia's [a] wretched chief
  What now, alas, remains!
 What, but to gaze upon his grief!
Of his fole fon, by his own arm bereav'd!

          O had

---

[a] Cucullin was called, by way of pre-eminence, the HERO OF CUALNIA, that being the name of his patrimony, which it ftill retains, in the county of Louth.

O had I died before this hour!—
    My loft, my lovely child!
Before this arm my Conloch's arm oppos'd;
Before this spear against him was addrest;
Before these eyes beheld his eye-lids clos'd,
And life's warm stream thus issuing from his breast!
Then, Death, how calmly had I met thy power!
Then, at thy worst of terrors, had I smil'd!

    Could fate no other grief devise?—
        No other foe provide?———
    Oh!—could no arm but mine suffice
        To pierce my darling's side!—
My Conloch! 'tis denied thy father's woe
Even the sad comfort of revenge to know!—
To rush upon thy murderer's cruel breast,
Scatter his limbs, and rend his haughty crest!—
While his whole tribe in blood should quench my rage,
And the dire fever of my soul assuage [b]!
The debt of vengeance, then, should well be paid,
And thousands fall the victims of thy shade!

E   Ultonian

---

[b] What a picture of a heart torn with sorrow is here exhibited, in these wild startings of passion!—the soul of a hero, pressed down with a weight of woe,—stung to madness by complicated aggravations of the most poignant grief, and struggling between reason, and the impatient frenzy of despair!—How naturally does it rave around for some object whereon to vent the burstings of anguish, and the irritations of a wounded spirit!

Ultonian knights[c]! ye glory of our age!
Well have ye 'fcap'd a frantic father's rage!
That not by *you* this fatal field is won!
That not by *you* I lofe my lovely fon!—
Oh, dearly, elfe, fhould all your lives abide
The trophies from my Conloch's valour torn;
And your RED-BRANCH, in deeper crimfon dy'd,
The vengeance of a father's arm fhould mourn!

O thou loft hope of my declining years!
O cruel winds that drove thee to this coaft!
  Alas! could Deftiny afford
  No other arm, no other fword,
 In Leinfter of the pointed fpears,
On Munfter's plains, or in fierce Cruachan's[d] hoft,
 To quench in blood my filial light,
And fpare my arm the deed, my eyes the fight!

 O had proud India's fplendid plain
  Beneath thy prowefs bled,
 There, funk on heaps of hoftile flain,
  Had thy brave fpirit fled,

That

---

[c] Thefe were the famous heroes of the RED-BRANCH.

[d] In Connaught.

That then Emania^e might the deed purſue,
And, for thy fate, exact the vengeance due!
Expiring millions had thy ranſom paid,
And the wild frenzy of my grief allay'd!

   O that to Lochlin's land of ſnows
      My ſon had ſteer'd his courſe!
   Or Grecian^f ſhores, or Perſian^g foes,
      Or Spain, or Britain's force!

There

---

^e By Emania he means the knights of the Red-branch, as a conſiderable part of that palace was occupied by this celebrated body. The part appointed for their reſidence was called *Teagh na Craoibhe-ruadh* (i. e. the palace of the Red-branch), where there was alſo an academy inſtituted for the inſtruction of the young knights, and a large hoſpital for their ſick and wounded, called *Bron-bhearg*, or the Houſe of the Warriors' Sorrow. See O'Hall. *Int. to the Hiſt. of Ireland*, p. 40. See alſo Keating.

The palace of Emania, or Eamania, ſtood near Armagh. Some ruins of it were remaining ſo late as the time of Colgan. Vide *Collect. de Reb. Hib.* vol. III. p. 341.

^{f g} The anti-hibernian critic will here exclaim—" What knowledge could Cucullin " poſſibly be ſuppoſed to have had of Greece, or Perſia, or of proud India's ſplendid " plain?—Does not the very mention baniſh every idea of the antiquity of this " poem, and mark it out at once as a modern production?" It is granted that this would indeed be the caſe, had our early anceſtors been *really* ſuch as modern writers repreſent them:—*Barbarians, deſcended from barbarians, and ever continuing the ſame*; but their Phœnician origin of itſelf ſufficiently accounts for their knowledge of the ſituation, inhabitants, manners, &c. of the various nations of the earth; ſince the Phœnicians, a maritime and commercial people, traded to every port, and were acquainted with every country.

Beſides this, the literary and intellectual turn of the ancient Iriſh, frequently ſent them, in queſt of knowledge, to different parts of the globe. " Our early writers " (ſays Mr O'Halloran) tell us, (and Archbiſhop Uſher affirms the ſame,) that

There had he fallen, amidſt his fame,
  I yet the loſs could bear;
Nor horror thus would ſhake my frame,
  Nor ſorrow be—Deſpair!—

Why was it not in Sora's barbarous lands
  My lovely Conloch fell?
Or by fierce Pictiſh chiefs[h], whoſe ruthleſs bands
  Would joy the cruel tale to tell;
Whoſe ſouls are train'd all pity to ſubdue;
Whoſe ſavage eyes unmov'd that form could view!

Rejoice, ye heroes of Albania's plains!
(While yet I live, my conquering troops to lead,)
  Rejoice, that guiltleſs of the deed
    Your happy earth remains!

                                              And

" the celebrated champion Conall Cearnach, Maſter of the Ulſter Knights, was
" actually at Jeruſalem at the time of the crucifixion of our Saviour, and related the
" ſtory to the King of Ulſter on his return." He alſo adds that one of our great
poets, in the fifth century, traverſed the eaſt, and dedicated a book to the Emperor
Theodoſius. Many ſimilar inſtances and proofs could alſo be here ſubjoined; but the
limits of my deſign oblige me to refer my readers to the learned works of O'Conor,
O'Halloran and Vallancey, names dear to every ſpirit of liberality and ſcience,
but by *Iriſhmen* peculiarly to be revered.

[h] The period, when the Picts firſt invaded North-Britain, has not (I believe) been
exactly aſcertained.—We *here* find that country divided between the Picts and the
Albanians, and the former mentioned as a bloody and cruel people.—It was not till
two centuries after this that a *third* colony from Ireland, under Carbry Riada, was
eſtabliſhed there.

And you, ye chiefs of Galia's numerous hoſt;
Bleſs the kind fate that ſpar'd your favour'd coaſt!

But what for me—for me is left!
Of more, and dearer far than life, bereft!
    Doom'd to yet unheard of woe!
A father, doom'd to pierce his darling's ſide,
    And,—oh! with blaſted eyes abide
To ſee the laſt dear drops of filial crimſon flow!

Alas!—my trembling limbs!—my fainting frame ᵏ!—
    Grief!—is it thou?——
    O conquering Grief!—I know thee now!
Well do thy ſad effects my woes proclaim!
Poor Victor!—ſee thy trophies, where they lie!—
Waſh them with tears!—then lay thee down and die!

Why

ⁱ I had nearly forgotten to acknowledge, that ſome ſtanzas of the original of this poem are omitted in the tranſlation; Cucullin, before this, enumerates the heroes of the RED-BRANCH; viz. Conal Cearnach, Loire Buahach, Cormac Conluingeas, Dubthach, Forbuidh, &c. &c. and tells them, one by one, that they happily eſcaped being guilty of the death of his ſon, and the vengeance that he would have exacted In ſome other copies of the poem I do not find theſe ſtanzas; I therefore took the liberty of leaving them out, as I thought they broke the pathos of the compoſition; and, beſides, they were (in point of poetry) rather inferior to the reſt of the piece.

ᵏ The beautiful lines, in my original, from which the three following ſtanzas are tranſlated, were not in Mr. O'HALLORAN's copy.

Why, why, O Aifè! was thy child
Thus cruelly beguil'd!
Why to my Conloch did'ſt thou not impart
The fatal ſecret of his father's art?
To warn him to avoid the deadly ſnare,
And of a combat on the waves beware[1].

Alas, I ſink!—my failing ſight
Is gone!—'tis loſt in night!
Clouds and darkneſs round me dwell!
Horrors more than tongue can tell!
See where my ſon, my murdered Conloch lies!
What further ſufferings now can fate deviſe!
O my heart's wounds! well may your anguiſh flow,
And drop life's tears on this ſurpaſſing woe!

Lo, the ſad remnant of my ſlaughter'd race,
Like ſome lone trunk, I wither in my place!—
No more the ſons of USNOTH to my ſight
Give manly charms, and to my ſoul delight!

No

---

[1] Some of our romances and poems aſcribe to Cucullin the property of being invulnerable in water, and in relating this circumſtance of his life, ſay, that (when hard preſſed by Conloch) he took the refuge of a ford, and *then* threw the fatal GATH-BOLG, with which he was ſure of killing his antagoniſt. The preceding poem makes no mention of this fable, perhaps through tenderneſs for the honor of Cucullin; and from this, and ſome other circumſtances, I am tempted to think they were not written by the ſame hand.

No more my Conloch shall I hope to see;
Nor son, nor kinsman now survives for me!
O my lost son!—my precious child, adieu!
No more these eyes that lovely form shall view!
No more his dark-red spear shall Ainle [m] wield!
No more shall Naoise thunder o'er the field!
No more shall Ardan sweep the hostile plains!—
Lost are they all, and nought but woe remains!—
Now, chearless earth, adieu thy every care:
Adieu to all, but Horror and Despair!

[m] Ainle, Naoise, and Ardan, were the three sons of Usnoth, whose tragical story is related in the notes to the preceding poem.

II.

MAGNUS THE GREAT:

A

POEM.

ADVERTISEMENT.

THE language of the following Poem, as it now stands, is certainly too modern to be ascribed to an earlier period than the middle ages;—but, whether it did or did not exist, prior to those times, in a dress more ancient than that in which we now find it, is a matter which I confess myself unqualified to determine: for, though there be many reasons to suppose that this is really the case; yet there are also some circumstances in the Poem, which seem to contradict the supposition. If, by the Magnus *of our Bard, he means the King of that name, who made some descents on Ireland about the latter end of the eleventh century, he is then guilty of a great anacronism, in synchronising heroes, who flourished at such different periods; and we must fix the date of his composition at some time in the twelfth, or thirteenth century. This, however, is mere conjecture, upon the strength of which, it would be unfair to judge, much less to condemn our Bard.* Magnus *is a name so common amongst the Northern princes, that it cannot determine our opinion.*

According to the accounts that Irish history gives of Danish Invasions in this kingdom, the earliest was about the end of the eighth century; we therefore cannot safely rest upon the credit of our Bards, who tell us of numberless descents, which that fierce and warlike people made upon our coasts, wherein they were opposed and beaten back by kings and heroes, who flourished here in the earliest ages of Christianity. Yet, small as is the faith to be placed in mere poetical authority, it ought not to be wholly disregarded: it seems to me that they must have had some foundation for their perpetual allusions to the early period of Danish depredations in Ireland; nor is the silence of our history a sufficient reason for concluding that all their accounts are founded in fiction only. The greater part of our historical records are lost, and, doubtless, amongst them, many authentic accounts of events much more interesting than this now in question; and which are not mentioned in the few of our annals that yet remain. Besides this, an invasion, such as that recorded by our Bard, might easily have passed unnoticed by either a concise or a careless historian. The Danes, under his hero, acquired no footing, gained no victory in our island; they were only just landed, and beaten back: so fruitless an attempt might have been purposely omitted by the historian, as not of sufficient consequence to take up room in his annals; or it may perhaps have been noticed in some of our more voluminous records, which are lost. Add to this, that numbers of the Latin writers (from the commencement of the fourth, to the close of the tenth and eleventh centuries) speak fully of an intercourse between the old Inhabitants of Ireland, and the Northern nations. All these circumstances considered, it is left to the judgment of the reader, whether to acquit our Bard of anachronism, or not.

There are numberless copies of this Poem in the hands of the learned and curious. The one from which I have translated is in the collection of Mr. Joseph C. Walker. The author (or perhaps only the modernifer of the piece) is said to have belonged to the family of the O'Neils; but, what his name was, I have not been able to learn.

MAGNUS

MAGNUS[a] THE GREAT:

A POEM.

OISIN. ST. PATRICK.

OISIN. I care not for thee, senseless clerk!
  Nor all thy psalming throng,
Whose stupid souls, unwisely dark,
  Reject the light of song:

Unheeding, while it pours the strain,
  With Finian glory swell'd;
Such as thy thought can scarce contain,
  Thine eye has ne'er beheld!

        PATRICK.

---

[a] Maguire is pronounced in the Irish, *Manos;* but the name being a foreign one, is here purposely written according to the spelling of the original. The Irish names are, in general, given in such spelling as will convey the sound of the original.

PATRICK.   O son of Finn! the Fenii's fame
                Thou gloriest to prolong;
            While I my heav'nly King proclaim,
                In psalm's diviner song.

OISIN.   Dost thou insult me to my face?
                Does thy presumption dare
            With the bright glories of my race
                Thy wretched psalms compare?

            Why did my folly let thee live,
                To brave too patient age,
            To see how tamely I forgive,
                And preach me from my rage!

PATRICK.   Pardon, great chief!—I meant no ill;
                Sweet is to me thy song;
            And high the themes and lofty skill
                Its noble strains prolong.

            Sing then, sweet bard! thy purpos'd tale,
                While gladly I attend,
            And let me on thy grace prevail
                Its lovely sounds to lend.

                                            OISIN.

OISIN. Once, while we chac'd the dark-brown deer [b],
Along the fea-girt plain,
We faw a diftant fleet appear,
Advancing on the main.

Quick ceas'd the hunt :—to eaft, to weft
Our rapid mandate hi'd;
With inftant march the Fenii preft
To join their leader's fide.

Beneath the chief of mighty fame,
Whom lovely Morna [c] bore,
Seven warlike bands [d] to join us came,
Collected on the fhore.

Then

[b] "Thefe hunting matches (fays O'CONOR) continued feveral days; and, in fome "feafons, feveral months: at night they encamped in woods, and repofed in booths, "covered with the fkins of the animals they hunted down." The chafe was alfo, to them, "a fort of military fchool, which rendered toil eafy, and annexed pleafure to "the rudeft fatigue. It gave them great mufcular ftrength, and great agility and "firmnefs againft the feverity of the moft rigorous feafons. It befides taught them "vigilance; fkill in archery, and great patience under long abftinence from food. "They came out of the foreft expert foldiers; and no nation could excel them in "rapid marches, quick retreats, and fudden fallies. By thefe means it was, that they "fo often baffled the armies of South-Britain, and the Roman legions, united." O'CONOR's *Differtations*, p. 71, 101.

[c] Morna, or Muirne monchaoimh, (i. e. the beloved maid, with the gentle, or engaging wiles,) was the mother of Finn, and it was in right of her that he poffeffed his palace of Almhain. Vide KEATING, p. 271.

[d] Thefe were the *Fiana Ereann*, the celebrated militia, fo renowned in the annals
of

> Then Finn, the foul of Erin's might,
> With fame and conqueſt crown'd;
> To deeds of glory to incite,
> Addrefs'd the heroes round.

" Which

this country, and in the fongs of her Bards. Dr. Warner gives the following account of that formidable body.——

" The conſtant number of this ſtanding army in times of peace, when there were
" no diſturbances at home, nor any want of their affiſtance to their allies abroad, were
" nine thouſand men, divided equally into three battalions. But in cafe of any appre-
" henſions of a conſpiracy, or rebellion againſt the monarch, or if there was any
" neceſſity for tranſporting a body of troops to Scotland, in order to defend their
" allies, the Dalriada's, it was in the power of Finn, the generaliſſimo, to encreaſe
" his forces to feven battalions, of three thouſand each. Every battalion was com-
" manded by a Colonel; every hundred men by a Captain; an officer, in the nature of
" a Lieutenant, was fet over every fifty; and a Serjeant, refembling the Decurio of
" the Romans, was at the head of every five and twenty. When they were drawn
" out for action, every hundred men were diſtributed into ten files, with ten (of
" courfe) in each; and the leader of the file gave the word to the other nine. As it
" was thought a great honor to be a member of this invincible body of troops, their
" General was very ſtrict in inſiſting on the qualifications neceſſary for admiſſion
" into it."

" The parents, (or near relations) of every candidate for the militia, were to give
" fecurity that they would not attempt to revenge his death, but leave it to his fellow-
" foldiers to do him juſtice. He muſt have a poetical genius, and be well acquainted
" with the twelve books of poetry. He was to ſtand at the diſtance of nine ridges
" of land, with only a ſtick, and a target; and nine foldiers were to throw their
" javelins at him at once, from which he was to defend himfelf unhurt, or be re-
" jected. He was to run through a wood, with his hair plaited, purfued by a com-
" pany of the militia, the breadth of a tree only being allowed between them at
" fetting out, without being overtaken, or his hair falling loofe about him. He was
" to leap over a tree, as high as his forehead; and eafily ſtoop under another that
" was as low as his knee. Thefe qualifications being proved, he was then to take

an

"Which of my chiefs the firſt will go
"To yon inſulted ſhore,
"And bravely meet the daring foe,
"Their purpoſe to explore!"

Then

"an oath of allegiance to the King, and of fidelity to Finn, his commander in
"chief.

"The reader will judge of the propriety of moſt of theſe qualifications; but this
"was not every thing that was required, in order for admiſſion into this illuſtrious
"corps. Every ſoldier, before he was enrolled, was obliged to ſubſcribe to the fol-
"lowing articles. That, if ever he was diſpoſed to marry, he would not conform to
"the mercenary cuſtom of requiring a portion with his wife; but, without regard to
"her fortune, he would chuſe a woman for her virtue, and courteous manners.
"That he would never offer violence to any woman. That he would be charitable
"to the poor, as far as his abilities would permit. And that he would not turn his
"back, nor refuſe to fight with ten men of any other nation.

"In the times of peace, they were required to defend the inhabitants againſt the
"attempts of thieves and robbers; to quell riots and inſurrections; to levy fines,
"and ſecure eſtates that were forfeited for the uſe of the crown; in ſhort, to ſup-
"preſs all ſeditious and traiterous practiſes in their beginning; and to appear under
"arms, when any breach of faith required it. They had no ſubſiſtence money from
"the monarchs but during the winter half year, when they were billeted upon the
"country, and diſperſed in quarters. During the other part of the year, from the
"firſt of May to November, they were encamped about the fields, and were obliged
"to fiſh and hunt for their ſupport. This was not only a great eaſe to the monarch
"and his ſubjects, but it inured the troops to fatigue, preſerved them in health and
"vigour, and accuſtomed them to lie abroad in the field: and in a country which
"abounded ſo much with veniſon, fiſh, and fowl, as Ireland did, it was no other
"hardſhip than what was proper to the life of ſoldiers, to be obliged to draw their
"ſubſiſtence in the ſummer ſeaſon from thoſe articles.

"They made but one meal in four and twenty hours, which was always in the
"evening; and beſides the common method of roaſting their meat before the fire,
"they had another very remarkable, and which they ſeem moſt to have practiſed.

"The

Then Conan [c] of the froward mind,
The bald M'Morni fpoke,
And as his fpleenful foul inclin'd,
His fneering accents broke.

" O chief

" The places, which they chofe to encamp in, were always in the neighbourhood of
" water, where great fires were made, in order to heat fome large ftones, for fod-
" dening of their meat; here large pits were dug, into which they threw a layer of
" ftones, when they were hot, and then a layer of flefh, covered up in fedges or
" rufhes; then another courfe of ftones, and another of flefh, till the pit was full,
" or their quantity of meat was finifhed. While their food was ftewing in this man-
" ner, they wafhed their heads, necks, &c. till they had cleanfed themfelves from the
" duft and fweat, occafion'd by hunting; and this contributed as much to take off
" their fatigue as it did to promote their health and cleanlinefs. When they were
" dreffed, and their meat was ready, they uncovered the pits, and took out their food,
" of which they eat large quantities with great chearfulnefs and fociability.

" If their exercife led them, as it often did, to too great a diftance to return to
" the camp, as foon as dinner was ended they erected little temporary tents or
" booths, in which their beds were laid out, and conftructed with great exactnefs.
" Next the ground were placed the fmall branches of trees, upon which was ftrewed
" a large quantity of mofs, and over all were laid bundles of rufhes, which made a
" very commodious lodging, and which, in the old manufcripts, are called ' The
" Three Beds of the Irifh Militia.' The marks of their fires continue deep in the
" earth, in many parts of the ifland, to this day; and when the hufbandman turns up
" the black burnt clay with his plow, he immediately knows the occafion of it; and
" even now that foil is called by the name of ' Fullacht Finn.' The militia were as
" much under difcipline, when encamped thus in the fummer, as when they were at
" quarters, and they were at ftated times obliged to perform their military exercife.
" Befides thefe regulations for the army, the celebrated Finn, who was as great a
" philofopher as a general, drew up feveral axioms of jurifprudence, which were incor-
" porated into the celeftial judgments of the ftate." WARNER's *Hift. of Ireland*, p. 289.

[c] Conan, wherever he is mentioned, or wherever he appears, always bears the fame
character for infolent perverfenefs; but, like Homer's Therfites, he was endured; and
probably for the fame reafon.

" O chief of Erin's batt'ling hoft!
" Whom fhould yon navy bring?—
" Haply fome Prince, or hero's boaft,
" To match our *wond'rous* King!

" Let Fergus, *peaceful* Bard, advance
" To meet their haughty lord;
" He, with accuftom'd art, perchance
" The threaten'd blow may ward [f]."

" Peace, tongue accurs'd, bald, froward fool!"
(The graceful Fergus cry'd)
" Think'ft thou I move beneath *thy* rule,
" To go or to abide?———

" Yet, for the Fenii, I will go
" To yon infulted fhore,
" And meet, for them, the daring foe,
" Their purpofe to explore."

Bright

---

[f] In the tranflation of this paffage, more is given than is abfolutely expreffed in the original, but not more than is implied: the words of Conan here are very few;—he only fays " Who, O mighty Finn of battles! who fhould there be but fome great " chief, or prince, coming againft thee?—let Fergus then, with his confummate art, " go and meet him; he is accuftomed to fuch errands." From the epithet *perverfe*, or *froward*, being beftowed on Conan, immediately before; and from the angry reply of the ufually gentle Fergus, I collected the full force of the intended irony, and underftood whatever my tranflation has added.

Bright in the glittering blades of war,
The youthful Fergus goes;
Loud founds his martial voice afar [f],
And greets the diftant foes.

" Whence are thofe hofts? Come they the force
" Of Finian arms to brave?—
" Or wherefore do they fteer their courfe
" O'er Erin's guarded wave?"

" Mac-Mehee, of the crimfon fhields [h],
" Fierce Magnus heads our bands,
" Who Lochlin's mighty fceptre wields,
" And mighty hofts commands."

" Why

---

[f] " With us (fays Mr. WALKER) as with the ancient Greeks, (Iliad, b. v.) before
" the ufe of trumpets was known in our armies, it was the bufinefs of thofe Herald-
" bards, (who had Stentoric lungs,) to found with the voice the alarm, and call the
" fquadrons together." *Hift. Mem. of Irifh Bards.*

A loud and well-toned voice was, indeed, peculiarly neceffary to the Bard; fince, without it, it was impoffible that the animated exhortations of his Rofg-cata could be heard, amidft the din of arms.

[h] The fhields of the Danes were ufually coloured crimfon. We find in HOLIN-SHED's Chronicle, where he defcribes the army led by Hafculphus againft Dublin, in the reign of Henry II. that " their fhields, bucklers and targets, were round, and " *coloured red*, and bound with iron." Perhaps, however, it is only in a figurative fenfe, that the *red fhield* is here mentioned by the poet, as having been often dyed in the blood of the enemy; it is in this fenfe that we frequently read of the *red fpear*, the *red fword*, &c.

" Why does he thus our coasts explore,
  " And hither lead his power?
" If peace conducts him to our shore,
  " He comes in happy hour."

The furious Magnus swift reply'd,
  With fierce and haughty boast,
(The King whose navy's speckled¹ pride
  Defied our martial host.)

" I come (he cried) from Comhal's son
  " A hostage to obtain;
" And, as the meed of conquest won,
  " His spouse and dog to gain ᵏ.

" His

---

¹ *Breac*, speckled.—I have nothing but conjecture to offer upon this epithet; and must leave it to those who are better versed in Northern antiquities, to determine what kind and degree of ornament is here meant.

ᵏ It is not certain, whether such a demand as that of " the spouse and dog" was usual, upon similar occasions, amongst the Scandinavian, or Celtic nations. Among the Asiatics and other ancients, it was the custom to demand " earth and water," as a token of submission. The " spouse and dog" are here insisted on, evidently in the same sense; and perhaps it was the practise of the Northerns to do so.

"His Bran[1], whose fleetness mocks the wind,
 "His spouse of gentle love:
"Let them be now to me resign'd,
 "My mightier arm to prove."

"Fierce will the valiant Fenii fight,
 "And thin will be their host,
"Before our Bran shall, in their sight,
 "Perform thy haughty boast;

"And Finn will swell green Erin's wave
 "With Lochlin's[m] blood of pride,
"Before his spouse shall be thy slave,
 "And leave his faithful side."

"Now by that generous hand of thine,
 "O Fergus! hear me swear,
"Though bright your Finian glories shine,
 "And fierce you learn to dare;

"Or

---

[1] This Bran is much celebrated in many of the Finian tales and poems, for fidelity and extraordinary endowments.

[m] Lochlin is the Gaelic name for Scandinavia in general.

"Or Bran shall soon the dark-brown deer
 "O'er Lochlin's hills pursue;
"Or soon this arm shall teach you fear,
 "And your vain pride subdue."

"Though strong that valiant arm you deem,
 "Whose might so loud you boast;
"And high those martial troops esteem,
 "Whose numbers hide our coast;

"Yet, never with thy haughty will
 "Shall Erin's chief comply;
"Nor ever deer, o'er Lochlin's hill,
 "Before our Bran shall fly."

Mild Fergus then, his errand done,
 Return'd with wonted grace;
His mind, like the unchanging sun*,
 Still beaming in his face.

Before

---

* The reader's attention is particularly called to the peculiar beauty of this image, and indeed of the whole preceding passage. How exquisitely is the character of Fergus supported! He greets the enemy with courtesy: he is answered with insolence; yet still retains the same equal temper, for which he is every where distinguished. We see his spirit rise, but it is with something more noble than resentment; for his reply to Magnus breathes all the calmness of philosophy, as well as the energy of the patriot, and the dignity of the hero.

Before bright Honor's generous chief,
   His noble fire, he goes;
And thus unfolds, in accents brief,
   The message of his foes.

" Why should I, from the valiant ear,
   " The words of death withhold;
" Since, to the heart that knows no fear,
   " All tidings may be told.

" Fierce Magnus bids thee instant yield,
   " And take the granted hour;
" Or soon the dire contested field
   " Shall make thee feel his pow'r;

" Fleet-bounding Bran, his deer to chase,
   " And prove his mightier arm;
" And thy soft love, his halls to grace,
   " And his fierce soul to charm;

" These are his proud, his stern demands,
   " Or soon, from shore to shore,
" His spear shall desolate thy lands,
   " And float thy fields with gore."

                                      " From

" From me shall my soft love be torn,
  " A stranger's halls to grace?—
" Or my fleet Bran away be borne,
  " A stranger's deer to chase?—

" Oh! first shall cease this vital breath,
  " And useless be this blade;
" And low in earth, and cold in death,
  " This arm be powerless laid!

" O Gaul! shall these redoubted bands
  " Stand cold and silent by;
" And hear such insolent demands,
  " And not to vengeance fly!

" Shall we not chase yon vaunting host,
  " With rout and death away,
" And make them rue their haughty boast,
  " And rue this fatal day?——"

" Yes, by that arm of deathful might,
  " O Comhal's noble son!
" Soon shall our swords pursue their flight,
  " And soon the field be won;

" Yon

" Yon King, whose ships of many waves
    " Extend along our coast,
" Who thus thy power insulting braves,
    " And dares our gallant host.

" Soon shall this arm his fate decide,
    " And, by this vengeful blade,
" Shall that fierce head of gloomy pride
    " In humble dust be laid!"

" Not so! (with eager warmth exclaim'd
        My generous son of Love)
" Yon King, though fierce, though widely fam'd,
    " Thy Osgur's arm shall prove!

" Soon his twelve Judges' tribe [p] before
    " My valiant troop shall flee;
" And their proud King shall fall, no more
    " His isle of boars to see."

" No,

---

[p] In the original, clan an ᴅa comajpleaċ ᴅeag. (tribe of the twelve Counsellers or Judges). "Odin, the conqueror of the North, established in Swe-
" den a supreme court, composed of twelve members, to assist him in the functions
" of the priesthood, and civil government. This, doubtless, gave rise to what was
" afterwards called the senate; and the same establishment, in like manner, took
" place in Denmark, Norway, and other Northern states. These senators decided,
" in the last appeal, all differences of importance; they were, if I may so say, the
                                                                        " assessors

"No, mine" (the famed Macluya [q] cry'd)
"Mine be yon vaunting foe!
"Mine be the talk to check his pride,
"And lay his glories low!

"Dark Norway's King myfelf will meet,
"And well his arm employ:
"For danger, in thy caufe, is fweet,
"And life is rifqu'd with joy."

"No, I to glorious fame will fpring!
(Brown Dermid [r] cry'd) "or die;
"Mine be to meet yon ftranger king,
"His boafted arm to try:

"Strong

"affeffors of the prince; and were in number twelve, as we are exprefsly informed
"by Saxo, in his Life of King Regner Lodbrog. Nor are there other monuments
"wanting, which abundantly confirm this truth. We find in Zealand, in Sweden,
"near Upfal, and, (if I am not miftaken) in the county of Cornwall alfo, large
"ftones, to the amount of twelve, ranged in the form of a circle, and, in the midft
"of them, one of fuperior heighth. Such, in thofe rude ages, was the hall of
"audience; the ftones that formed the circumference were the feats of the fenators;
"that in the middle was the throne of the King." MALLET's *Northern Antiquities*,
p. 44, note [e].

[q] Mac Luigheach.

[r] For an account of Dermid; fee notes on *The Chafe*.

" Strong though it be, it foon fhall yield,
" While in thy caufe I fight;
" Or foon thefe eyes, on yonder field,
" Shall clofe in endlefs night."

" My vifion now I call to mind!
(The ftarting Fallan* cry'd)
" I dream'd that with the Moorifh ᵗ King,
" Alone the fight I try'd:

" At length, methought, one lucky aim
" Struck off his gloomy head;
" And thence my foul forebodes our fame,
" And fees our glories fpread!"

" Bleft be your fouls, ye arms of war ᵘ!
(The blooming Finn exclaim'd)
" May victory bear your triumphs far,
" To diftant nations fam'd!

" But,

* Fœlan.

ᵗ ꀞᵫᵹ ċꀂꀃꀄ ꀅꀆ ꀇꀈꀉꀊ ꀋꀌꀍꀎꀏꀐ.—Literally " the King of the country of the Moors." This feems a ftrange paffage, and I muft confefs myfelf unable to conjecture whence it could have taken rife, or what connection there could have been between the Irifh and the Moors.

ᵘ How natural and how beautiful is this burft of feeling! We fee the affections of Finn exult ftill more in the attachment of his heroes, than his pride does in their prowefs.

" But, my brave troops! your chief alone,
" Shall chief in danger be;
" And Magnus shall be all my own,
" Whate'er the fates decree.

" Strong though his arm, the war to wage,
" I mean that arm to try;
" Nor from his might, nor from his rage,
" Shall Erin's chieftain fly [x]."

Then, girding on each warlike blade,
And glorying in their might,
Our martial host advanc'd, array'd,
And ardent for the fight.

Auspicious arms around us blaz'd [y],
Each thigh its weapon grac'd;
And, on each manly shoulder rais'd,
A spear of war is plac'd.

Each

---

[x] There is not one of the heroes who speaks with so much modesty as Finn, the greatest of them all. The rest promise, with confidence, a certain success to their valour; he alone speaks without a boast, and is modest, though determined.

[y] The pagan Irish had a custom, which was introduced by the Tuatha-de-Danans, of using charms, to enchant their weapons, previous to their going to battle; but perhaps, by the word *auspicious*, the poet only means that their weapons had been tried and victorious in fight.

Each chief with ardent valour glows,
 To prove the faith he fwore;
And forth we march, to meet the foes
 Encamp'd upon the fhore.

No mirth conducts the night along;
 No wax² illumes our board:
Nor faffron³, banquet, wine or fong,
 The darkfome hours afford.

At length we fee grey morning rife
 Upon its early dew;
And the firft dawn of eaftern fkies
 Gives Lochlin's hoft to view.

Before us, on the crouded fhore,
 Their gloomy ftandard rofe,
And many a chief their navy bore,
 And many princely foes.

And

---

[2] It appears ftrange to meet with *wax-lights* amongft the antient Irifh, but thofe mentioned in this paffage were probably a part of the plunder of the Roman provinces.

[3] I cannot conjecture the reafon why *faffron* is here introduced, and muft therefore difmifs the paffage without any thing more than a faithful adherence to my original.

And many a proud and bossy shield,
And coat of martial mail [b],
And warlike arms of proof they wield,
To guard, or to assail.

And

---

[b] We here see a marked difference between the arms and appearance of either host. The troops of Magnus are covered with steel; but we meet with no *coats of mail* amongst the chiefs of the Fenii.

"It should seem (says Mr. WALKER) that body armour of any kind was unknown to the Irish previous to the tenth century, as we find King Muirkertach, in that century, obtaining the ascititious name of *Muirkertach na geachall croceann*, for so obvious an invention as that of the leathern jacket. Yet coats of mail are mentioned in the Brehon laws, and the word *mail* is supposed to be derived from *mala* in Irish. Though the poets* of the middle ages describe the heroes of Oisin, as shining in polished steel, no relic of that kind of armour has escaped the wreck of time in Ireland; nor has there even a specimen of the brass armour, in which it is said the Danes so often met the Irish, fallen under my observation. Smith indeed tells us that corselets of pure gold were discovered on the lands of Clonties in the county of Kerry[†]; but these might have been left there by the Spaniards, who had a fortification called *Fort del Orè*, adjoining those lands.

"That the bodies of Irishmen should have been totally defenceless with respect to armour, during their several bloody contests with the Danes, I am neither prepared to admit nor deny; but I confess myself inclined to think, that their inflexible attachment to their civil dress would not yield to the fashion of the martial garb of their enemies, though it gave those people an evident advantage over them in the field of battle. It is however certain that the English did not find them cased in armour [‡]." *Hist. Essay on the Dress and Armour of the Irish*, p. 106.

* The poet before us is, however, (as well as many others) an exception.

[†] *Nat. and Civ. Hist. of Kerry*, p. 187. One of these corselets was purchased by Mr. O'HALLORAN, the gold of which was so ductile, as to roll up like paper. *Introd. to Hist. of Ireland*, p. 210.

[‡] Vide SPENCER's *State of Ireland*.

And many a sword with studs engrav'd [c]
In golden pomp was there;
And many a silken standard wav'd
Its splendid pride in air.

And many a chief in fight renown'd,
Finn of the banquets led,
And many a helmet [d] darkly frown'd
On many a valiant head.

And

[c] I am not certain whether these four lines relate to the troops of Magnus, or those of Finn, and have therefore purposely given to the translation, the same ambiguity which is found in the original. It is, however, most probable that the poet here speaks of the Fenii, because the two lines from which this verse is translated begin a stanza in the original, and in the third line, " Finn of the banquets" comes in. However, " Golden-hilted swords have been found in great abundance in this kingdom; and " we are told, in the Life of St. Bridget, that the king of Leinster presented to Dub- " tachus, her father, a sword ornamented with many costly jewels, which the pious " virgin purloined from Dubtachus, and sold for the charitable purpose of relieving " the necessities of the poor." *Hist. Essay on the Dress and Armour of the Irish*, p. 118.

[d] At what period helmets were first worn in Ireland, is a matter of mere con- jecture. That they were in use, previous to the tenth century, is certain, from some coins, discovered in the Queen's county, in the year 1786; (*Transf. of the Royal Irish. Acad.* 1787. See also SIMON's *Essay on Irish Coins.*) But how much earlier, or of what kind of metal they were formed, I have never been able to discover. Mr. WALKER's memoirs of our ancient armour, give an account of a golden helmet, which was found in the county of Tipperary; it is described as resembling in form a huntsman's cap, with the leaf in front divided equally, and elevated, and the scull encompassed with a ribband of gold crimped. Golden helmets are sometimes, but seldom, mentioned in the Irish poems which have fallen under my observation; but with helmets of some sort, all their warriors are armed. *Clogad* in general they are
called,

And many a warlike axe[e] was there,
To hew the ranks of fight;
And many a glittering spear[f] in air
Arose with stately height.

And

called, but hardly ever described; and when they are, it is in such figurative language, that one can neither determine on the form, nor the material of which they are composed. " The strong helmet," and " The dark frowning helmet," are the most common; but sometimes we meet with " The golden helmet," " The helmet enwreathed with " gold," and " The helmet blazing with gems of the East." These latter are in general described as a part of the armour of foreigners, not of Irish.

[e] The Irish were particularly expert in the use of the Tuaċ-ċaċa, or battle-axe. Cambrensis, in speaking of this dreadful weapon, as wielded by our countrymen, says, " They make use of but one hand to the axe, when they strike, and extend their " thumb along the handle, to guide the blow, from which neither the crested helmet " can defend the head, nor the iron folds of the armour, the body; whence it has " happened, in our time, that the whole thigh of a soldier, though cased in well- " tempered armour, hath been lopped off by a single blow of the axe, the whole " limb falling on one side of the horse, and the expiring body on the other."

[f] A great number, and a variety of spear-heads have been found, in different parts of this kingdom. The *Collectanea de Rebus Hibernicis* has furnished drawings of several, and several more are given in Mr. WALKER's *Memoir on the Armour of the Irish.*

STANIHURST has described the dexterous manner in which the Irish use the spear or lance. " They grasp (says he) about the middle, heavy spears, which they do not " hold pendant at their sides, under their arms, but hurl with all their strength over " their heads." In spight of the incommodious length of these weapons, HARRIS tells us, that the Irish usually cast them with such might, as no Haubergeon or coat of mail were proof against their force, but were pierced through on both sides. *Hibern.* p. 52.

I

And many [g] a chief of martial fame,
And prince of mighty sway,
All rang'd beneath our banners came
That memorable day.

Bright waving from its staff, in air,
Gall-grena [h] high was rais'd,
With gems that India's [i] wealth declare,
In radiant pomp it blaz'd.

The

The helmet, the sword, the axe, and the spear, are the only arms with which the poet before us has furnished the Irish troops [*], though to the enemy he has given coats of mail, and shields; and this circumstance so far confirms the most correct ideas that we have been enabled to form of the arms of our ancient countrymen. This, however, does not invalidate the authority and antiquity of other poems, in which we find some of the most distinguished chiefs of the Fenii possessed of shields; not the wicker target, but of metal, and sometimes embossed with gold. These we may very well suppose were trophies borne away from vanquished enemies, and therefore, though we should find them still more frequently mentioned, it would not be a matter of wonder.

[g] The repetition of the word *many* is exactly literal; it had an admirable effect in the original, and, I thought, also, appeared well in an English dress.

[h] *The blazing sun.*—This was the celebrated standard of the Finian general.

[i] The words in the original are clocaıb tıpe anoıp, i. e. precious stones from the country of the east.

[*] Even the target is not mentioned; but this appears only an omission of the poet, for it is certain that it was universally in use amongst the antient Irish.

The next in rank, and next in name,
   Gaul's *Fuillaing-torrigh* [j] rose,
Attendant on its master's fame,
   And dreadful to his foes;

Oft, while the field of death he brav'd,
   Triumphant in his might,
High o'er the ranks its beauty wav'd,
   And led the rage of fight!

At length we mov'd;—then was the shock!
   Then was the battle's roar!
Re echoing shouts from rock to rock
   Resounding, shook the shore!

With tenfold might each nerve was strung;
   Each bosom glow'd with flame!
Each chief exulting, forward sprung,
   And rush'd to promis'd fame!

The foe recoil'd?—fierce on we prest,
   For freedom or for death!—
Each arm to vengeance was addrest,
   And victory gasp'd for breath.

[j] The standard of the tribe of Morni.

Almost the bloody field was won,
  When through the ranks of fight,
Dark Lochlin's king, and Comhal's son,
  Rush'd forth, like flame, to fight.

Round on their falling hosts, their eyes
  With rage and grief they threw;—
Then, swift as bolts from angry skies,
  They fierce to vengeance flew!

Each Chief, with the collected rage
  Of his whole host was fir'd;
And dire was the suspence, O Sage!
  That dreadful fight inspir'd!

As when two sinewy sons of flame
  At the dark anvil meet;
With thundering sound, and ceaseless aim
  Their mighty hammers beat:

Such are the fierce contending kings!
  Such strokes their fury sends;
Such thunder from their weapons rings,
  And sparkling flame ascends!

Dire

Dire was the rending rage of fight,
 And arms that stream'd with gore;
Until dark Lochlin's ebbing might
 Proclaim'd the combat o'er.

Beneath the conq'ring Finn he lay,
 Bound[1] on the blood-stain'd field;
No more to boast his martial sway,
 Or hostile arms to wield.

Then, base of soul, bald Conan spoke—
 " Hold now the King of Spears,
" Till, with one just and vengeful stroke,
 " I ease our future fears!"

" Ungenerous chieftain that thou art!
 (The hapless Magnus cry'd)
" With thee no mercy can have part;
 " No honor can abide!

" Not

---

[1] From this, and many similar passages, it appears that our ancient countrymen, in their martial contests, thirsted rather for honor than for blood. In the heat and confusion of a mixed engagement, numbers were necessarily slaughtered; but, where-ever mercy could be shewn, we find that the conqueror spared the life of even his bitterest enemy, and was content with the honor of laying him " bound on the " field."

" Not for thy favour e'er to call
  " My foul fhall I abafe;
" Beneath a hero's arm I fall,
  " Beneath a hero's grace."

" Since then to me the glory fell
  " Thy valour to fubdue,
" My arm fhall now thy foes repel,
  " Nor injure thofe who fue.

" For thou thyfelf an hero art [m],
  " Though Fortune on thee frown;
" Rife therefore free, and free depart,
  " With unimpair'd renown.

" Or chufe, ftrong arm of powerful might!
  " Chufe, Magnus, now thy courfe:
" With generous foes in peace unite,
  " Or dare again their force.

" Better

---

[m] The ancient Irifh have been repeatedly ftigmatifed with the name of *Barbarians*. Their fouls, their manners, and their language, were thought alike incapable of any degree of refinement. The reader will eafily judge how little of the marks of barbarifm appear in the paffage before us; yet this poem has been the favourite of many centuries; and its antiquity has never been queftioned, though the date cannot be exactly afcertained. Here, however, it may be urged, that we do not contend for its being of prior date to the middle ages. Does *this* then invalidate the proof? and were we lefs barbarians, when torn with civil broils, and foreign invafions, than when we were a conquering and flourifhing people?

" Better our friendship to engage,
" And be in peace ally'd,
" Than thus eternal warfare wage,
" Defying and defy'd."

" O never more my arm, through life,
" Against thee, Finn, shall rife!
" O never such ungrateful strife
" Shall Mchee's son devife!

" And O! that on their hills of snow
" My youths had still remain'd,
" Nor thus against a generous foe
" Unprofperous war maintain'd!

" Exulting in their confcious might,
" And glorying in their fame,
" And gay with spoils of many a fight,
" And flush'd with hope they came!

" (O fad reverfe! O fatal hour!
" In mangl'd heaps to die!)
" Too mighty Erin! to thy power,
" Pale victims, here they lie."

Thus

Thus was the mighty battle won
   On Erin's founding shore;
And thus, O Clerk! great Comhal's son
   The palm of valour bore!

Alas! far sweeter to my ear
   The triumphs of that day,
Than all the psalming songs I hear,
   Where holy zealots pray.

Clerk, thou hast heard me now recite
   The tale of Lochlin's shame,
From whose fierce deeds, and vanquish'd might,
   The battle took its name.

And by that hand, O blameless sage!
   Hadst thou been on the shore,
To see the war our chiefs could wage;
   The sway their prowess bore:—

From Laogare's sweetly flowing stream [a],
   Had'st thou the combat view'd,
The Fenii then thy thoughts would deem
   With matchless force endued.——

                                         Thou

---

[a] In hopes of being able to ascertain the scene of this battle, I have endeavoured to find which of our rivers was anciently called by the name of *Laogare's Stream*, but

Thou haft my tale,—Tho' memory bleeds,
  And forrow waftes my frame,
Still will I tell of former deeds,
  And live on former fame!

Now old,—the ftreams of life congeal'd,
  Bereft of all my joys!
No fword this wither'd hand can wield,
  No fpear my arm employs°.

Among thy clerks, my laft fad hour
  Its weary fcene prolongs;
And pfalms muft now fupply the pow'r
  Of victory's lofty fongs.

but in vain. I can difcover nothing more of it than what the poem points out, that it is near to and within fight of the fea.

° How beautifully pathetic is the clofe of this poem! Surely every reader of fenfibility muft fympathife with a fituation fo melancholy, and fo very feelingly defcribed!

III.

THE CHASE:

A

POEM.

ADVERTISEMENT.

My curiosity respecting the Poem of The Chase, was first awakened by a long extract from it, which I saw in Mr. Walker's Memoirs of the Irish Bards. I accordingly wrote to that Gentleman, to request an entire copy of it, and also his opinion respecting the age in which it was composed; together with any anecdotes upon the subject, which his knowledge of Irish Antiquities might enable him to afford me. To this request I received an answer, from which I have obtained Mr. Walker's permission to give the following extract, as an introduction to the Poem.

" I am happy to find that my work has been the means of intro-
" ducing the Poem of The Chase to your notice. It is indeed eminently
" deserving of the judgment you have passed upon it. The story is ex-
" tremely interesting, and admirably well conducted; and for brilliancy
" of fancy, and powers of description, we may almost rank the author
" with Ariosto himself."

" I am sorry I cannot afford you all the information I could wish
" upon the subject of this beautiful Poem: indeed I have little more to
" offer than vague conjecture."

" The legend which either gave rise to, or was taken from the Poem
" of The Chase, is frequently alluded to, in many of the written, as
" well

" well as traditional tales of the Irish. It is also ingeniously interwoven
" with the romance of Feṛ τιξϵ Canajn. Of its antiquity I cannot
" speak with any certainty; all my enquiries concerning the author, and
" the age in which it was written, have been unsuccessful. Nor can
" we give it (at least in its present dress,) either to Oisin, or to any
" other poet of the age in which he lived. The marks of a classical
" hand appear frequently throughout the whole; and the mention of
" bells also seem to bring it forward to more modern times; so that
" I fear we should risk an error in ascribing it to any period earlier than
" the middle ages."

" I have never had an opportunity of visiting the scene of this
" Poem, though I often saw Slieve Guillen, at some distance, as I
" travelled through the county of Armagh. But a friend, whose
" business often leads him to that mountain, drew up, at my request, the
" following description of it, in which you will find mention of the
" lake where the poet tells us the gallant Finn paid so dearly for
" his complaisance, when he fought the Enchantress's ring; and also
" of the cave whence she issued, when pressed by the Finian heroes to
" restore their beloved chief to his pristine form."

' I am tenant to a lady for Slieve Guillen, (says my correspondent,)
' and often visit it, during the summer, to see my cattle. In July last,
' (1788) I went over the extent of this mountain: From bottom to top it
' is reckoned two miles. On the summit there is a large heap of stones,
' which is called CAILLEACH Birrn's House; in which it is said that
' Finn Mac Cumhal lies buried; and, at an hundred paces distance, on

' nearly

' nearly the same level, there is a circular lake, the diameter of which
' is about one hundred feet ; and is about twenty deep. On one side of
' this lake, another heap of stones is piled ; and round it, at all fea-
' sons, is a beaten path, leading to the Old Lady's, or Witch's House.
' Lately, some peasants, expecting to find out this old woman, (who,
' however, has at no time thought proper to appear,) threw down her
' house, and came to a large cave, about twenty feet long, ten broad,
' and five deep, covered with large flags, in which either the dame,
' or money was expected, but only a few human bones were found.
' From the summit of this mountain, if the day happens to be clear, you
' command an extensive view of Lough-Neagh, and all the circum-
' jacent country.'

Mr. Walker, *after this description of the mountain by his friend,
adds his regret that he was not possessed of a complete copy of* The
Chase ; *but I afterwards procured one from* Maurice Gorman, *of
this city (a professor of the Irish language), and from that copy I have
made my translation.*

THE CHASE:

A POEM.

[a] OISIN.   ST. PATRICK.

OISIN.   O SON of Calphruin!—sage divine!
Soft voice of heavenly song,
Whose notes around the holy shrine
Sweet melody prolong;

Did

---

[a] There are numberless Irish poems still extant, attributed to Oisin, and either addressed to St. Patrick, or like this, composed in the form of a dialogue between the Saint and the Poet. In all of them, the antiquary discovers traces of a later period than that in which Oisin flourished; and most of them are supposed to be the compositions of the eighth, ninth and tenth centuries. But be they of what age they may, as productions abounding with numberless beauties, they plead for preservation, and recommend themselves to taste: and as, (at the very latest period to which it is possible to ascribe them,) they must certainly relate to an age of much antiquity,

Did e'er my tale thy curious ear
   And fond attention draw,
The story of that Chase to hear,
   Which my fam'd father saw?

The Chase, which singly o'er the plain,
   The hero's steps pursu'd;
Nor one of all his valiant train
   Its wond'rous progress view'd.

PATRICK.   O royal bard, to valour dear,
   Whom fame and wisdom grace,
It never was my chance to hear
   That memorable Chase.

But let me now, O bard, prevail!
   Now let the song ascend;
And, thro' the wonders of the tale,
   May truth thy words attend!

OISIN.

and reflect much light on manners, customs and events that, in consequence of modern pyrrhonism, have been doubted to have ever existed, they surely have a high and serious claim to attention, and call equally upon the poet, the historian, and the public-spirited, to preserve these reliques of ancient genius amongst us! But *Irishmen* —all of them at least who would be thought to pride themselves in the name, or to reflect back any part of the honor they derive from it;—*they* are *particularly* called upon, in favour of their country, to rescue these little sparks from the ashes of her former glory.

OISIN.   O Patrick!—to the Finian race
              A falsehood was unknown;
           No lie, no imputation base
              On our clear fame was thrown;

           But by firm truth, and manly might
              That fame establish'd grew,
           Where oft, in honorable fight [b],
              Our foes before us flew.

           Not thy own clerks, whose holy feet
              The sacred pavement trod,
           With thee to hymn, in concert sweet,
              The praises of thy God;

           Not thy own clerks in truth excell'd
              The heroes of our line,
           By honor train'd, by fame impell'd
              In glory's fields to shine!

           O Patrick of the placid mien,
              And voice of sweetest sound!
           Of all thy church's walls contain
              Within their hallow'd round,

---

[b] The heroes of ancient Ireland were sworn never to attack an enemy at any disadvantage. O'HALLORAN.

Not one more faithful didst thou know
Than Comhal's noble son,
The chief who gloried to bestow
The prize the bards had won [c]!

Were Morni's valiant son [d] alive,
(Now in the deedless grave,)
O could my wish from death revive
The generous and the brave!

[c] In all these poems, the character of Oisin is so inimitably well supported, that we lose the idea of any other bard, and are for a time persuaded it is Oisin himself who speaks. We do not seem to read a narration of events, wherein the writer was neither a witness, nor a party:—it is the *Son,*—the *Father,*—the *Hero,*—the *Patriot* who speaks; who breathes his own passions and feelings on our hearts, and compels our sympathy to accompany all his griefs; while, in a strain of natural and impassioned eloquence, he descants on the fame and virtues of a parent whom he describes as at once so amiable, and so great; and bewails the loss of all his former friends, kindred, and companions, and laments his own forlorn and disconsolate state, in apostrophes that pierce the very soul of pity!—Besides passages which occur in this, and the two poems of MAGNUS and MOIRA BORB, the agallam oisin ⁊ patruig exhibits a very pathetic instance, where, lamenting the loss of his father and his celebrated Fenii, he exclaims, " To survive them is my depth of woe! the banquet and " the song have now no charms for me! Wretched and old.—the poor solitary rem- " nant of the Fenii! Why,—O why am I yet alive?—Alas, O Patrick! grievous is my " state!—the last of all my race!—My heroes are gone! my strength is gone!— " Bells I now hear, for the songs of my birds; and age, blindness and woe are all " that remain of Oisin!"

[d] The celebrated Goll, or Gaul Mac Morni. He is a favourite hero, in most of the Fian tales; and is in general ranked next to Finn Mac-Cumhal, and equal to Osgur, in point of prowess. Great as is Oisin's partiality in favour of the heroes of his own race, yet we find him, on all occasions, doing ample justice to the cha-

racter

Or Mac-O'Dhuivne[e], graceful form,
　Joy of the female fight;
The hero who would breast the storm,
　And dare the unequal fight.

Or he whose sword the ranks defy'd,
　Mac-Garra, conquest's boast,
Whose valour would a war decide,
　His single arm an host[f],

Or could Mac-Ronan[g] now appear,
　In all his manly charms;
Or—Oh my Osgur[h]! wert thou here,
　To fill my aged arms!

Not

racter and valour of a chief, who was not allied to his family, and whose tribe had even, at different times, been their very bitterest enemies.

[e] Diarmad, or Dermot Mac O'Dhuivne. This hero was celebrated for his extraordinary beauty, and the graces of his form:—but we find he was not less brave than beautiful.

[f] Possibly this was the Mac Garraidh Mac Morni, king of Connaught, mentioned in the War-Ode to Osgur at the battle of Gabhra. His having been, at that time, the enemy of the Fenii, would not be a reason sufficient to prevent the poet from making Oisin speak thus highly of him here;—on the contrary, the Irish heroes were instructed, from their youth, to respect a brave enemy; and made it a point of honor to speak of them in honorable terms. It is very seldom that an instance to the contrary occurs, as the attentive reader will perceive, through the whole course of these poems.

[g] Caoilte Mac Ronain; he is a very distinguished chief amongst the Fenii, and a favourite with all their poets.

[h] Osgur, the son of Oisin, who was killed at the battle of Gabhra.

Not then, as now, should Calphruin's son,
   His sermons here prolong;
With bells, and psalms, the land o'er-run,
   And hum his holy song!

If Fergus[i] liv'd, again to sing,
   As erst, the Fenii's fame;
Or Daire[k], who sweetly touch'd the string,
   And thrill'd the feeling frame;

Your bells, for me, might sound in vain,
   Did Hugh the little, live[l];
Or Fallan's[m] generous worth remain,
   The ceaseless boon to give;

                                          Or

---

[i] Fergus, the brother of Oisin, and chief poet of the Fenii. See *Diss. on the* WAR-ODE.

[k] We find nothing particular related of this Daire, further than his skill in music. This enchanting science, as well as poetry, was cultivated by the chiefs of antient Ireland.

[l] Hugh, or Aodh beag Mac-Finn.

[m] We meet this hero again, in the poem of Magnus.

Or Conan bald [n], tho' oft his tongue
    To rage provok'd my breaſt;
Or Finn's ſmall dwarf [o], whoſe magic ſong
    Oft lull'd the ranks to reſt.

Sweeter to me their voice would ſeem
    Than thy pſalm-ſinging train;
And nobler far their lofty theme,
    Than that thy clerks maintain!

PATRICK. Ceaſe thy vain thoughts, and fruitleſs boaſts;
    Can death thy chiefs reſtore?—
Son of the King of mighty hoſts,
    Their glories are no more.

---

[n] For the character of Conan, ſee the notes on the preceding poem.

[o] It is not eaſy to determine whether the poet, here, only means, that this dwarf had a voice of that particular cadence, as naturally to incline his hearers to ſleep; or whether he means to aſcribe to him the actual powers of magic. Upon the ſubject of the dwarf, I have only conjecture to offer. In the learned and curious work of Monſ. MALLET, we find that, amongſt the nations of the North, the Laplanders were conſidered as dwarfs, on account of the comparative lowneſs of their ſtature; and alſo, that their extreme ingenuity in the mechanic arts, which a diſpoſition of mind, naturally pacific, gave them leiſure and inclination to purſue, had acquired them the reputation of being ſkilled in magic. Perhaps the little Being here mentioned might have been one of thoſe. Oiſin, we ſee, piqued at the inſinuation of St. Patrick, takes pains to ſhew him, that, from the firſt of the heroes, down to the laſt; even the very dwarf that belonged to Finn, was dearer, and more acceptable to him than he was.

Confide in him whose high decree
    O'er-rules all earthly power;
And bend to him thy humble knee,
    To him devote thy hour;

And let thy contrite prayer be made
    To him who rules above;
Entreat for his almighty aid,
    For his protecting love!

Tho' (with thy perverse will at strife,)
    Thou deem'st it strange to say,
He gave thy mighty father life,
    And took that life away.

OISIN. Alas! thy words sad import bear,
    And grating sounds impart;
They come with torture to mine ear,
    And anguish to my heart!

Not for *thy* God these torrents spring,
    That drain their weeping source,
But that my Father, and my King,
    Now lies a lifeless corse!

Too much I have already done,
  Thy Godhead's smile to gain;
That thus each wonted joy I shun,
  And with thy clerks remain!

The royal robe, the social board,
  Musick and mirth are o'er,
And the dear art I once ador'd
  I now enjoy no more;

For now no bards, from Oisin's hand,
  The wonted gift receive [p];
Nor hounds, nor horn I now command,
  Nor martial feats atchieve!

O Innisfail!

[p] All Irish Histories, Chronicles and Poems, concur in testimony of the high respect in which the office of the Bard, and the favours of the Muse, were formerly held in this kingdom. Oisin, at once a Hero and a Bard, is supposed to have felt equally for both; as a Bard, to have felt the dignity and importance of those talents, which had power to confer the immortality of fame, that, as a Hero, he so ardently desired. We, therefore, are not to wonder if we find him frequently recurring with a pleased, yet melancholy retrospection, to those happy days, when he joined, to the luxury of bestowing, the glory of encouraging an art, of which he was himself a master.

O Innisfail! thy Oisin goes
To guard thy ports no more [q];
To pay with death the foreign foes
Who dare insult thy shore [r]!

I speak

[q] Dr. HAMMER, in his Chronicle, gives us a long list of the chieftains, under the command of Finn-Mac-Cumal, *[Cumhal]* who were particularly appointed to the care of the harbours of Ireland; at the end of which he adds, " These were the chiefe commanders " by direction from Fin M'Koyll, who tooke farther order that beacons should be set " up in sundrie places of the land, where, in time of danger, they might have " direction for reliefe, and to draw a head for their defence.

[r] We find Oisin, in this passage, does not appear so old, or so infirm, as he is represented in many other of the Fian Poems; on the contrary, he laments—not his inability—but the religious restraints which detain him from the field. Perhaps the poet here means to shew the over strained zeal of the early Christian missionaries, who, finding the Irish chiefs so passionately devoted to military glory; so haughty, high spirited and impatient of injury; thought it impossible ever to bow their minds to the doctrine of meekness, without carrying it absolutely to an extreme, that exceeded the reasonable bounds prescribed by its divine Teacher. They were, however, successful:—the same enthusiasm that led our heroes to the field, soon after plunged them into cloisters. Still it was a sense of duty; the object only was changed; through an unhappy error, they thought themselves performing an acceptable service to heaven, by contradicting the very purposes for which heaven designed them; by refusing to fulfil the obligations of active life, and withdrawing alike from the spheres of domestic and public duty, to devote themselves to the austerities of secluded penitence, productive only of *individual*, instead of *general* advantage. Still, however, they were impelled by an ardour to perform, in its fullest extent, that service which they conceived to be their duty; and therefore, for the consequences of such a mistake, they were more to be pitied than condemned.

Of the same nature were the motives that influenced the hosts of Israel (considering only the *letter* of the law,) to submit themselves tamely to the swords of their enemies, rather than defend their lives, at the hazard of offending heaven, by what,

they

  I speak not of the fast severe
  Thy rigid faith has taught;
  Compar'd with all the rest I bear,
  It is not worth a thought.

PATRICK. O! Oisin of the mighty deed!
  Thy folly I deplore;
  O! cease thy frenzy thus to feed,
  And give the subject o'er.

---

they conceived, would be a breach of the sabbath day. But Mattathias, and his heroic sons, more enlightened—not less religious than their mistaken countrymen, stood forth and said, " If we all do as our brethren have done, and fight not for our " lives and our laws, against the heathen; they will now quickly root us out of " the earth. Whoever shall come to make battle with us, on the sabbath day, we " will fight against him; neither will we die all, as did our brethren!"—And the consequence was, that " the work prospered in their hands, and they recovered the law " out of the hands of the Gentiles, and out of the hands of Kings, and suffered " not sinners to triumph." *Maccabees*, b. 1. ch. 2.

 But the Irish, less instructed in the *spirit* of true religion than the sons of Israel had been, did not so soon perceive, and recover from their error; an error to which, Mr. O'HALLORAN thinks, we may in part attribute the success of Danish invasions, and of English arms in Ireland; for, while such numbers of their princes and chiefs abandoned the government, and the defence of their country, for the barren duties of a cloister, the remaining patriots, who said, " Let us fight for our lives and our laws " against the heathen," were not always sufficient to the task. Those of their princes and nobility, who were led away by a noble, but unhappy mistake, had they entertained the true sense of what Christian duty demanded, would have been the bravest defenders, the firmest friends of their country; but, deprived of them, she remained, for the most part, a prey to foreign invaders; or else, torn by the tumults of her own factious sons,—too few of her nobler offspring remaining for her defence.

Nor Finn, nor all the Finian race,
 Can with his power compare,
Who to yon orbs affigns their place,
 And rules the realms of air!

For man yon azure vault he fpreads,
 And clothes the flow'ry plains;
On every tree foft fragrance fheds,
 And blooming fruit ordains!

'Tis he who gives the peopl'd ftream,
 Replete with life to flow;
Who gives the Moon's refplendant beam,
 And Sun's meridian glow!

Would'ft thou thy puny King compare
 To that Almighty hand,
Which form'd fair earth, and ambient air,
 And bade their powers expand?

OISIN.   It was not on a fruit or flower
 My King his care beftow'd;
He better knew to fhew his power
 In honor's glorious road.

To load with death the hoſtile field;
In blood, his might proclaim;
Our land with wide protection ſhield,
And wing to heaven his fame!

In peace, his tranquil hours to bleſs,
Beneath ſoft beauty's eye;
Or, on the chequer'd field of cheſs [s],
The mimic fight to try;

Or

---

[s] Fjċċjll, is the Iriſh name for Cheſs. "I have not been able to find the Iriſh names of the *men* of this game, but it was univerſally played by the ancient nobility of Ireland. Dr. HYDE ſays, the old Iriſh were ſo greatly addicted to cheſs, that, amongſt them, the poſſeſſion of good eſtates has been often decided by it: and, adds he, there are ſome eſtates, at this very time, the property whereof ſtill depends upon the iſſue of a game at cheſs. For example, the heirs of two certain noble Iriſh families, whom we could name, (to ſay nothing of others,) hold their lands upon this tenure, viz. that one of them ſhall encounter the other at cheſs, in this manner; that which ever of them conquered, ſhould ſeize and poſſeſs the eſtate of the other. Therefore, (ſays the doctor,) I am told they manage the affair prudently among themſelves; once a year they meet, by appointment, to play at cheſs; one of them makes a move, and the other ſays, I will conſider how to anſwer you next year. This being done, a public notary commits to writing the ſituation of the game; by which method, a game that neither has won, has been, and will be continued for ſome hundred of years.

"I find, in the old BREHON LAWS, that one tax, levied by the Monarch of Ireland, on every province, was to be paid in cheſs-boards, and complete ſets of men: and that every *bruigh* (or inn-holder of the ſtates,) was obliged to furniſh travellers with ſalt proviſions, lodging, and a cheſs-board, *gratis*." VALLANCEY's *Iriſh Grammar, Eſſay on the Celtic Lang.* p. 85.

Or Sylvan sports [t], that well beseem
    The martial and the brave;
Or, plung'd amid the rapid stream,
    His manly limbs to lave.

But, when the rage of battle bled !———
    Then—then his might appear'd,
And o'er red heaps of hostile dead
    His conquering standard rear'd !

Where was thy God, on that sad day,
    When, o'er Ierne's wave,
Two heroes plough'd the wat'ry way,
    Their beauteous prize to save ?

From Lochlin's King of Ships, his bride,
    His lovely Queen they bore,
Through whom unnumber'd warriors dy'd,
    And bath'd in blood our shore [u].

Or

---

[t] See O'Conor's *Dissertations*, p. 101.

[u] A note for this passage was furnished from Laoɼò Aiɼʒeaɲ móiɼ, (i. e. the Poem of Airgean the Great) in the collection of J. C. Walker, Esq; the story of which is briefly this.

Two heroes, (Mac-Connacher and Ainle,) were forgotten by Finn at his feast: They resented the neglect of their chief, deserted from his standard, and went over to that of his enemy, Airgean, King of Lochlin.

Or on that day, when Tailk's [x] proud might
Invaded Erin's coaſt;
Where was thy Godhead in that fight,
And where thy empty boaſt?

While

The graceful beauty of Ainlè's form, inſpiring the young Queen of Lochlin with a guilty and fatal paſſion, ſhe fled with him and his friend to Ireland, whither they were purſued by the furious King, who determined, if poſſible, to ſacrifice all the Fenii, for the crime of a ſingle hero. The poet expreſsly tells us, that Finn would have compelled the guilty pair to make all the reparation which the nature of the caſe would admit of; and further, offered from himſelf ſuch conditions of peace, as he thought might prevent the neceſſity of his fighting in ſo diſhonorable a cauſe:—but his overtures were rejected with diſdain, and he was conſtrained to the iſſue of a battle. The ſlaughter on each ſide was dreadful; the Iriſh, in the end, were victorious. Ainlè himſelf was killed in the engagement; but the poet does not deign to take any further notice of the unhappy partner of his crimes.

[x] Tailk or Taile Mac Trein.—A Poem on this ſubject is in the ſame collection with that of *Airgean the Great*; there is alſo another copy of it, entitled ⱅⱁⱍⱅⱁ ⱍⱀⱁⱌ ⱇⱁⱃⱅ (i. e. the Poem of the Hill of Slaughter). It contains ſome beauties, but, upon the whole, is ſcarce worth tranſlation. The ſtory, however, is here extracted, to gratify any curioſity that may be excited by the line to which this note refers.

A Grecian Princeſs flies, in diſguſt, from the brave, but fierce and deformed Tailk Mac Trein, whom her father had compelled her to marry, and ſolicits the protection of the Finian commander. He grants it, of courſe, but his generoſity coſts him dear. Tailk purſues his wife, and fights the Fians, who refuſe to give her up to him. After an incredible ſlaughter, he is at length ſubdued, and killed by Oſgur, the grandſon of Finn.

The Princeſs beholds the havoc ſhe has occaſioned, and overcome by the emotions of grief, terror, and ſuſpence, which ſhe had ſuffered, during the conflict, and ſhocked to ſee the numbers of her generous protectors, that had fallen in her defence, ſhe ſinks beneath the preſſure of her feelings, and expires in the midſt of her ſurviving deliverers.

While round the bravest Fenii bled,
  No help did he bestow;
'Twas Osgur's arm aveng'd the dead,
  And gave the glorious blow!

Where was thy God, when Magnus came [y]?
  Magnus the brave, and great;
The man of might, the man of fame,
  Whose threat'ning voice was fate!

Thy Godhead did not aid us then;—
  If such a God there be,
He should have favour'd gallant men,
  As great and good as he!

Fierce Anninir's wide-wasting son,
  Allean [z], of dreadful fame,
Who Tamor's treasures oft had won,
  And wrapt her walls in flame;

Not by thy God, in single fight,
  The deathful hero fell;
But by Finn's arm, whose matchless might
  Could ev'ry force repel!

---

[y] Vide Poem of *Magnus the Great*.

[z] No connected, or probable account, has been learned of this hero, and his conquests.

  In ev'ry mouth *his* fame we meet,
   Well known, and well believ'd;—
  I have not heard of any feat
   Thy cloudy King atchiev'd.

PATRICK. Drop we our speech on either side,
   Thou bald and senseless fool [a]!
  In torments all thy race abide [b],
   While God in heaven shall rule.

OISIN.

[a] It must be owned, this railing is rather of the coarsest; but our poet seems more partial to his heroes than to his saints, or he would hardly have put this language into the mouth of the good bishop.

[b] In the *Agallam Oiṡ,ṅ ⁊ Pádruig* (i. e. Dialogue between Oisin and St. Patrick), the Saint gives his reason for supposing what he here asserts.

 P. Iṡ aingeall le meadair na ccon,
   S'le ṗiaṡ na ṡluaġ gaċ lá,
  Aguṡ gan ṡmuaineaḋ ar Ḋia,
  Atá Fjon na bḟjan alaṡiṅ.

  Tá ṡe niġriġoṅ alaṡiṅ,
  An ḟear buḋ ṡaiṅ ag broṅaḋ oir.
  A neiṁe easuṁubaiṡ air Ḋia,
  Tá ṡe attiġ na bpiaṅ ṡa broṅ.

In English,—" It is because his whole time, and delight, were engrossed by the plea-
" sures of the chase, and the pomp of warlike hosts; and because he never bestowed a
" thought upon God, that Finn of the Fenii is in thraldom.—He is now confined in
               " torment;

OISIN.   If God then rules, why is the chief
          Of Comhal's gen'rous race
          To fiends confign'd, without relief
          From juftice, or from grace?

          When, were thy God himfelf confin'd,
          My King, of mild renown,
          Would quickly all his chains unbind,
          And give him back his crown.

For

" torment; nor does all his wealth, or generofity avail him, for the want of piety to-
" wards God:—for this he is now in forrow, in the Manfion of Pain."

To thefe lines, immediately follows a paffage, that very much refembles this part of *The Chafe.*

Da maireaḋ faolan, aguf Goll,
Djarmujd don, aguf Ofgur aiġ,
Aġ tṙine, no aġ Dja
Ni beiṫ fjon na byjan alajm!

Da maireaḋ clanna Mojrne ftiġ,
No clanna baoifġne fir ba tṙean,
Do beartſif fjon amaċ,
No beiṫ an teaċ aca fein!

In Englifh,—" If Fallan and Gaul now furvived, Dermot of the dark-brown
" locks, and Ofgur of the mighty arm;—nor man,—no nor even Deity, fhould have
" power to detain their King in bondage!——If the tribe of Morni yet lived, or the
" heroes of Boifhne's gallant race;—forth from thence their mighty Finn would they
" bring, or rend the infernal dominion from its immortal ruler!"

For never did his generous breast
Reject the feeling glow;
Refuse to succour the distrest,
Or slight the captive's woe.

His ransom loos'd the prisoner's chains,
And broke the dire decree;
Or, with his hosts, on glory's plains,
He fought to set them free [c]!

O Patrick! were I senseless grown,
Thy holy clerks should bleed,
Nor one be spar'd, to pour his moan
O'er the avenging deed!

Nor books, nor crosiers should be found,
Nor ever more a bell [d],
Within thy holy walls should sound,
Where prayers and zealots dwell.

---

[c] What a beautiful idea of the character of Finn, these wild stanzas convey?

[d] "Small bells, (such, we mean, as were appended to the tunic of the Jewish
"high priest, and afterwards employed by the Greeks and Romans, for various reli-
"gious purposes, but particularly to frighten ghosts and demons from their temples,)
"—were undoubtedly introduced with Christianity into this kingdom; being then
"universally, as now, tingled occasionally at the altars of the Roman Catholics, by
"the officiating priest. Their use amongst the Christian clergy is supposed to be
"coeval

PATRICK. O Oisin, of the royal race!
The actions of thy sire,
The king of smiles, and courteous grace,
I, with the world, admire;

Thy

" coeval with their religion; and the missionaries who were sent to convert the
" pagan Irish, would not omit bringing with them an appendage of their profession
" which is still thought so necessary.

" But the period at which large bells, for belfries, were first used here, is not so
" easy to determine. Primate Usher informs us, that bells were used in the churches
" of Ireland in the latter end of the seventh century; but as he does not ascertain
" the size of the bells, nor mention belfries, we may conclude he only means the
" small bells alluded to above. Sir John Hawkins, on the authority of Polyd.
" Virgil, ascribes the above invention of such bells as are suspended in the towers,
" or steeples of churches, to Paulinus of Nola, about the year 400; but W. Strabo
" assures us, that large suspended bells were in his time (in the ninth century) but
" a late invention. Now, as the persecuted Christians, in the infancy of the church,
" dared not openly avow their profession, much less publicly summon a congregation
" by the sound of a bell, we are inclined to lean to Strabo's assurance; so that we
" cannot venture to give an higher antiquity to large suspended bells in this kingdom,
" than the calm which immediately succeeded the expulsion of the Danes; at which
" time, according to Walsh, the Christian clergy converted the round towers into
" steeple-houses, or belfries; ' from which latter use of them (continues he,) it is, that
' ever since, to this present time, they are called, in Irish, *Cloghteachs*; that is,
' belfries, or bell-houses, *cloc* and *clog* signifying a bell, and *teach*, a house, in
' that language." *Hist. Mem. of the Irish Bards*, p. 93.

Of the large suspended bell, Mr. WALKER certainly supposes the poet to speak, when
he says, that " the mention of bells seems to bring the poem forward to more modern
" times." But this gentleman, not having the original of the passage now before us to
consult, did not perfectly recollect the precise words that must determine the distinction.
There is not the least mention of a steeple or belfry;—the words are simply
these—no clog na trát an do éill (literally) " nor a bell of prayer time in
" thy church;" Trát is in the genitive case, yet I conceive that it must mean
" a bell *at* prayer time," (*of* or *during the* time of prayer). The reader is, however,
at liberty to decide.

> Thy ſtory therefore I await,
>   And thy late promiſe claim,
> The Chaſe's wonders to relate,
>   And give the tale to fame.

OISIN.
> O Patrick! tho' my ſorrowing heart
>   Its fond remembrance rend,
> I will not from my word depart,
>   Howe'er my tears deſcend!

> Full joyous paſt the feſtive day
>   In Almhain's ſtately hall ᵉ,
> Whoſe ſpears, with ſtudded ſplendours gay,
>   Illum'd the trophy'd wall.

The

ᵉ Almhain, or Almhuin (pronounced Alwin) the palace of Finn Mac-Cumhal, in Leinſter: It was built on the top of the hill called, from it, "The Hill of Allen," in the county of Kildare.

In the *Oiſle Oiſin* (i. e. Rhapſody of Oiſin) wherein he gives an account of the ſeven celebrated battalions of the Fenii, there is a paſſage, partly deſcriptive of the palace of Almhain, its œconomy, feaſts, &c.

> Do conairc ſe mo ṫiġ,
> aiġe ſion ſe ġaċ nol,
> deiċ cceᴅ copn ġo byleaġ
> ſo na ccneaſriḃ oſir.

Do

The feaft was for the Fenii fpread [r];
Their chiefs, affembled round,
Heard the fong rife to praife the dead,
And fed their fouls with found.

Or

*Do bí da bṗnġṁ deaġ
ṡa leḃp aṁeao aṅouṅ.
aġ mac ṁġṁe ċajoṡ,
O aliṁojṁ na bẏjaṁ up.*

*Do bí da ṡé ċejṁce
ġo cjṁce aṁ ṡġaċ cjġ,
ṡeap 7 ceao ġaṁ ġaṁe
ṡa ġaċ cejṁe ḋjob ṡjṁ.*

In Englifh,—" I have feen, when I banqueted in the halls of Finn, at every
" banquet, a thoufand cups, (copṁ) bound with wreaths of wrought gold.

" There were twelve palaces, filled with the troops of the fon of the daughter of
" Tages, at Almhain of the noble Fenii.

" Twelve conftant fires flamed in each princely houfe; and each fire was fur-
" rounded by an hundred of the mighty Fenii."

Many of our romances, and poems, give accounts of fplendid entertainments at
this palace of Almhain.

[r] In this defcription of the feaft at Almhain, the poet accords exactly with the
accounts which our hiftory and annals have given, of the manner in which the early
Irifh held their entertainments. See O'Conor on this fubject. " Conformable
" (fays he) to the fpirit of hofpitality, their entertainments were frequent, and
" rational; feldom diforderly. Every fubject of the *Fileacht* entered into their con-
" vivial affociations; peace, and war; fcience, and law; government, and morals.
" Thefe ferious fpeculations gave way, in their turn, to fports and paftimes, wherein
" they fung the actions of their anceftors, and the exploits of their heroes. Nothing
" could

Or on the chequer'd fields of chefs
  Their mimic troops beftow'd;
Or round, to merit or diftrefs,
  Their ample bounty flow'd.

At length, unnotic'd of his train,
  The Finian king [g] arofe,
And forth he went where Almhain's plain
  With neighbouring verdure glows.

There, while alone the hero chanc'd
  To breathe the fragrant gale,
A young and beauteous doe advanc'd,
  Swift bounding o'er the vale.

He call'd his fleet and faithful hounds,
  The doe's light fteps to trace;
Sgeolan and Bran [h] obey'd the founds,
  And fprung upon the chafe.

                                                  Unknown

"could animate their youth more. From thefe recitations they derived intrepidity of mind, and many noble feelings, which counteracted the treachery and malevolence to which our human nature is otherwife fubject." O'Conor's *Differtations on the Hift. of Ireland*, p. 100.

[g] Finn was not a king, though, indeed, few kings were poffeffed of more authority and power. Ríg na bFían (king of the Fenii,) means no more than general, or military fovereign over that formidable body.

[h] Sgeolan, and Brann, were the two famed and favourite dogs of Finn.

Unknown to us, no friend to aid,
 Or to behold the deed;
His dogs alone, and Luno's blade [i],
 Companions of his speed.

Swift on to steep Slieve Guillin's foot [k],
 The doe before him flew;
But there, at once, she mock'd pursuit,
 And vanish'd from his view!

He knew not whether east or west
 She past the mountain's bounds,
But east his random course he prest,
 And west his eager hounds!

At

[i] In the original, Mac an Luin, (the son of Luno). This sword, tradition tells us, was made by a smith of Lochlin, named Luno, and therefore it was called after him, poetically, the son of Luno. What makes this account the more probable is, that we do not find the swords of the Irish heroes distinguished by names, as amongst those of the northern nations, and also of ancient Britain.

Anecdotes have been sought for, in vain, of this famous Lun, or Luno; but, from the wonders recited, of the product of his art, it seems probable that he was one of those people, whom the Norwegians denominated dwarfs, and complimented with the reputation of Magic. See *Northern Antiquities*, vol. ii. p. 46.

"Give me out of the tomb, (says Hervor) the hardened sword, *which the dwarfs made* for Suafurlama." *Five Pieces of Run. Poetry*, p. 13.

[k] Here the muse has led our poet and his hero a very long dance indeed; and so beguiled the way with the melody of her song, that he appears to have been quite insensible of the distance between Almhain in Leinster, and Slieve Guillin in Ulster, and in the county of Armagh.

At length he ftopp'd,—he look'd around,
    To fee the doe appear;
When foft diftrefs, with plaintive found,
    Affail'd his gentle ear.

The plaintive found, quick to his breaſt,
    With wonted influence fped;
And on he follow'd in its queſt,
    Till to Lough-Shieve it led.

There he beheld a weeping fair,
    Upon a bank reclin'd,
In whofe fine form, and graceful air,
    Was every charm combin'd.

On her foft cheek, with tender bloom [1],
    The rofe its tint beſtow'd;
And in her richer lip's perfume,
    The ripen'd berry glow'd.

---

[1] The Iriſh poets, both antient and modern, abound, and excel in defcriptions of female beauty. The one before us, though exquifitely charming, is not *fingly* fo; for the collection of fongs, contained in this volume, exhibit many inſtances of the fame fpecies of excellence; and many more are to be found in other fongs and poems, in the Iriſh language.

Her neck was as the blossom fair,
 Or like the cygnet's breast,
With that majestic, graceful air,
 In snow and softness drest:

Gold gave its rich and radiant die,
 And in her tresses flow'd [m];
And like a freezing star, her eye
 With Heaven's own splendour glow'd [n].

Thyself, O Patrick! hadst thou seen
 The charms that face display'd;
That tender form, and graceful mein,
 Thyself had lov'd the maid!

My

---

[m] A learned friend remarked, on this passage, that the poet here drew from his store of Eastern imagery, for that golden hair was unknown in these cold climates. It is certain that the mention of yellow, or golden hair, though it sometimes occurs, yet is not very common in the descriptions of our poets;—the " fair waving tresses" are most general; sometimes we are told of " hair like the raven's wing," and often of locks " of shining brown," which, from the brightness ascribed along with the colour, we may conclude to have been auburn.

[n] For this description of eyes, the poet has indeed left our world—and every one in it—far behind him.

In one of CAROLAN's songs, composed for Miss Mary O'Neil, he has given the following beautiful simile, which, though indeed not equal to the above, is yet well entitled to preservation.—" Her eyes (says he) are, to her face, what a diamond is " to a ring, throwing its beams around, and adorning the beauty of the setting."

My king approach'd the gentle fair,
   The form of matchless grace.——
" Hast thou, sweet maid of golden hair!
   " Beheld my hounds in chafe?"

" Thy chafe, O king, was not my care;
   " I nothing of it know;
" Far other thoughts my bosom share,
   " The thoughts, alas, of woe!"

" Is it the husband of thy youth,
   " O fair-one, that has died?
" Or has an infant pledge of truth
   " Been torn from thy soft side?

" White-handed mourner! speak the grief
   " That causes thy distress;
" And, if it will admit relief,
   " Thou may'st command redress°."

° We cannot too much admire the elegance and delicacy of this address!—Such tender refinement could not surely have existed amongst a nation of barbarians. The character of the Finian commander appears uniformly the same in all the Irish poems; and whether our bards, when they gave it, drew a faithful picture, or not, it is still a proof that they must have had *some* good and perfect models before them, to shew what Nature ought to be; since, in their favourite character, we see all the mildness and tenderness of female disposition, united with the ardour of the warrior, the firmness of the patriot, and the calmness of the philosopher. In the son of Comhal we see every quality that is either interesting, amiable, or great.

"Alas, my ring, for whose dear sake
 "These ceaseless tears I shed,
"Fell from my finger in the lake!"
(The soft-hair'd virgin said).

"Let me conjure thee [p], generous king!
 "Compassionate as brave,
"Find for me now my beauteous ring,
 "That fell beneath the wave!"

Scarce was the soft entreaty made,
 Her treasure to redeem,
When his fair form he disarray'd,
 And plung'd into the stream.

At

---

[p] It has been already shewn that, amongst the ancient Irish, each knight was bound, by his military vows, to the protection and respectful service of the fair: this is expressly recorded by our history; and our poetry and romances throw further light on the subject. According to them, no danger or difficulty was to deter an hero from the assistance of a distressed female, and her request was to be á law.

In the romance of ᚛ᚐᚅ ᚈᚔᚌᚓ ᚉᚐᚅᚐᚔᚅ᚜, where the story of this poem is related, Finn tells his chieftains, that he had a kind of instinctive horror at the thoughts of entering that lake; yet he instantly obeyed the injunction of the damsel, "for (says he) "it was a matter that no hero could refuse." Many similar instances of this respect and devotion to the fair occur in our old romances and poems.

At the white-handed fair's requeſt,
 Five times the lake he try'd;
On ev'ry ſide his ſearch addreſs'd,
 Till he the ring deſcry'd.

But when he ſought the blooming maid,
 Her treaſure to reſtore;
His powers were gone,—he ſcarce could wade
 To reach the neareſt ſhore!

That form where ſtrength and beauty met,
 To conquer, or engage,
Paid, premature, its mournful debt
 To grey and palſied age^q.

While

---

^q Our Iriſh poets inform us that Finn was married extremely young; yet even ſo, he muſt have been advanced in life at this period, ſince we find his grandſon Oſgur introduced in the following pages of the poem: 'Tis true he is mentioned only as a boy: yet ſtill, one would think his *grandfather* old enough to be grey, without the operation of ſorcery, to make him ſo. At the very leaſt, he muſt have been now, ſome years above fifty; yet he is repreſented as retaining all the bloom, as well as the ſtrength and activity, of youth. But we may well overlook a few faults of inadvertance, in favour of the numerous beauties with which this poem abounds. Our magical bard conjures up ſuch delightful enchantments, that our attention ſhould be too much engroſſed by the grace and grandeur of his images, to count the knots on his poetical wand.

While magic thus our king detain'd,
    In hateful fetters bound;
We in fair Almhain's halls remain'd,
    And feſtal joy went round.

The mirthful moments danc'd along
    To muſic's charming lore;
And, to the ſons of lofty ſong,
    Wealth pour'd her bounteous ſtore!

Thus fled the hours, on heedleſs wing,
    From every care releas'd;
Nor thought we of our abſent king,
    Nor miſs'd him from the feaſt:

Till Caoilte, ſtruck with ſudden dread [r],
    Roſe in the Hall of Spears:
His words around ſtrange panic ſpread,
    And wak'd miſgiving fears!

                           " Where

---

[r] We learn, from Iriſh romance, that the Fenii, and the chiefs of the Dananian race, were enemies, (ſee ⨍ℯℐſ ⨼ℐȼ̆ ℭᴀⁿᴀⁿ,); and as theſe people were ſuppoſed to be ſkilful in magic, the heroes of Finn were naturally alarmed for the ſafety of their general, when they miſſed him from the feaſt, and recollected the determined enmity and ſupernatural power of the Tuatha de Danans.—Caoilte, in the paſſage before us, ſeems to apprehend that Finn was ſnatched away by enchantment from amongſt them. For a particular account of theſe Tuatha de Danans, the reader is referred to the antient Hiſtory of Ireland.

"Where is the noble Comhal's son,
  "Renown'd assembly! Say?—
"Or is our arm of conquest gone,—
  "Our glory pass'd away!"

We stood aghast.—Conan alone,
  The rash Mac Morni, spoke;
"O joyful tidings! I shall groan
  "No more beneath his yoke.

"Swift Caoilte[1], of the mighty deed!
  "On this auspicious day,
"I, to his fame and power, succeed,
  "And take the sovereign sway."

We laugh'd to scorn his senseless boast,
  Tho' with a grieving heart;
And Almhain saw our numerous host,
  With headlong haste depart.

The van myself and Caoilte led,
  The Fenii in the rear;
And on our rapid march we sped,
  But saw no king appear.

[1] Caoilte was remarkable for his speed in running.

We follow'd, where he led the chase,
  To steep Slieve Guillin's foot;
But there we could no further trace,
  And stop'd the vain pursuit.

North of the mount our march we stay'd,
  Upon a verdant plain,
Where conquest once our arms array'd¹,
  Tho' bought with heaps of slain!

Hope threw each eager eye around,
  And still'd attention's ear,—
In vain,—for neither sight or sound
  Of our lov'd chief was near.

But, on the borders of a lake,
  A tall old man we spy'd,
Whose looks his wretched age bespake
  To want and woe ally'd!

Bare wither'd bones, and ghastly eyes,
  His wrinkl'd form display'd;
Palsy'd and pale, he scarce could rise,
  From age and strength decay'd.

---

¹ The battle here alluded to is described in a Poem, entitled *Laoj̇b an Ďṽb mac tjc̄ṅjb*.—The terrible Mac-Dirive, after an obstinate combat, is at last slain by the hand of Osgur.

We thought, perchance, that famine gave
    That wan and wasted frame,
Or that from far, adown the wave,
    A fisherman he came.

We ask'd him, had he seen in chase,
    Two hounds that snuff'd the gale,
And a bold Chief, of princely grace,
    Swift bounding o'er the vale.

The head of age in silence hung,
    Bow'd down with shame and woe,
Long e'er his hesitating tongue
    The cruel truth could shew [u].

At length, to Caoilte's faithful ear,
    The fatal change he told,
And gave our raging host to hear
    The dreadful tale unfold!

---

[u] It is but proper to acquaint the reader, that in this passage, the sense of the poem is a little extended, and brought nearer to that of the romance.—In the poem, we are only told that Finn, when questioned by his chieftains, did not, at first, give a direct answer; but, after some time, imparted the secret to the ear of Caoilte. In the romance, Finn himself tells the story, and says, that " he *felt it grievous to his heart* to acquaint them, that he was the object of their search; nevertheless, when his faithful bands surrounded him, he at last informed them of his fatal adventure.

With horror struck, aghast and pale,
 Three sudden shouts we gave.—
Affrighted badgers fled the vale,
 And trembling sought the cave!

But Conan glory'd in our grief;
 Conan the bald, the base;
He curs'd with rage the Finian chief,
 And all the Finian race.

" O, were I sure (he fiercely said)
 " Thou wert that heart of pride,
" Soon should this blade thy shaking head
 " From thy old trunk divide!

" For never did thy envious mind
 " Bestow my valour's meed;
" In secret has thy foul repin'd
 " At each heroick deed.

" I grieve not for thy strength decay'd,
 " Shrunk form, and foul disgrace;
" But that I cannot wave my blade
 " O'er all thy hated race.

        " Oh,

"Oh, were they all like thee this day,
"My vengeance, as a flood,
"Should sweep my hated foes away,
"And bathe my steel in blood!

"Since Comhal of the Hosts was slain [x]
"Upon the ensanguin'd field,
"By Morni's son, who ne'er in vain
"Uprear'd his golden [y] shield;

"Since then, our clan in exile pine,
"Excluded from thy sight;
"And the fam'd heroes of our line
"But live in thy despight."

CAOILTE.

---

[x] Comhal, or Cumhal, the father of Finn. He was killed in a battle against the tribe of Morni; we find, however, that this tribe were afterwards reconciled to the Fenii, and obedient to their chief, who treated them with the utmost kindness. This complaint of Conan's is therefore to be ascribed to his own perverse humour, and not to any injustice that he or his clan had met with from the Finian general.

[y] Here we find mention of a golden shield; but it is not supposed that such were common in Ireland, because they do not often occur in our MSS. and very few of them have been found in our bogs. But we are not, from this, to conclude that the metal itself was scarce in the kingdom.—CAMBRENSIS and STANIHURST bear testimony to the riches of our mines. Doctor BOAT also, in his *Natural History*, mentions the gold and silver mines of Ireland; and DONATUS, Bishop of Fesulæ, a poet of the 7th century, in a beautiful description of our island, does not omit to celebrate the natural wealth of its soil.

CAOILTE. " Did not my foul too keenly fhare
  " In our great caufe of woe,
  " On aught like thee [2] to wafte its care,
  " Or any thought beftow;

  " Bald, fenfelefs wretch! thy envy, foon
  " This arm fhould make thee rue;
  " And thy crufh'd bones, thou bafe buffoon,
  " Should bear thy folly's due!"

OSGUR. " Ceafe thy vain bab'ling, fenfelefs fool!
  " Bald boafter [3], ftain to arms,
  " Still forward to promote mifrule,
  " But fhrink at war's alarms!"

CONAN.

---

[1] The Leabap Lecan, (or Book of Sligo) informs us, that in the reign of Tighearmas was firft introduced the boiling and refining of gold; that the refiner's name was Inachadan, and he carried on the art at the eaft fide of the Liffey. Befides the teftimony of foreign writers, and our domeftic annals; numbers of utenfils, arms, collars, chains, &c. of pure gold, have been dug up in different parts of the kingdom. But it would be endlefs to multiply proofs upon this fubject. If the reader wifhes any further teftimonies, he will find them at large in Mr. O'HALLORAN's *Introduction to the Hift. and Antiq. of Ireland*.

[2] We are here, at once, let into the character of Conan, and fee that contempt alone is the caufe of the forbearance with which his infolence is fuffered to pafs.

[3] We could wifh that this dialogue were not fo coarfely conducted; but the heroes of Homer are ftill lefs acquainted with good breeding, than thofe of our Irifh Bard; and Conan is only the *Therfites* of Oifin. In juftice, however, to the Finian chiefs,
it

CONAN. " Cease thou, vain youth [b], nor think my soul
"Can by thy speech be won,
"Servile to stoop to the controul
"Of Oisin's beardless son.

"Even Finn, who, head of all thy line,
"Can best their boasts become,
"What does he do, but daily dine,
"Upon his mangl'd thumb [c].

"'Twas not the sons of Boishne's clan,
"But Morni's gallant race,
"That thunder'd in the warlike van,
"And led the human chase.

" Oisin,

[a] it should be observed, that it is the insolent folly of Conan which provokes abusive language, because they will not raise their arm against an idiot. To an enemy they are never abusive; but, on the contrary, polite to a degree that might afford improved example, even to modern refinement. See *Magnus*.

[b] Conan, afraid to reply to Caoilte, yet ventures to discharge his spleen upon "Oisin's beardless son."

[c] This strange passage is explained by some lines in the Poem of Ɖub-ɱac-ᴅıṡɲıḃ, where Finn is reproached with deriving all his courage from his fore-knowledge of events, and chewing his thumb for prophetic information. The reader will easily perceive the source of this ridiculous mistake of the wonder-loving multitude; a habit taken up, when deep in thought, was construed into divination; and we may conclude how great that wisdom, and that heroism, must have been, which was supposed no other way to be accounted for, than by gifting the possessor with inspiration.

"Oisin, this silken son of thine,
  "Who thus in words excels,
"Will learn of thee the psalming whine,
  "And bear white books and bells [d].

"Cease Osgur, cease thy foolish boast,
  "Not words, but deeds decide;
"Now then, before this warlike host,
  "Now be our valour try'd!"

My son high rais'd his threat'ning blade,
  To give his fury sway;
But the pale Conan shrunk dismay'd,
  And sprung with fear away:

Amid

In the romance of ᚛ᚓᚔᚄ ᚈᚔᚌᚓ ᚉᚐᚅᚐᚌᚔᚅ᚜, among other curious particulars, Finn is said to have derived a portion of his knowledge from the waters of a magical fountain, in the possession of the Tuatha-de-danans; a single draught of which was sold for three hundred ounces of gold.

[d] From this passage, it appears, that Oisin was supposed to have been won over, at least in part, by some of the missionaries who preceded the arrival of St. Patrick in Ireland.—Here also we seem to have proof that the bells, mentioned in the course of the poem, were not, nor could have been, the large suspended ones; but only the smaller ones, that were borne by the priests, and tingled at the altars, in the very first ages of Christianity. Conan could not possibly mean any other than these, when he says that Osgur would learn in time to *bear* or carry them;—that is, leaving the profession of arms, to become a priest, by which he plainly intends to reproach him with cowardice, as desirous to excel in *words alone*.

Amid the fcoffing hoft he fprung,
   To fhun th' unequal ftrife;
To 'fcape the forfeit of his tongue,
   And fave his worthlefs life.

Nor vainly did he importune;
   The hoft, as he defir'd,
Engag'd my fon to give the boon
   His cowardice requir'd.

Once, twice, and thrice, to Erin's chief
   The forrowing Caoilte fpoke:
" O fay, lov'd caufe of all our grief!
   " Whence came this cruel ftroke?

" What curft Tuathan's [e] direful charm
   " Has dar'd that form deface?
" O! who could thus thy force difarm,
   " And wither ev'ry grace?"

                                          " Guillen's

---

[e] In the original, Tuaṫa ᴅe (i. e. Tuatha-de-danan). Moft of the Irifh Romances are filled with Dananian enchantments; as wild as the wildeft of ARIOSTO's fictions, and not at all behind them in beauty.

" Guillen's fair daughter, (Finn reply'd,)
" The treacherous snare design'd ¹,
" And sent me to yon magic tide,
" Her fatal ring to find."

Conan who, penitent of tongue,
Would now his guilt revoke,
Forward, with zeal impatient sprung,
And vengeful ire bespoke.

" May

¹ This apparent malice, and ingratitude of the Enchantress, is fully accounted for in the romance. Finn had ever been the servant and protector, and of course, the favourite of the fair: he is scarce ever mentioned, without some epithet, expressive of amiable attraction, such as " the majestic—the graceful—the courteous—the generous—the gentle—the smiling—the blooming—son of Comhal." He surpassed his cotemporaries as much in the manly beauty, and majestic graces of his countenance and form, as he did in the superior strength of his arm, and the extraordinary endowments of his mind.

Miluachra, and Aine, the two fair daughters of Guillen Cualgne, of the Dananian race, saw, and fell in love with him. Miluachra was jealous of her sister's charms; and hearing her, one day, take an oath, that she would never marry any man whose hair was grey, she determined, if possible, to make this rash vow a bar to her union with Finn. She assembled her friends of the Tuatha-de-danans; and, by the power of their enchantments, they called forth a magical lake, on the side of Slieve-Guillen, which had the property of rendering any person grey-headed, who should enter the waters thereof. This done, she assumed the form of a beautiful doe, and appeared to Finn, as already related: then followed the chase; but the romance gives only three days and nights to the destruction of the Enchantress's cave; the poem gives eight. Also, in the romance, the magical cup, which restored our hero to his former shape, endowed him, at the same time, with added wisdom, and knowledge. His hair, however, remained grey; but the Enchantress, after acknowledging, in much confusion and terror, the reason of the trick she had played him, offered to restore that also: this offer, we are told, he declined, chusing to continue grey; but the reason of his refusal does not appear.

" May never from this hill (he cry'd,)
" Our homeward steps depart,
" But Guillen [g] dearly shall abide
" Her dark and treacherous art!"

Then our stout shields with thongs we bound [h],
  Our hapless King to bear;
While each fond chieftain press'd around,
  The precious weight to share.

North of the mount, to Guillen's cave,
  The alter'd form we bore;
Determin'd all her art to brave,
  And his lost powers restore.

Eight nights and days, without success,
  We tore the living tomb,
Until we pierc'd the last recess
  Of the deep cavern's gloom.

---

[g] Her name, as we have seen, was Miluachra, though she is here called Guillen, as being daughter to the Enchantress Guillen.

[h] This passage seems to throw some light on the size of the Irish shield.—It is spoken of in the plural number here, by which it should seem that it must have been the target; for, otherwise, one alone would have been sufficient to have borne Finn from the field.

Then forth the fair Enchantress came,
  Swift issuing to the light,
The form of grace, the beauteous dame,
  With charms too great for sight.

A cup quite full she trembling bore
  To Erin's alter'd chief,
That could his pristine form restore,
  And heal his people's grief.

He drank.—O joy! his former grace,
  His former powers return'd;
Again with beauty glow'd his face,
  His breast with valour burn'd.

Oh, when we saw his kindling eye
  With wonted lustre glow,
Not all the glories of thy sky
  Such transport could bestow!

The Hero of the Stately Steeds,
  From magic fetters free,
To Finian arms, and martial deeds
  Thus—thus restor'd to see!—

Scarce could our souls the joy sustain!—
 Again three shouts we gave;
Again the badgers fled the plain,
 And trembling sought the cave!

Now, Patrick of the scanty store,
 And meager-making face!
Say, did'st thou ever hear before
 This memorable Chase?

IV.

MOIRA BORB:

A

POEM.

ADVERTISEMENT.

THE original of this poem is in the hands of Maurice Gorman: *there is also another copy in* Mr. Walker's *collection, but not altogether so perfect as the one from which this translation has been made. Neither of these copies are dated, nor can we discover the author. Like most of the* Finian *poems, it is ascribed to* Oisin; *but, though it may, possibly, have originated with him, it has certainly assumed, since that period, a different form from any that he could have given it. The poetry, indeed, breathes all the spirit of the* Finian Bard; *but the language is evidently not earlier than that of the middle ages.*

MOIRA BORB:

A POEM.

A Tale of old,—of Finian deeds I sing:
Of Erin's mighty hosts, the mighty King!
Great Comhal's son the lofty strain shall swell,
And on his fame the light of song shall dwell.

Oft have I seen his arm destruction wield;
Oft, with its deadly prowess, sweep the field!
Then did the world his matchless deeds proclaim,
And my ear drank the musick of his fame.

Once, while the careless day to sport we gave,
Where fierce Mac-Bovar[a] rolls his headlong wave,

With

---

[a] The words of the original are Ꝑaſ pꞃáḋ mac boḃaꞃ na mojll, literally, *the fiercely rushing Cataract, deafening son of the heap!* This is a very beautiful

fall

With deaf'ning clamour pours upon the plain,
Foams o'er his echoing banks, and feeks the main.

Carelefs we rang'd along the founding fhore,
And heard the tumbling of the torrent's roar;
Thin was our hoft, no thought of danger nigh,
When the near ocean caught our roving eye.

A white fail'd boat, that fwiftly fought the fhore,
On its light plank, a lovely female bore;
To meet our hoft her rapid courfe was bent,
And much we queftion'd on this ftrange event.

Fifty brave chiefs, around their braver King.—
Ah, why to mind, their deeds, their glories bring!
Since anguifh muft on bleeding memory wait,
Comparing former fame with prefent fate.

Alas! with them is quench'd the hero's flame,
And glory, fince, is but an empty name!
Oh, after them, 'tis Mifery's dire decree
The chiefs of thefe degenerate days to fee.

---

fall of the river Erne, at Ballyfhannon, and the principal falmon leap in Ireland. The fcenery is extremely picturefque; a bold coaft of perpendicular rocks is covered to the very edge with the richeft verdure, and projects, in unequal promontories, as it opens to the fea. This falmon leap is let at 400l. a year.

Oh, loſt companions! once your mighty ſway
Made the proud princes of the earth obey;
Your conq'ring powers through every region led,
And wide around victorious triumphs ſpread!

But to my tale.—Our wondering chiefs aroſe,
To ſee the bark its beauteous freight diſcloſe:
Swift glanc'd its courſe through the divided wave,
And the near ſtream a ready harbour gave.

As morn from ocean lifts her lov'ly light,
Freſh from the wave, with gentle ſplendours bright;
So roſe the maid, as ſhe approach'd the ſhore,
And her light bark to land its burden bore.

Deck'd by ſoft Love with ſweet attractive grace,
And all the charms of mind-illumin'd face;
Before our hoſt the beauteous ſtranger bow'd,
And, thrown to earth, her eyes their glories ſhroud.

Her ſoft ſalute return'd, with courteous air,
Finn, by the hand of ſnow, conducts the fair.
Upon his left, the valiant Gaul was plac'd,
And on his right, her ſeat the ſtranger grac'd.

And, oh, to tell the charms her form array'd!
The winning sweetness that her face display'd!
On her alone we could or think, or gaze,
And our rapt souls were lost in sweet amaze!

" Soft Mariner! (the son of Comhal cry'd,)
" What chance has torn thee from protection's side?
" Why com'ft thou here, and from what happy earth?
" And whose the noble race that gave thee birth?"

" Truth, O great chief! my artless story frames:
" A mighty King [b] my filial duty claims.
" But princely birth no safety could bestow;
" And, royal as I am, I fly from woe.

" Long have I look'd that mighty arm to see,
" Which is alone of force to set me free:
" To Erin's far fam'd chief for aid I fly,
" And on that aid my trembling hopes rely."

" Say,

---

[b] This passage is not translated literally, as it was difficult to know what turn to give it: the words in Irish are *Af mé inġean ríġ fo ċuinn*. *I am the daughter of the King under Waves:* or it may be rendered, *King of Waves*, or *King of Ton*, (in the genitive) *Tuin*. Literally, *a wave;* but it may also mean some country, anciently called by that name; or possibly it may be a metaphorical phrase, to imply either an island, or some of the low countries.

" Say, wherefore, lovelieſt! art thou thus diſtreſt?
" Whom do'ſt thou fly?—by whom art thou oppreſt?
" Why do'ſt thou ſeek me, o'er the rolling ſea,
" And from what peril ſhall I ſet thee free?"

" And art thou, then, that gen'rous ſon of fame,
" Whoſe aid the wretched, and the helpleſs claim?
" O then, to me that needful aid extend!
" And, oh, thy ſtrength to guard my weakneſs lend!"

With ſoothing ſpeech, the pitying King reply'd,
" Fear not, ſweet maid! thy cauſe to me confide.
" Speak but thy ſorrows! whom do'ſt thou accuſe?
" Who perſecutes thee, Fair One?—who purſues?"—

" O! I am follow'd o'er the rolling wave!
" O! mighty Finn! thy trembling ſuppliant ſave!
" The ſon of Sora's ᶜ King with wrath purſues,
" The Chief of Spears, whoſe arm the hoſt ſubdues!

" Dark

ᶜ Tradition inform us, that *Meira*, or (as ſome write it) *Beiry Borb*, was a Luſitanian Prince, of great fame and prowefs, but cruel, and extremely fierce, as the word *berb* (i. e. *fierce*) implies. This admitted, it follows, of courſe, that *Sora* (in the original, *Sorcha*,) muſt have been, anciently, the Iriſh name for Portugal.

" Dark Moira-borb is his tremendous name,
" And wide o'er earth extends his dreadful fame!
" From him I fly, with thefe unhappy charms,
" To fhun the horror of his hateful arms!

" To one delay his fullen foul agreed,
" Nor can he from his promife now recede;
" He will not force me to become his bride,
" Until thy pow'r fhall in my caufe be try'd."

Then fpoke my Ofgur, Erin's lovely boaft,
Pride of her fame, and glory of her hoft!
With generous zeal his youthful bofom glow'd;
His fervent fpeech with rapid ardour flow'd.

" Fear not (he cry'd) no power fhall force thee hence;
" My arm, my life, O maid! is thy defence!
" No hateful union fhall thy vows compel,
" Nor fhalt thou with the dreadful Sora dwell!"

Then, by his fide, the fon of Morni rofe;
Each champion equal to an hoft of foes!
Proudly they ftrode, exulting in their might,
The fierce, triumphant Deities of fight!

Before

Before the hoſt they ſtood, in arms array'd,
To guard, from her approaching foe, the maid;
For now, ſwift riding on the ſubject wave,
A wond'rous chief to fight his terrors gave!

In the ſame path the princeſs took, he came,
And more than human ſeem'd his monſtrous frame;
A magic ſteed its giant burden bore,
And ſwiftly gain'd upon the trembling ſhore!

Fierce did he ſeem, as one in fight renown'd;
Dark on his head a gloomy helmet frown'd:
Emboſs'd with art, he held a mighty ſhield,
And well his arm its ponderous orb could wield!

Two ſpears of victory, on its front engrav'd,
Stood threat'ning, as if every foe they brav'd!
Never our eyes had ſuch a fight beheld,
Nor ever chief ſo dreadfully excell'd!

His heavy ſword, of more than monſtrous ſize,
Next ſtruck with wonder our admiring eyes;
When, bending forward, from his mighty thigh
He drew, and wav'd its maſſy weight on high!

Of princely fway the cloudy champion feem'd,
And terror from his eye imperial ftream'd!
A foul of fire was in his features feen,
In his proud port, and his impetuous mien!

His wond'rous fteed was like the torrent's force;
White as its foam, and rapid as its courfe!
Proud, the defyer of our hoft he bore,
And fprung with fury to the hoftile fhore.

A fight like this had never met our eyes,
Or ftruck our fenfes with a like furprize;
To fee a fteed thus courfing on the wave,
And his fierce rider thus the ocean brave!

My King, whofe arm would every peril dare,
Then calm demanded of the trembling fair,
" Is this the chief of whom thy terror fpoke,
" Againft whofe power thou didft our aid invoke?"

" O that is he! that is my deadly foe!
" Too well, alas! his dreadful face I know!
" O Comhal's generous fon! I grieve for thee,
" Againft thy hoft that at al arm to fee!

"He comes! he comes to tear his victim hence!
"No power, alas, can now be my defence!
"No force, no courage can that sword abide,
"And vainly will your generous aid be try'd!"

While thus to Comhal's noble son she spoke,
Fierce through the host, the foreign champion broke!
Glowing with rage, in conscious might array'd,
Forward he rush'd, and seiz'd the trembling maid!

Swift flew the spear of Morni's wrathful son,
And to the foe unerring passage won:
Through his pierc'd shield the aim its fury guides,
Rends its proud bosses, and its orb divides.

Impatient Osgur glow'd with ardent fire,
With raging scorn, and with indignant ire;
And, darting fate from his impetuous hand,
He stretch'd the dying courser on the strand!

Unhors'd, and furious for his wounded steed,
And breathing tenfold vengeance for the deed;
With wrath augmented the fierce champion burn'd,
And mad with rage, on his assailants turn'd.

Dauntlefs he ftood, with haughty ire inflam'd,
And loud defiance to our hoft proclaim'd:
Againft us all his fingle arm he rais'd,
While in his hand the dreadful faulchion blaz'd!

Enrag'd, our hofts the proud defiance hear,
And rufh to vengeance with a fwift career.
Finn and myfelf alone our arms withhold,
And wait to fee the ftrange event unfold.

When lo! amazement to our wondering eyes!
In vain each fpear with rapid fury flies!
In vain with might, the nearer fwords affail,
No fpears can wound, no weapons can prevail.

Thofe chiefs, who every foe till then excell'd,
Foil'd by his force, his fingle arm repell'd.
Low on the blood-ftain'd field with fhame they lay,
Bound by his hand, and victims of his fway!

Great Flan Mac-Morni fell beneath his fword;
By valour, friendfhip, and by fong deplor'd!
Of all the champions who his arm fuftain'd,
Not one unwounded on the field remain'd.

Had

Had not our chiefs been all well arm'd for fight,
They all had funk beneath his matchlefs might!
Or had each, fingly, met his dreadful force,
Each, in his turn, had fall'n a mangled corfe!

Now Gaul's brave bofom burns with frantic ire,
And terror flafhes from his eyes of fire!
Rending in wrath, he fprings upon the foe!
High waves his fword, and fierce defcends its blow!

Dire as when fighting elements engage,
Such is the war the dreadful champions wage!
Whoever had that fatal field beheld,
He would have thought all human force excell'd.

Loud was the clafh of arms that ftream'd with gore,
And deep the wounds each dauntlefs bofom bore!
Broke are their fpears, and rent each maffy fhield,
And fteel, and blood beftrew the deathful field!

Never again fhall two fuch chiefs contend,
Nor ever courage, as did theirs, tranfcend!
So great the havock of each deadly blade!
So great the force each valiant arm difplay'd!

At length they flack'd the fury of the fight,
And vanquish'd Sora own'd superior might :
No more he could the sword of Gaul sustain,
But gash'd with wounds, he sunk upon the plain.

Woe was the day in which that strife arose,
And dy'd with blood the harbour of his foes !
Woe to the champions of that lovely dame !
Woe to the land to which her beauty came [d] !

The valiant Sora by the stream we laid,
And while his last and narrow house we made,
We on each finger plac'd a glitt'ring ring [e],
To grace the foe, in honor of our King.

Thus fell the foreign champion on our coast,
And gave a dear-bought conquest to our host.
The royal maid our courtesy embrac'd,
And a whole year the Finian palace grac'd.

Six

---

[d] It is probable that this passage alludes to some subsequent consequences of the death of Moira-borb.

[e] It has not been found that any particular custom of antiquity is here alluded to : the passage is translated literally, and it appears that, by placing rings on the fingers of Moira-borb, they meant to shew the generosity of their chief, in honouring a gallant foe.

Six following months, beneath the leeches hand,
The wounds of Gaul our constant care demand:
The valiant Gaul, unvanquish'd in the fight,
Gaul of the weapons of resistless might.

With Finn, the chief of princely cheer, he lay,
Whose friendly tendance eas'd the tedious day.
Finn, who was ever to the brave a friend,
Finn, who the weak would evermore defend [f]!

But

---

[f] In the *baile Oisin*, (Rhapsody of Oisin) we find the following beautiful character, and personal description of this celebrated hero.

    Fjonn ꞅa ꞃꞅjnꞅ ꞅjál
    baꞃ ꞅaiꞃꞅe ꞅheaꞃꞃib ꞅájl
    ꞃjꞅ móꞃðalać cóojn.
    ꞅa móꞃ aðjol ðán.

    Aćꞃojðe oꞅꞅajlꞇe meaꞃ.
    aꞅhjan ꞅa móꞃ.
    ꞅjoñ ꞅjoꞃꞅljce ꞅajð
    a aꞅa ꞅa móꞃ bꞃan.

    ꞅa ꞅlan ꞅoꞃm aꞃoꞅꞅ.
    ꞇo bj aꞅholꞇ maꞃ a nóꞃ.
    ꞃꞅejm ꞃjꞅ ꞅa bꞃan
    ꞇo bj aꞅꞃuajð maꞃ an ꞃóꞅ.

    Ðo bj ꞅać bean lan ða ꞅeaꞃꞇ
    aćneꞃ maꞃ an ccajlc bajn.
    mac Ꝋjꞃme ꞅa cóojn.
    ꞅjonn, ꞃjꞅ na naꞃm najꞅ.

In

But why of heroes should I now relate?
Chang'd is my form, and chang'd is my estate!
These alter'd looks, with age and sorrow pale,
Should warn to cease from the heroic tale!

In English,—" Finn of the large and liberal soul of bounty; exceeding all his
" countrymen in the prowess and accomplishments of a warrior. King of mild
" majesty, and numerous bards.

" The ever-open house of kindness was his heart; the seat of undaunted courage!
" great was the chief of the mighty Fenii; Finn of the perfect soul, the consummate
" wisdom; whose knowledge penetrated events, and pierced through the veil of futu-
" rity. Finn of the splendid and ever-during glories.

" Bright were his blue-rolling eyes, and his hair like flowing gold! Lovely were
" the charms of his unaltered beauty, and his cheeks like the glowing rose.

" Each female heart overflowed with affection for the hero whose bosom was like
" the whiteness of the chalky cliff, for the mild son of Morna; Finn, the king of
" the glittering blades of war."

ODES.

AN
INTRODUCTORY DISCOURSE
TO THE
WAR ODE.

THE military Odes of the ancient Celtæ have been noticed by numberless historians; nothing amongst those people was left unsung: Poetry was their darling science, and they introduced it into every scene, and suited it to every occasion. One of the duties of the Bard was, to attend his chief to battle, and there exert his poetic powers, according to the fluctuations of victory, and the fortune of the fight. This fact is well attested by antient Greek and Roman writers; also, Du Cange, Mezeray, and many other antiquaries and historians affirm, that this custom continued amongst the Gauls, many centuries after their dereliction by the Romans. Even at the battle of Hastings, the troops of Normandy were accompanied by a Bard, animating them to conquest with warlike odes. The great number of Troubadours retained by the French noblesse, in the different invasions of the Holy Land, prove how well this custom was supported by civilized nations of the middle ages.

But it will, no doubt, appear singular, that, while France and Germany suffered no ruin or subversion of their states, from that epocha, yet so little care has been taken, by their antiquaries, for the preservation of antient documents, that it is affirmed, there is not one of these Odes now extant amongst them; while Ireland,—harrassed by war and rapine; and her records plundered by foreign invaders, and envious policy,—yet still has preserved a number of these original productions, which throw many rays of light on the obscurest periods of Celtic antiquity.

But the WAR ODE was not peculiar to the Celtæ alone; Scandinavia, too, sent her Scalds to battle, and her Chiefs were animated by their military songs; although indeed many centuries later than the period in which we find our Bards possessed of this office in Ireland. " Hacon, Earl of Norway (says Monf.
" MALLET) had five celebrated poets along with him in that
" famous battle of which I have been speaking, when the war-
" riors of Jomsbourg were defeated; and history records that
" they sung each an Ode, to animate the soldiers, before they
" engaged [a,b]."

WE

[a] See TORF. BARTHOLIN, p. 172, who produces other instances to the same purpose; particularly that of Olave, king of Norway, who placed three of his scalds

We see here a remarkable difference between the Scandinavian and Celtic poet, in the execution of this military duty: The Ode of the Scald was compofed for the purpofe, and fung *before the engagement*: while the Irifh Bard, glowing with the joint enthufiafm of the poet, and the warrior, frequently rufhed amidft the ranks, and following his Chief through all the fury of the fight, continued, to the laft, thofe fublime and elevating ftrains, which, infpired by the fight of heroic valour, and called forth by, and fuited to the inftant occafion, wrought up courage to a pitch of frenzy, and taught the warrior to triumph even in the pangs of death. But it was only when victory was doubtful, and occafion required the Bards to exert all their powers, that we find them thus rufhing through the carnage of the field. At other times " marching at the head of the armies, " arrayed in white flowing robes, harps glittering in their hands, " and their perfons furrounded with ORFIDIGH, or inftrumental " muficians; while the battle raged, they *ftood apart*, and " watched in fecurity (for their perfons were held facred) every action

fcalds about him to be eye-witneffes of his exploits: thefe bards compofed, each of them, a fong upon the fpot, which BARTHOLIN has printed, accompanied with a Latin verfion. Other fongs of the fame kind may be found in the fame author.

Here is one inftance wherein we find a Scandinavian war ode compofed (as it appears) either *during*, or *after* the engagement; but their eftablifhed cuftom was, to fing the ode (as is related above) *before* the battle joined.

᛫ *North. Antiq.* vol. i. p. 386.

"action of the Chief, in order to glean subjects for their "lays ⁵."

INDEED, the enthusiastic starts of passion; the broken, unconnected, and irregular wildness of those Odes which have escaped the wreck of ancient literature in this kingdom, sufficiently and inconteſtibly point out their true originality to every *candid* reader. It need not here be objected, that the character in which we find the copies now extant of these Odes, is different from that which was in use among the pagan Irish, and that the language of them, also, is too intelligible to be referred to so remote an æra. With the beauties of these singular compositions, every Irish reader, of every age, must have been eager to acquaint himself; and when acquainted with them, to communicate to others the knowledge, and the pleasure they afforded him: of course, when a word became too obsolete to be generally understood, it was changed for one more modern; and, for the same reason, when the ancient character was exploded, every ensuing copy of these Odes was written in the character of the times. Indeed there are still a sufficient number of obsolete words among them, to make the language extremely difficult; but I conceive that it is in the ſtructure of the compositions, and the ſpirit which they breathe, rather than in a few unintelligible epithets, that we are to look for the marks of their antiquity.

THE

---

⁵ WALKER's *Hiſt. Mem. of the Iriſh Bards*, p. 10.

THE copies from which the two following Odes are tranflated, I procured from Maurice Gorman; there is alfo a copy of them in the collection of Mr. O'Halloran of Limerick, and another, as I am informed, in the College collection. An accomplifhed proficient in the learning and antiquities of this country, whofe name (had I permiffion) I fhould be proud to reveal, made the following elegant, and fpirited remarks, on a literal tranflation of the firft of thefe Odes, upon which I had requefted his judgment. " It is (fays he) in my opinion, a very fine fpecimen of
" that kind of poetry, and carries genuine originality on the face
" of it. It feems not only to have been compofed on the occa-
" fion, but as if it was actually fung by the bard during the
" heat of the battle; which fuppofition is quite confonant with
" the accounts we have of the antient Celtic warriors, and the
" office of their Bards. The extreme fimplicity of it is no fmall
" part of its merit, and has more in it of the true fublime, than
" all the flowers and images with which a modern poet would
" have embellifhed it. Imagination may follow it through all
" the changes that may be fuppofed to have attended an obfti-
" nate engagement, in which the hero was exerting his valour
" to the utmoft; with his bard ftanding clofe at his back,
" exhorting him to perfevere, and giving, as it were, frefh
" energy and effect to every ftroke of his fword."

IT may appear ftrange to fee a Bard rufhing, fearlefs and unhurt, through the midft of contending warriors; his hand encumbered with the harp, and unprovided with any arms for

either

either defence or attack: but the character of the *Filea* was held so sacred amongst the ancient Celtæ, that they wanted no other defence, and were so protected and revered by foes, as well as friends, that even " the very whirl and rage of fight" respected the person of the Bard.

IRISH history, indeed, affords one, and *but one*, instance of a sort of sacrilege offered to the life of a Bard; the circumstances, however, which accompany the fact, as well as the manner in which it is told, present us with the strongest idea of the horror that so unusual a crime then excited. The Leabaɲ Lecan, (or *Book of Sligo*) has thus preserved the relation: Fierce wars were carried on, about the middle of the fourth century, between Eochaidh, Monarch of Ireland, and Eana, the King of Leinster. Cetmathach, the Monarch's laureat, had satyrized so severely the enemy of his King, as to provoke the bitterest resentment of Eana, who vowed unsparing revenge. In the battle of Cruachan, the Monarch was defeated; and Cetmathach, pursued by the furious King of Leinster, fled for safety amidst the troops of the victor, who, though the enemies of Eochaidh, would have protected his Bard: but the brutal Eana was not to be appeased, and the life of the laureat fell a sacrifice to his art. Eana, for this atrocious deed, was ever after branded with the opprobrious name of *Cin-falach*, (foul, or dishonorable head). It has descended down, through his immediate posterity, to the present day; numbers of his race, of the name of *Cin* or *Kin-falah*, now existing in Ireland.

OF

Of the first of the following Odes, Ofgur, the son of Oisin, is the hero, but we are not told who the Bard was that composed it. We have, however, sufficient reason to conclude, that it was sung by Fergus, the uncle of Ofgur; first, because he was the appointed ARD-FILEA of the Fenii; and also because that, in an ancient poem on the battle of Gabhra, he is introduced as exhorting the troops, on that occasion, to the fight, surrounded by his *Orfidigh*, or band of musicians.

> bj ᘎeapᴣuſ ſjle,
> aᴣuſ opſjceach na ſlaċa,
> ᴅaꞃ mbpoſcaḃ ſan mjonᴣṁ
> ᴅol ᴅjoṅſojᴣ an chaċa.

Mr. WALKER, in his MEMOIRS OF THE IRISH BARDS, takes particular notice of Fergus. " Oisin (says he) was not Finn's chief
" Bard, or Ollamh-re-dan. This honorable station was filled by
" Fergus *Fibbeoil*, (of the sweet lips) another son of the great
" Finian commander; a Bard on whom succeeding poets have
" bestowed almost as many epithets, as Homer has given to his
" Jupiter.—In several poems, still extant, he is called Fergus
" *Fir-glic*, (the truly ingenious); *Fathach*, (superior in know-
" ledge); *Focal-geur*, (skilled in the choice of words) &c. &c.
" So persuasive was his eloquence, that, united with his rank, it
" acquired him an almost universal ascendency.

" But

"But it was in the field of battle that Fergus' eloquence
"proved of real utility. In a fine heroic Poem [a] called
"the Cat ᚌᚔᚏ-ᚈᚏᚐᚷᚐ (The battle of Ventry), Finn is often
"reprefented as calling on Fergus, to animate the droop-
"ing valour of his officers, which the Bard never fails to do,
"effectually. In this battle, Oifin was beginning to yield in
"fingle combat; which being obferved by Fergus, he addreffed
"fome encouraging ftrains to him, in a loud voice : Thefe were
"heard by Oifin, and his foe fell beneath his fword [b].

"Several admirable poems, attributed to Fergus, are ftill ex-
"tant; Dargo, a poem [c], written on occafion of a foreign prince
"of that name invading Ireland. Dargo encountered the Fenii,
"and was flain by Goll, the fon of Morni.—Cat ᚌᚐᛒᚏᚐ (the
"battle of Gabhra). This battle was fought by the Fenii againft
"Cairbre, the monarch of Ireland, whofe aim in provoking it,
"was

---

[a] This compofition is not written in verfe, but it does indeed abound with all the ornaments of poetry.

[b] O'Halloran's *Hift. Irel.* vol. i. p. 275.

[c] A copy of this poem is now in my poffeffion, and it glows with all the fire of genius; but at the fame time is debafed by fuch abfurd impoffibilities, that, as I could not venture to omit any part of the piece, I did not think it would an-fwer for tranflation. From the character given of this poem, I am tempted to fup-pofe that my copy is a corrupt and bad one; perhaps a future day may enable me to procure a better.

" was to fupprefs the formidable power of that legion. Cairbre's
" life fell a facrifice to this bold attempt.

" THESE Poems abound with all the imagery, fire, and glow-
" ing defcription of the ancient Gäelic, and juftify the praifes
" beftowed on Fergus. Each poem concludes with Fergus' at-
" teftation of his being the author. Befides thefe, there are, A
" Panegyric on Goll, the fon of Morni [d], and another on Ofgur [e].
" In the latter, the poet has interwoven an animating harangue
" to the hero, who is the fubject of it, in the battle of Gabhra."

IN moft of the Finian poems that I have feen, Fergus is ho-
norably noticed, both for his poetical powers, and the peculiar
fweetnefs of his temper and difpofition: Thus in THE CHASE,

" Did Fergus live, again to fing,
" As erft, the Fenii's fame!"

Alfo in MAGNUS.

" Mild Fergus then, his errand done,
" Return'd with wonted grace;
" His mind, like the unchanging fun,
" Still beaming in his face [f]."

THE

[d] See the fecond War Ode in this collection.

[e] This I fuppofe is the fame with the original of the following Ode.

[f] Probably this extreme gentlenefs of Fergus' temper, was the reafon why he was chofen ARD-FILEA, or chief poet to the Fenii, though his brother Oifin was fo eminently

The Annals of Innisfallen, and other ancient records, and poems, inform us, that the battle of Gabhra was fought in the year of our Lord 296. The cause of this battle (as well as I can collect from various accounts) was pretty nearly as follows:—The celebrated body of the Fenii had grown to a formidable degree of power. Conscious of the defence they afforded their country, and the glory they reflected upon it, they became overweening and insolent, esteeming too highly of their merits, and too meanly of their rewards; and this the more, as they perceived the Monarch disposed to slight their services, and envy their fame.

It would be tedious here to relate the various causes assigned by different writers for the discontents which occasioned this battle: Historians, in general, lay the chief blame upon the Fenii; and the poets, taking part with their favourite heroes, cast the whole odium upon Cairbre, then Monarch of Ireland. The fault

---

nently distinguished for his poetical talents. Oisin, most likely, would not have accepted of the laureatship: his high and martial spirit would not be confined to the duties of that station, as they would often have necessarily withheld him from mixing in the combat, and taking a *warrior*'s share in the victory. The character of Fergus was much more adapted than that of Oisin, to fill the place he held, even supposing the poetic powers of Oisin superior to those of his brother.—Oisin, like the Caractacus of the inimitable Mason, felt too much of

" —————————— the hot tide
" That flushes crimson on the conscious cheek
" Of him who burns for glory!"

And he would never have borne to hold the harp, in battle, while able to wield a sword.

fault moſt likely was mutual, and both parties ſeverely ſuffered for it. Cairbre himſelf was killed in the action, and a dreadful ſlaughter enſued among his troops; but thoſe of the Fenii were almoſt totally deſtroyed[h]; for, relying upon that valour which they fondly deemed invincible, they ruſhed into the field againſt odds, that madneſs alone would have encountered. In an ancient poem upon this ſubject, Oiſin, relating the events of the battle to St. Patrick, tells him, that " few in number were the Fenii, " on that fatal day, oppoſed to the united forces of the king- " dom, headed by their Monarch! Finn and his heroes were " not there to aſſiſt them; they were abſent on a Roman expe- " dition."—Oſgur, the grandſon of Finn, commanded the little body that remained, and led them on to the attack; fired with the hope of encreaſing glory, and wrought up to a frenzy of valour, by the animated exhortations of his Bard, he performed prodigies, he ſlew numbers, and Cairbre himſelf at length fell by his hand. Victory then ſeemed to declare for the Fenii, till Oſgur, covered with wounds, ſunk upon the field. He died; with him died the hopes of his adherents. And Epic ſtory gives no further account of the few who ſurvived the field.

SEVERAL poems have been compoſed upon the ſubject of this battle. I have never yet ſeen that one which is ſaid to have been written by Fergus; but I have now before me two that bear the name

---

[h] *The Book of Heath* affirms, that they were *all* deſtroyed, Oiſin excepted; and that he lived till the arrival of St. Patrick, to whom he related the exploits of the Fenii.

name of Oisin, and are possessed of considerable merit: I would gladly, with the following Ode, have given a translation of one of the many poems which this celebrated battle gave rise to; but as I am told there are more perfect copies extant, than those in my possession, I am unwilling to give an inferior one to the public.

I.

WAR ODE

TO

OSGUR.

WAR ODE
TO
OSGUR, THE SON OF OISIN,
IN THE FRONT OF THE BATTLE OF GABHRA.

 RISE, might of Erin! rise[a]!
O! Osgur, of the generous soul!
Now, on the foe's astonish'd eyes,
 Let thy proud ensigns wave dismay!
Now let the thunder of thy battle roll,
And bear the palm of strength and victory away!

  Son of the fire, whose stroke is fate[b],
   Be thou in might supreme!
  Let conquest on thy arm await,
   In each conflicting hour!

Slight

---

[a] Eirigh! literally, *arise!*—It means here, *rouse thyself! exert all thy powers!*

[b] Oisin, the father of Osgur, was as much celebrated for his valour, as for his poetical talents.

Slight let the force of adverfe numbers feem,
Till, o'er their proftrate ranks, thy fhouting fquadrons pour!

O hear the voice of lofty fong!—
    Obey the Bard!——
Stop—ftop M'Garaidh^c! check his pride,
And rufh refiftlefs on each regal foe!
Thin their proud ranks, and give the fmoaking tide
    Of hoftile blood to flow!
Mark where Mac-Cormac^d pours along!—
    Rufh on—retard
His haughty progrefs!—let thy might
    Rife, in the deathful fight,
    O'er thy prime foe fupreme,
    And let the ftream
    Of valour flow,
Until thy brandifh'd fword
Shall humble ev'ry haughty foe,
And juftice be reftor'd^e.

                                 Son

---

^c This fon of Garaidh was then King of Connaught, and he led a chofen band to the battle of Gabhra.

^d Cairbre, Monarch of Ireland; he was fon to Cormac, the preceding Monarch, and it was in his quarrel that the allied Princes were affembled in this day's battle, againft the little band of the Fenii. He was alfo nearly related to the chiefs of the party he oppofed, his fifter having been the wife of Fiun-Mac-Cumhal.

^e Injuftice was the complaint, and the caufe of quarrel, affigned both by the King's forces, and the Fenii: *The Book of Houth* has preferved a fpeech of Ofgur's on this

Son of the King of spotless fame [f],
    Whose actions fill the world!
Like his, thy story and thy name
    Shall fire heroick song,
And, with the prowess of this day, the lofty strain prolong!
Shall tell how oft, in Gabhra's plain,
    Thy dreadful spear was hurl'd [g]:
How high it heap'd the field with slain,
    How wide its carnage spread,
Till gorg'd upon the human feast, the glutted ravens fed.

---

this occasion; probably just as authentic as most other speeches of the kind, that history gravely tells us have been spoken at such times. It sets forth the gross injustice and ingratitude with which they had been treated by the Monarch; and that they only fought to maintain those privileges which they had honorably won, and which were granted to their ancestors by those faithless Princes, now in arms against them. That they and their predecessors had been the guardians of the nation, protecting its harbours, and repelling its invaders; and also increasing its glory by the splendour of foreign conquests, and the rich trophies of foreign tributes to its power; but that now, after so many battles fought, and so many honors and advantages derived to the Monarch by their valour, he wished to acquit himself of the obligation, by putting his benefactors to the sword, or banishing them for ever from the land.

[f] It is uncertain, here, *what* King the poet means, whether the father, or the grandfather of his hero; either of them might have been called *King* by the Bard, as the word *Righ* is frequently made use of for any great commander, or military sovereign; and Osgur might have been stiled *son* to either, because *Mac* (son) signifies also grandson, and often only a descendant.

[g] The poets tell us of an incredible slaughter, made in this battle by the sword of Osgur: the brave and fierce Mac-Garaidh, King of Connaught, of the tribe of Morni, and Cairbre, Monarch of Ireland, besides numbers of inferior chieftains, fell by his single arm.

Resistless as the spirit of the night,
  In storms and terrors drest,
Withering the force of ev'ry hostile breast,
  Rush on the ranks of fight!—
    Youth of fierce deeds, and noble soul!
    Rend—scatter wide the foe!—
Swift forward rush,—and lay the waving pride
    Of yon high ensigns low!
Thine be the battle!—thine the sway!—
On—on to Cairbre hew thy conquering way,
And let thy deathful arm dash safety from his side!
    As the proud wave, on whose broad back
      The storm its burden heaves [h],
      Drives on the scatter'd wreck
        Its ruin leaves;
    So let thy sweeping progress roll,
      Fierce, resistless, rapid, strong,
Pour, like the billow of the flood, o'erwhelming might along!

  From king to king [i], let death thy steps await,
      Thou messenger of fate,
  Whose awful mandate thou art chosen to bear:

Take

---

[h] It is impossible that the utmost stretch of human imagination and genius could start an image of greater sublimity than this!—Had Fergus never given any further proof of his talents than what is exhibited in the ode now before us, this stanza alone had been sufficient to have rendered his name immortal!

[i] The monarch, and the provincial kings, who were united against the Fenii.

Take no vain truce, no respite yield,
'Till thine be the contested field;
O thou, of champion'd fame the royal heir!
Pierce the proud squadrons of the foe,
And o'er their slaughter'd heaps triumphant rise!
Oh, in fierce charms, and lovely might array'd!
Bright, in the front of battle, wave thy blade!
Oh, let thy fury rise upon my voice!
Rush on, and glorying in thy strength rejoice!
Mark where yon bloody ensign flies [k]!
Rush!—seize it!—lay its haughty triumphs low!

Wide around thy carnage spread!
Heavy be the heaps of dead!
Roll on thy rapid might,
Thou roaring stream of prowess in the fight!
What tho' Finn be distant far [l],
Art thou not *thyself* a war?—

Victory

[k] The taking of the enemy's standard was, we find, an object of great importance; for we see the bard repeatedly point it out in the battle, and urge his hero to the capture of it. The striking of a standard among the Irish troops was in general a token of defeat. See O'Halloran.—" The duty of the hereditary standard-bearer " was, to preserve the royal banner; to be amongst the foremost of the troops in " action, and in the rear on a retreat; for the troops had ever their eye on the " standard, and when the prince was killed (for their princes seldom survived a " defeat) the standard was struck, which was the signal for a retreat." Thus, had Osgur been able to seize upon the enemy's banner, they might have mistaken its disappearing for the usual signal, and so been thrown into confusion.

[l] Finn, at the time of this battle, was absent on a Roman expedition, and Cairbre took advantage of this circumstance, to hasten the issue of the contest. A beautiful

and

Victory shall be all thy own,
And this day's glory thine, and thine alone!
Be thou the foremost of thy race in fame!
So shall the bard exalt thy deathless name!
So shall thy sword, supreme o'er numbers, rise,
And vanquish'd Tamor's [n] groans ascend the skies!

Tho'

and most affecting poem (ascribed to Oisin) on this subject, informs us, that Finn, with his troops, returned on the eve of the battle, and that he arrived just time enough to take a last adieu of his dying grandson. Their meeting is described, and is deeply pathetic. The poet also adds, that " Finn never after was known to " smile: Peace, after that, had no sweets, nor war any triumphs that could restore " joy to his breast, or raise one wish for ambition or for glory, even though the " empire of Heaven itself were to be won by his arm, or were offered to his ac-
" ceptance!"

[n] Tamor, or Teamor, the royal seat of the monarch of Ireland. " Its chief
" court, (says O'Conor) was three hundred feet in length, thirty in height, and
" fifty in breadth. It had access by fourteen doors, which opened on their several
" apartments, fitted up for the kings and deputies of each province: The royal seat
" was erected in the middle of the house, where the monarch sat in state, with his
" *Afionn*, or imperial cap on his head. The kings of the two Munsters took their
" seats on his left; those of Ulster, on his right; the king of Leinster, in his
" front; and the king of Connaught, together with the *Ollamhain*, behind the
" throne. The particular reasons for such a disposition are not set down in any
" MSS. come to our hands.

" This high court of convention was surrounded by four other large houses, fitted
" up for the lodging and accommodation of the several provincial kings and deputies,
" during the session; close to these were other houses; one for state prisoners, ano-
" ther for Fileas, and another for the princesses, and the women who attended at
" court.

" Teamor was the royal seat of the kings of Ireland, and the principal court of
" legislation, from the days of Ollamh Fodla, down to the reign of Dermod Mac
Cervaill;

Tho' unequal be the fight,
Tho' unnumber'd be the foe [n],
No thought on fear, or on defeat beftow,
For conqueft waits to crown thy caufe, and thy fuccefsful might!
Rufh, therefore, on, amid the battle's rage,
Where fierce contending kings engage,
And powerlefs lay thy proud opponents low!

O lovely warrior! Form of grace,
Be not difmay'd [o]!
Friend of the Bards! think on thy valiant race!
O thou whom none in vain implore,

Whofe

"Cervaill; fo that the Fees of Teamor continued, from time to time, through a feries of more than eleven hundred years." *Differtations on the Hift. of Ireland*, p. 108.

The fear of extending this note to too great a length has obliged me, though reluctantly, to give only extracts from Mr. O'CONOR's defcription. For a more enlarged account of this celebrated palace, fee *Collectanea*, vol. i.

[n] The Fenii were greatly out-numbered in this battle. In another poem on the fubject, attributed to Oifin, and addrefied to St. Patrick, we find this paffage. "There was Cairbre Liffecar, at the head of Erin's mighty hofts, marching againft our forces, to the field of Gabhra, the battle of fatal ftrokes! There was alfo Mac Garaidh, and a thoufand champions, afiembled againft the powers of my fon:—Nine battalions alfo from Ulfter, and the Munfter troops, againft our Leinfter legion; befides the king of Connaught, and his valiant bands, who joined with the monarch againft us, in that day's engagement. Unfair, and unequal was that divifion of our forces, for finall was the band of the Fenii."

[o] Here it appears that Ofgur begins for a moment to yield; but quickly after, animated, and renovated by the exhortations of his bard, we find him again dealing death around.

Whose soul by fear was never sway'd,
Now let the battle round thy ensigns roar!

Wide the vengeful ruin spread!
Heap the groaning field with dead!
Furious be thy griding sword,
Death with every stroke descend!
Thou to whose fame earth can no match afford;
That fame which shall thro' time, as thro' the world, extend!

Shower thy might upon the foe!
Lay their pride, in Gabhra, low!
Thine be the sway of this contested field!
To thee for aid the Fenii fly [p];
On that brave arm thy country's hopes rely,
From every foe thy native land to shield!

Aspect of beauty! pride of praise!
Summit of heroic fame!
O theme of Erin! youth of matchless deeds!
Think on thy wrongs! now, now let vengeance raise
Thy valiant arm!—and let destruction flame,

Till

---

[p] The Irish in general were frequently called *Fenians*, or *Phenians*, from their great ancestor *Phenius Farsa*, or, perhaps, in allusion to their Phœnician descent. But the Leinster legions proudly arrogated that name entirely to themselves, and called their celebrated body, exclusively, *Fenii*, or *Fiana Eireann*.

'Till low beneath thy sword each chief of Ulster lies!
O prince of numerous hosts, and bounding steeds!
Raise thy red shield, with tenfold force endu'd!
Forsake not the fam'd path thy fathers⁋ have pursu'd!
But let, with theirs, thy equal honours rise!

Hark!—Anguish groans!—the battle bleeds
Before thy spear!—its flight is death!—
    Now, o'er the heath,
    The foe recedes!
  And wide the hostile crimson flows!—
  See how it dyes thy deathful blade!—
See, in dismay, each routed squadron flies!
Now!—now thy havoc thins the ranks of fight,
  And scatters o'er the field thy foes!—
O still be thy encreasing force display'd!
Slack not the noble ardour of thy might!
Pursue—pursue with death their flight!—
    Rise, arm of Erin!—Rise!—

⁋ All of the tribe of Boishne were particularly famed for prowess, and celebrated by our ancient poets.

II.

ODE

TO

GAUL.

Y

ADVERTISEMENT.

TO throw light on the subject of the following Ode, I have endeavoured, in vain, to procure a copy of the legend of bruighan beag na h'almuine, *mentioned in* Mr. WALKER's Irish Bards; *in which, he says, is related the* "celebrated contention for precedence between "Finn *and* Gaul, *near* Finn's *palace at* Almhain. *The attending* "Bards, *(continues he) observing the engagement to grow very* "sharp, were apprehensive of the consequences, and determined, if "possible, to cause a cessation of hostilities. To effect this, they shook "The Chain of Silence, and flung themselves among the ranks, ex- "tolling the sweets of peace, and the atchievements of the combatants' "ancestors. Immediately both parties, laying down their arms, listened, "with mute attention, to the harmonious lays of their Bards, and in "the end rewarded them with precious gifts [a]."

I regret much that I have never seen this legend, and therefore can only conjecture that the Ode before us was composed, or rather recited, extempore, upon the same occasion. There is frequent mention made, in our romances and poems, of a memorable contest between the rival tribes of Morni *and* Boihne, *of which* Gaul *and* Finn *were the leaders; and that, by the mediation of the Bards, it was finally concluded in peace: but I have never seen any particular account of the dispute, or description of the combat: nor been able to obtain any further information upon the subject, than the little I have here given to the public.*

---

[a] *Hist. Mem. Irish Bards*, p. 44. The legend here alluded to is not in the possession of Mr. WALKER; if it was, his politeness and public spirit would not have suffered him to refuse it.

ODE TO GAUL,

THE SON OF MORNI.

H IGH-minded Gaul, whose daring soul
Stoops not to our Chief's [a] controul!
Champion of the navy's pride [b]!
 Mighty ruler of the tide!
 Rider of the stormy wave,
 Hostile nations to enslave [c]!

Shield

---

[a] Finn Mac-Cumhal, then general of the Irish militia.

[b c] " Besides their standing armies, we find the Irish kept up a considerable naval
" force, whereby, from time to time, they poured troops into Britain and Gaul,
" which countries they long kept under contribution. To this, however, many
" objections have been made; as if a people who invaded Ireland in thirty large
" ships could ever be condemned to make use of noevogs, and currachs!—Their
" migrations from Egypt to Greece, and from thence to Spain, have also been
" doubted, from the supposed difficulty of procuring shipping; whilst at the same
" period of time no objections have been made to the accounts of the Phœnicians,
" the

Shield of freedom's glorious boaſt!
Head of her unconquer'd hoſt!
Ardent ſon of Morni's might!
Terror of the fields of fight!
Long renown'd and dreadful name!
Hero of auſpicious fame!
Champion, in our cauſe to arm!
Tongue, with eloquence to charm!
With depth of ſenſe, and reach of manly thought;
With every grace, and every beauty fraught!

  Girt with heroic might,
When glory, and thy country call to arms,
Thou go'ſt to mingle in the loud alarms,
   And lead the rage of fight!
  Thine, hero! thine the princely ſway
   Of each conflicting hour;

Thine

" the Tyrians, and, after them, the Greeks, having very conſiderable fleets, and mak-
" ing very diſtant ſettlements." O'HALL. *Introd. to the Hiſt. and Antiq. of Ireland*,
p. 125.

The ſame learned author proceeds to bring forward ſuch proofs of the naval power of our early anceſtors, as muſt do away every doubt, in minds of any reaſon or candour; but a quotation of them at large would exceed the limits of a note; my readers are therefore referred to the valuable work from which the above is taken. In many parts of Colonel VALLANCEY's ineſtimable *Collectanea*, they may alſo find proofs of the knowledge of the early Iriſh in naval affairs:—indeed, the aſtoniſhing number of names (no leſs than between forty and fifty) for a ſhip, in the Iriſh language, appears to give ground for concluding that there muſt have been *ſome* degree of proportionable variety in their ſtructure.

Thine ev'ry bright endowment to difplay,
The fmile of beauty, and the arm of pow'r!
Science, beneath our hero's fhade,
Exults, in all her patron's gifts array'd:
Her Chief, the foul of every fighting field!
The arm,—the heart, alike unknown to yield!

Hear, O Finn! thy people's voice!
Trembling on our hills ᵈ we plead;
O let our fears to peace incline thy choice!
Divide the fpoil ᵉ, and give the hero's meed!
For bright and various is his wide renown,
And war and fcience weave his glorious crown!

Did all the hofts of all the earth unite,
From pole to pole, from wave to wave,

Exulting

ᵈ This alludes to a cuftom which prevailed, amongft the early Irifh, of holding all their public meetings, and frequently their feafts, on the tops of lofty eminences. In the few prefatory lines, annexed to this ode, I have hazarded a conjecture that it was one of the extemporaneous compofitions, fo celebrated in the romance of bruʒđa n beaʒ na b' aɫınıujne; yet this paffage feems an objection, unlefs we fuppofe that an entertaiment, or a peaceable meeting, ended in a battle, (which indeed might have been the cafe) for the mention of " hills" here, implies peace, and the quotation from the romance exprefsly tells us, that the ode was fung *at the combat*.

ᵉ Poffibly it might have been about the divifion of the booty, gained in fome Britifh, or perhaps Continental expedition, that the tribes of Morni and Boifhne were at variance: at leaft it appears by this paffage that a part of their difcontents arofe from fome fuch occafion.

Exulting in their might:
His is that monarchy of foul
To fit him for the wide controul,
　　The empire of the brave!

Friend of learning! mighty name!
Havoc of hosts, and pride of fame!
Fierce as the foaming strength of ocean's rage,
　When nature's powers in strife engage,
　　So does his dreadful progress roll,
　　And such the force that lifts his soul!

Fear him, chief of Erin's might!
　And his foe no longer be;
Sun of honor's sacred light,
　Rending storm of death is he!

Finn of the flowing locks ^f, O hear my voice!
　No more with Gaul contend!
Be peace, henceforth, thy happy choice,
　And gain a valiant friend!

　　　　　　　　　　　　　Secure

---

^f The natural and beautiful ornament of *hair* was much cherished and esteemed amongst the ancient Irish. I know not whence the idea of their *matted* locks (so often mentioned by English chroniclers) had its rise:—certain it is that we meet with no such expression, in any of our Irish annals, legends, or poems:—on the contrary, the epithets "flowing,—curling—waving locks," perpetually occur, and are apparently esteemed as essential to the beauty of the warrior, as to that of the fair.

Secure of victory, to the field
His conquering standard goes;
'Tis his the powers of fight to wield,
And woe awaits his foes!

Not to mean infiduous art [s]
Does the great name of Gaul its terrors owe;
But from a brave, undaunted heart
His glories flow!

Z   Stature

---

[s] "What added luftre to the native valour, was, the extreme opennefs, candour, and fimplicity of this people (the Irifh); not even to gratify that infatiable thirft for power, the fource of fuch devaftations, do we often read of indirect or difhonorable means ufed. Heralds were fent to denounce fair, open war, and the place, time and action were previoufly fettled. If any unforefeen accident difappointed either party, as to the number of troops, &c. notice was fent to his opponent, and a further day was appointed, and generally granted." O'HALL. *Int. to the Hift. and Antiq. of Ireland*, p. 223.

Indeed, for a fpirit of honor, and a natural rectitude of mind, the Irifh were remarked even by the writers of a nation, once their bitter enemies. Their love of juftice, and attachment to the laws, was thus acknowledged by Baron FINGLAS, in the days of Henry the Eighth. "The laws and ftatutes made by the Irifh, on their hills, they keep firm and ftable, without breaking them for any favour or reward." Baron FINGLAS's *Breviate of Ireland*. Sir JOHN DAVIS too, (Attorney General in the reign of James the Firft) acknowledges that "there is no nation under the fun that love equal and indifferent juftice better than the Irifh; or will reft better fatisfied with the execution thereof, although it be againft themfelves." DAVES's *Hift. of Ireland*. Alfo COOKE, treating of our laws, fays, "For I have been informed by many of them that have had judicial places there, and *partly of mine own knowledge*, that there is no nation of the Chriftian world, that are greater lovers of juftice than they are; which virtue muft of neceflity be accompanied by many others." COOKE's *Inftitutes*, chap. 76.

Stature sublime [h], and awful mien!
Arm of strength, by valour steel'd!
Sword of fate, in battle keen,
Sweeping o'er the deadly field!

Finn of the dark-brown hair! O hear my voice!
No more with Gaul contend!
Be peace sincere henceforth thy choice,
And gain a valiant friend!
In peace, tho' inexhausted from his breast
Each gentle virtue flows,
In war, no force his fury can arrest,
And hopeless are his foes.

Leader of the shock of arms,
Loudest in the loud alarms!
Friend of princes, princely friend,
First in bounty to transcend!
Patron of the schools [i] encrease!
Sword of war, and shield of peace!

Glory

---

[h] Amongst our early ancestors, not only personal strength, and courage, but also beauty,—a graceful figure, an elegant address, and majestic stature, were requisite in the candidates for knighthood. See O'HALLORAN. KEATING.

[i] To be esteemed the patrons of science, was (next to military renown,) the chief object of ambition, with the princes, and chieftains of the ancient Irish.

Glory of the fields of fame!
Pride of hosts! illustrious name!
Strength of pow'r! triumphant might!
Firm maintainer of the fight!
Fierce in the conflicting hour;
Bulwark of the royal pow'r!

O generous charm of all-accomplish'd love!—
Locks of bright redundant shade!
Breast where strength and beauty strove!
White as the hue the chalky cliffs display'd [k]!
To thee glad Erin should her homage pay,
And joy to own thy glorious sway!
Spirit resolute to dare!

Aspect

---

[k] " The breast like the chalky cliff."—" The hero with the breast of snow."—" The side, white as the foam of the falling stream,"—frequently occur in our Irish poets' descriptions of their youthful warriors. The ideas which these passages convey, are rather inconsistent with the disgusting ones that must be conceived of the early Irish, by those who give credit to the accounts of writers who tell us, *they were shirts dyed in saffron, for the convenience of hiding the dirt,* and further add, that *they never pulled them off until fairly worn out.*—In this case, whatever nature might have done in the blanching of their skins—habit must have counteracted all her good intentions. Whence then did the bard derive his idea?—So false a compliment, one would think, must rather have drawn resentment upon him than thanks, by reminding his slovenly heroes what filthy creatures they were. But indeed the assertion seems too absurd for argument, and is most worthily answered by a smile. The fact is, that the antient Irish were so *remarkably cleanly,* as never to rest from fatigue, or sit down to meat, after exercise, until they had first refreshed and cleansed themselves by ablutions. See KEATING, WARNER, &c.

Aspect sweet beyond compare,
Bright with inspiring soul! with blooming beauty fair!
Warrior of majestic charms!
High in fame, and great in arms!
Well thy daring soul may tow'r,
Nothing is above thy pow'r!

Hear, O Finn! my ardent zeal,
While his glories I reveal!
Fierce as ocean's angry wave [1],
When conflicting tempests rave;
As still, with the encreasing storm,
Increasing ruin clothes its dreadful form,
Such is the Chief, o'erwhelming in his force,
Unconquer'd in his swift, resistless course!

Tho' in the smiles of blooming grace array'd,
And bright in beauty's every charm;
Yet think not, therefore, that his soul will bend,
Nor with the Chief contend;
For well he knows to wield the glittering blade,
And fatal is his arm!

Bounty

---

[1] Here we find a repetition of the same image that occurs a few stanzas before: the language is indeed a little varied, yet still the image is the same. I have already apologized for this frequent repetition, and entreat my readers to recollect what has been said upon the subject. But an extemporaneous composition, like this, ought to be exempt from that severity of criticism which may with justice be exercised on the productions of study, and the labours of time.

Bounty in his bosom dwells;
High his soul of courage swells!
Fierce the dreadful war to wage,
Mix in the whirl of fight, and guide the battle's rage!
Wide, wide around triumphant ruin wield,
Roar through the ranks of death, and thunder o'er the field!

Many a chief of mighty sway
Fights beneath his high command;
Marshals his troops in bright array,
And spreads his banners o'er the land.

Champion of unerring aim!
Chosen of Kings, triumphant name!
Bounty's hand, and Wisdom's head,
Valiant arm, and lion soul,
O'er red heaps of slaughter'd dead,
Thundering on to Glory's goal!

Pride of Finian fame, and arms!
Mildness [m] of majestic charms!
Swiftness of the battle's rage!
Theme of the heroic page!

Firm

---

[m] "The knowledge of arms was but a *part* of the education of the Celtic warrior. In Ireland, they were well informed in history, poetry, and the polite arts; they were sworn to be the protectors of the fair, and the avengers of their wrongs; and to be polite in words and address, even to their greatest enemies." O'HALLORAN.

Firm in purpose! fierce in fight!
Arm of slaughter! foul of might!
Glory's light! illuftrious name!
Splendour of the paths of fame!
Born bright precedent to yield,
And fweep with death the hoftile field!

Leader of Sylvan fports; the hound, the horn,
    The early melodies of morn!—
Love of the fair, and favourite of the mufe [n].
In peace, each peaceful fcience to diffufe:
Prince of the noble deeds! accomplifh'd name!
Increafing bounty! comprehenfive fame!

Ardent, bold, unconquer'd Knight!
Breaker of the bulwark's might!
Chief of war's refiftlefs blade,
With fpears of wrath, and arms of death array'd!
Heroic Gaul! beneath thy princely fway,
The earth might bend, and all her hoft obey!

Hear, O Gaul! the poet's voice!
O be peace thy gen'rous choice!

Yield

---

[n] Irifh hiftory informs us, that thofe of their Monarchs or Chiefs who, befides the accuftomed patronage of fcience and fong, were *themfelves* poffeffed of the gifts of the mufe, obtained, on that account, from their Fileas, and from their countrymen in general, a diftinguifhed portion of honor, refpect and celebrity.

Yield thee to the Bard's defire!
Calm the terrors of thine ire!
Ceafe we here our mutual ftrife;
And peaceful be our future life!

GAUL. I yield, O Fergus! to thy mild defire;
   Thy words, O Bard! are fweet;
   Thy wifh I freely meet,
   And bid my wrath expire.
  No more to difcontent a prey,
  I give to peace the future day:
   To thee my foul I bend,
   O guilelefs° friend!
The accents of whofe glowing lip well know that foul to fway.

BARD. O fwift in honor's courfe! thou generous name!
   Illuftrious Chief, of never dying fame!

° A character ᵹan çheall, (without *guile* or *deceit*,) was efteemed the higheft that could be given, amongft the ancient Irifh: and the favourite panegyric of a Bard, to his favourite hero, would be, that *he had a heart incapable of guile*.

III.

ODE

ON A

SHIP.

ADVERTISEMENT.

THE following descriptive Ode was written by a gentleman of the name of Fitz-Gerald, *in the reign of* Elizabeth, *as appears from passages in some other pieces, composed by the same author. The subject of it, we see, is a voyage to* Spain; *but the idea of thus celebrating the subject, was probably suggested by the third Ode of* Horace: *for though the* Irish *poet can by no means be said to have copied the* Roman *one, yet he seems to have, in some measure, adopted his design.*

I should be accused of treason to the majesty of Horace, *did I say that he is surpassed by our* Irish *bard upon this subject:—I shall not, therefore, risk the censure:—but, my readers are at liberty to do it, if they please.*

For the original of the following Ode I am indebted to Mr. O'Flanagan *of* Trinity College.—*There is also another copy of it in* Mr. O'Halloran's *collection.*

ODE, BY FITZ-GERALD,

Written on his setting out on a VOYAGE to SPAIN.

BLESS my good ship, protecting pow'r of grace!
And o'er the winds, the waves, the destin'd coast,
Breathe benign spirit!—Let thy radiant host
    Spread their angelic shields!
Before us, the bright bulwark let them place,
And fly beside us, through their azure fields!

    O calm the voice of winter's storm!
    Rule the wrath of angry seas!
The fury of the rending blast appease,
Nor let its rage fair ocean's face deform!
    O check the biting wind of spring,
        And, from before our course,
    Arrest the fury of its wing,
        And terrors of its force!
So may we safely pass the dang'rous cape,
And from the perils of the deep escape!

                        I grieve

I grieve to leave the splendid feats
Of Teamor's ancient fame!
Mansion of heroes, now farewell!
Adieu, ye sweet retreats,
Where the fam'd hunters of your ancient vale,
Who swell'd the high heroic tale,
Were wont of old to dwell!
And you, bright tribes of sunny streams, adieu!
While my sad feet their mournful path pursue,
Ah, well their lingering steps my grieving soul proclaim!

Receive me now, my ship!—hoist now thy sails,
To catch the favouring gales.
O Heaven! before thine awful throne I bend!
O let thy power thy servants now protect!
Increase of knowledge and of wisdom lend,
Our course, through ev'ry peril to direct;
To steer us safe through ocean's rage,
Where angry storms their dreadful strife maintain;
O may thy pow'r their wrath assuage!
May smiling suns, and gentle breezes reign!

Stout is my well-built ship, the storm to brave,
Majestic in its might,
Her bulk, tremendous on the wave,
Erects its stately height!

From

From her strong bottom, tall in air
  Her branching masts aspiring rise;
Aloft their cords, and curling heads they bear,
And give their sheeted ensigns to the skies;
While her proud bulk frowns awful on the main,
And seems the fortress of the liquid plain!

  Dreadful in the shock of fight,
    She goes—she cleaves the storm!
Where ruin wears its most tremendous form
    She sails, exulting in her might;
On the fierce necks of foaming billows rides,
    And through the roar
Of angry ocean, to the destin'd shore
    Her course triumphant guides;
As though beneath her frown the winds were dead,
And each blue valley was their silent bed!

  Through all the perils of the main
She knows her dauntless progress to maintain!
  Through quicksands, flats, and breaking waves,
    Her dang'rous path she dares explore;
  Wrecks, storms, and calms, alike she braves,
And gains, with scarce a breeze, the wish'd-for shore!
    Or in the hour of war,
    Fierce on she bounds, in conscious might,
      To meet the promis'd fight!
        While, distant far,

                                            The

The fleets of wondering nations gaze,
And view her courſe with emulous amaze,
    As, like ſome champion'd ſon of fame,
    She ruſhes to the ſhock of arms,
And joys to mingle in the loud alarms,
Impell'd by rage, and fir'd with glory's flame.

Sailing with pomp upon the watery plain,
    Like ſome huge monſter of the main,
    My ſhip her ſpeckl'd boſom laves,
And high in air her curling enſigns waves;
Her ſtately ſides, with poliſh'd beauty gay,
And gunnel, bright with gold's effulgent ray.

    As the fierce Griffin's dreadful flight
      Her monſtrous bulk appears,
    While o'er the ſeas her towering height,
And her wide wings, tremendous ſhade! ſhe rears.
Or, as a champion, thirſting after fame,—
The ſtrife of ſwords,—the deathleſs name,—
So does ſhe ſeem, and ſuch her rapid courſe!
    Such is the rending of her force;
When her ſharp keel, where dreadful ſplendours play,
Cuts through the foaming main its liquid way.
Like the red bolt of Heaven, ſhe ſhoots along,
Dire as its flight, and as its fury ſtrong!

                                    God

God of the winds! O hear my pray'r!
    Safe paſſage now beſtow!
Soft, o'er the ſlumbering deep, may fair
    And proſperous breezes blow!
O'er the rough rock, and ſwelling wave,
    Do thou our progreſs guide!
Do thou from angry ocean ſave,
    And o'er its rage preſide.

Speed my good ſhip, along the rolling ſea,
O Heaven! and ſmiling ſkies, and favouring gales' decree!
  Speed the high-maſted ſhip of dauntleſs force,
  Swift in her glittering flight, and founding courſe!
      Stately moving on the main,
      Foreſt of the azure plain!
      Faithful to confided truſt,
      To her promis'd glory juſt;
      Deadly in the ſtrife of war,
      Rich in ev'ry gift of peace,
        Swift from afar,
      In peril's fearful hour,
Mighty in force, and bounteous in her power,
    She comes, kind aid ſhe lends,
    She frees her ſupplicating friends,
And fear before her flies, and dangers ceaſe!

Hear, bleſt Heaven! my ardent pray'r!
My ſhip—my crew—O take us to thy care!
   O may no peril bar our way!
Fair blow the gales of each propitious day!
Soft ſwell the floods, and gently roll the tides,
While, from Dunboy, along the ſmiling main
We ſail, until the deſtined coaſt we gain,
And ſafe in port our gallant veſſel rides!

ELEGIES.

ADVERTISEMENT.

OF the Irish Majnbna, or Funeral Elegy, I have been able to procure but few good originals; however, there are, doubtless, many of them still extant; as also, many other beautiful compositions of our ancient country-men, which I have never seen.

The Irish language, perhaps beyond all others, is peculiarly suited to every subject of Elegy; and, accordingly, we find it excel in plaintive and sentimental poetry. The Love Elegies of the Irish are exquisitely pathetic, and breathe an artless tenderness, that is infinitely more affecting than all the laboured pomp of declamatory woe.

The public are here presented with a few specimens of both kinds. To the following, on the Daughter of Owen, the foremost place is assigned, because (though without a date) it bears the appearance of belonging to an earlier period than any other of the Elegies contained in this volume. The original of it is in the hands of Mr. O'Flanagan, who has in vain endeavoured to procure some anecdotes of the author, and of the fair subject: that it was written by a poet of the name of O'Geran, is all that can be collected from enquiry.

In the Irish, it is one of the most beautiful compositions I have ever seen: it is, of all my originals, the one I most wished to give in its expressions, as well as its thoughts, to the English reader; but in this, notwithstanding all my efforts, I am conscious that I have failed.

Either

Either I am very unhappy in my choice of words, or it is next to impossible to convey the spirit of this poem into a literal translation; I tried, to the utmost my power, but, to my extreme regret, I found myself unequal to the task, though I chose an irregular measure, that I might be more at liberty to adhere closely to the expressions of my original, which are comprehensive, and striking, beyond the power of any one to conceive, who is unacquainted with the genius of the Irish language. In some passages, a single word conveys the meaning and force of a sentence; it was, therefore, impossible to translate it without periphrasis, and, of course, many of its native graces are lost: I shall be most happy to see some abler pen restore them, as I really lament sincerely my inability to do all the justice I wished, to that tender simplicity, and those beautiful expressions, which I read with so much delight.

Determined, however, to give the Poem, in the best manner I could, to the public, I have conveyed its thoughts into the following version; and, for those passages wherein the language is thought to be too diffuse, I rely on the candour of my readers to accept of this apology.

In the original there are some repetitions, and also a few entire lines, which are not given in the English version. I apprehended it might, otherwise, be too long, and have therefore omitted what I thought could best be spared.

I.
ELEGY
TO THE
DAUGHTER OF OWEN.

DAUGHTER of Owen! behold my grief!
 Look soft pity's dear relief!
Oh! let the beams of those life-giving eyes
 Bid my fainting heart arise,
  And, from the now opening grave,
   Thy faithful lover save!

Snatch from death his dire decree!
What is impossible to thee?
Star of my life's soul-cheering light!
Beam of mildness, soft as bright!
Do not, like others of thy sex,
Delight the wounded heart to vex!

But hear, O hear thy lover's sighs,
And with true pity, hither turn thine eyes!
   Still, tho' wasted with despair,
     And pale with pining care,
Still, O soft maid! this form may meet thy sight,
No object yet of horror, or affright.

   Long unregarded have I sigh'd,
     Love's soft return deny'd!
   No mutual heart, no faithful fair,
   No sympathy to soothe my care!
   O thou, to every bosom dear!
   Universal charmer!—hear!—
No more sweet pity's gentle power withstand!
   Reach the dear softness of thy hand!
O let it be the beauteous pledge of peace,
To bless my love, and bid my sorrows cease!

Haste, haste!—no more the kind relief delay!
Come, speak, and look, and smile my woes away!
   O haste, e'er pity be too late!
   Haste, and intercept my fate!
Or soon behold life, love, and sorrow end,
And see me to an early tomb descend!—
For, ah, what med'cine can my cure impart,
Or what physician heal a broken heart?

'Tis thine alone the fovereign balm to give,
Bind the foul's wound, and bid the dying live!
'Tis thine, of right, my anguifh to affuage,
If love can move, or gratitude engage!
For thee alone, all others I forfake!
For thee alone, my cares, my wifhes wake,
O locks of Beauty's bright redundant flow,
Where waving foftnefs, curling fragrance grow!

Thine is the fway of foul-fubduing charms,
That every breaft of all defence difarms!
With thee my will, enamour'd, hugs its chain,
And Love's dear ardours own thy potent reign!
Take then the heart my conftant paffion gave,
Cherifh its faith, and from its anguifh fave!
T. the poor trembler to thy gentle breaft,
And hufh its fears, and foothe its cares to reft!

For all I have, in timid filence borne,
For all the pangs that have this bofom torn,
   Speak now the word, and heal my pain,
      Nor be my fufferings vain!
For now, on life itfelf their anguifh preys,
And heavy on my heart the burden weighs!

   O firft, and faireft of thy fex!
Thou whofe bright form the fun of beauty decks!

Once more let Love that gentle bosom sway,
  O give the dear enchantment way!
Raise,—fondly raise those snowy arms,
  Thou branch of blooming charms!
Again for me thy fragrance breathe,
And thy fair tendrils round me wreath!

Again be soft affection's pow'r display'd,
While sweetly wand'ring in the secret shade:
Reach forth thy lip,—the honey'd kiss bestow!
Reach forth thy lip, where balmy odours grow!
Thy lip, whose sounds such rapture can impart,
Whose words of sweetness sink into the heart!

  Again, at gentle Love's command,
    Reach forth thy snowy hand!
  Soft into mine its whiteness steal,
    And its dear pressure let me feel!
Unveil the bashful radiance of thine eyes,
(Bright trembling gems!) and let me see them rise.
Lift the fair lids where their soft glories roll,
And send their secret glances to my soul!

O what delight, thus hand in hand to rove!
  To breathe fond vows of mutual love!
To see thee sweet affection's balm impart,
And smile to health my almost broken heart!
Ah! let me give the dear idea scope!
Ah! check not yet the fondly-trembling hope!—

Spent

Spent is the rock by which my life was fed,
And spun by anguish to a sightless thread!
A little more,—and all in death will end,
And fruitless pity o'er my grave will bend!

When I am dead, shun thou my cruel fate,
Lest equal harms on equal perils wait.
Hear my last words, their fond request declare,
For even in death, thy safety is my care!
No more, O maid! thy polish'd glass invite,
To give that fatal beauty to thy sight!
Enough one life its dangers to inthrall!
Enough that I its hapless victim fall!—
O thou, more bright, more cheering to our eyes,
Than the young beams that warm the dawning skies!

Hast thou not heard the weeping muse relate
The mournful tale of young Narcissus' fate?—
How, as the Bards of ancient days have sung,
While fondly o'er the glassy stream he hung,
Enamour'd he his lovely form survey'd,
And dy'd, at length, the victim of a shade.

Sweet! do not thou a like misfortune prove!
O be not such thy fate, nor such thy love!
Let peril rather warn, and wisdom guide,
And from thyself thy own attractions hide!

No more on that bewitching beauty gaze,
Nor truſt thy fight to meet its dazzling blaze!

Hide, hide that breaſt, ſo ſnowy fair!
Hide the bright treſſes of thy hair!
And oh! thoſe eyes of radiant ruin hide!
What heart their killing luſtre can abide?
Slow while their ſoft and tender glances roll,
They ſteal its peace from the unwary ſoul!

Hide the twin berries of thy lip's perfume,
Their breathing fragrance, and their deepening bloom;
And thoſe fair cheeks, that glow like radiant morn,
When ſol's bright rays his bluſhing eaſt adorn!
No more to thy incautious fight diſplay'd,
Be that dear form, in tender grace array'd!
  The roſy finger's tap'ring charms;
  The ſlender hand, the ſnowy arms;
  The little foot, ſo ſoft and fair;
  The timid ſtep, the modeſt air;
No more their graces let thine eyes purſue,
But hide, O hide the peril from thy view!

  This done,—in ſafety may'ſt thou reſt,
    And peace poſſeſs thy breaſt.
  For who can with thy charms compare,
  And who but thee is worth a care?—
                            O! from

O! from thyself thine eyes, thy heart protect,
And none beside, thy quiet can affect.

For thee, while all the youths of Erin sigh,
   And, struck beneath thine eye-beam, die;
  Still peace within thy bosom reigns,
    Unfelt by thee their pains!
O graceful meekness! ever new delight!
Sweet bashful charm of captivated sight!
Why, while my heart (fond subject!) bless'd thy sway,
Why did'st thou steal its vital soul away?
Ah! with the theft the life of life is fled,
And leaves me almost number'd with the dead!

While thus, in vain, my anguish I bewail,
    Thy peace no fears assail;
  None in my hapless cause will move;
Each partial heart is fetter'd to thy love!
Thou whose fair hand bids the soft harp complain,
Flies o'er the string, and wakes the tender strain,
Wilt thou not some—some kind return impart,
For my lost quiet, and my plunder'd heart?

    O thou dear angel-smiling face!
    Fair form of fascinating grace!

Bright as the gentle moon's soft splendours rise,
To light her steps of beauty through the skies!
O turn!--on me those tender glances roll,
And dart their cheering lustre on my soul!
Be dear compassion in their beams exprest,
And heal with love the sorrows of my breast!

ADVERTISEMENT.

THE original of the following pathetic little elegy, was taken down from the dictation of a young woman, in the county of Mayo, *by* Mr. O'Flanagan, *who was struck with the tender and beautiful simplicity which it breathes. No account can be obtained, either of the writer, or of the period in which it was written.*

This elegy was translated long since, without any view to publication, and the language is, therefore, rather more diffuse, than that of my other translations.

II.

E L E G Y.

WHEN oaths confirm a lover's vow,
  He thinks I believe him true :—
Nor oaths, nor lovers heed I now,
  For memory dwells on you!

The tender talk, the face like fnow
  On the dark mountain's height;
Or the fweet bloffom of the floe,
  Fair blooming to the fight!

But falfe as fair, alas, you prove,
  Nor aught but fortune prize;
The youth who gain'd my heart's firft love,
  From truth—to wealth he flies!

Ah that he could but still deceive,
  And I still think him true!
Still fondly, as at first, believe,
  And each dear scene renew!

Again, in the sequester'd vale,
  Hear love's sweet accents flow,
And quite forget the tender tale,
  ~~That~~ [Had] fill'd my heart with woe!

See this dear trifle,—(kept to prove
  How I the giver prize;)
More precious to my faithful love,
  Than all thy sex's sighs!

What tears for thee in secret flow,
  Sweet victor of the green!—
For maiden pride would veil my woe,
  And seek to weep unseen.

Return ye days to love consign'd,
  Fond confidence, and joy!
The crouded fair, where tokens kind
  The lover's cares employ!

Return once more, mine eyes to blef
　Thou flower of Erin's youth!
Return sweet proofs of tendernefs,
　And vows of endlefs truth!

And Hymen at Love's altar ftand,
　To fanctify the fhrine,
Join the fond heart, and plighted hand,
　And make thee firmly mine,

Ere envious ocean fnatch thee hence,
　And—Oh!—to diftance bear
My love!—my comfort!—my defence!—
　And leave me—to defpair!

Yes,—yes, my only love thou art!
　Whoe'er it may difpleafe,
I will avow my captive heart,
　And fpeak its mafter's praife!

Ah, wert thou here, to grace my fide
　With dear, protecting love!
Envy might rage, and fpight deride,
　And friends in vain reprove!

May

May pangs unnumber'd pierce the breast
    That cruel envy arms,
That joys in constancy distress'd,
    And sports with its alarms!

Bright star of love-attracting light!
    For thee these terrors sway;
Grief steeps in tears the sleepless night,
    And clouds the joyless day!

Ah God!—ah how, when thou art gone,
    Shall comfort reach my heart!
Thy dwelling, and thy fate unknown,
    Or where thy steps depart!

My father grieving at my choice!
    My mother drown'd in woe!
While friends upbraid, and foes rejoice
    To see my sorrows flow!

And thou, with all thy manly charms,
    From this sad bosom torn!
Thy soothing voice,—thy sheltering arms,
    Far—far to distance borne!

Alas!—my dim and sleepless eyes
　　The clouds of death obscure!
And nature, in exhausted sighs,
　　No longer can endure!

I can no more!—sad world farewell!
　　And thou, dear youth! adieu!
Dear, tho' forsworn!—yet, cruel! tell
　　Why falshood dwells with you?

ADVERTISEMENT.

THE following Elegy *was written, nearly a century ago, by a very celebrated perfonage, of the name of* Edmond Ryan, *concerning whom many ftories are ftill circulated, but no connected account has been obtained, further than that he commanded a company of thofe unhappy free booters, called* Rapparees, *who, after the defeat of the Boyne, were obliged to abandon their dwellings and poffeffions,* " hoping *(fays* Mr. O'Halloran) " *for fafety within the precincts of the* Irifh *quarters; but they were too numerous to be employed in the army, and their miferies often obliged them to prey alike upon friend and foe: at length fome of the moft daring of them formed themfelves into independent companies, whofe fubfiftence chiefly arofe from depredations committed on the enemy.*

" *It was not choice, but neceffity, that drove them to this extreme; I have heard ancient people, who were witneffes to the calamities of thofe days, affirm, that they remembered vaft numbers of thefe poor* Ulfter Irifh, *men, women and children, to have no other beds but the ridges of potatoe-gardens, and little other covering than the canopy of heaven; they difperfed themfelves over the counties of* Limerick, Clare *and* Kerry; *and the hardnefs of the times at length fhut up all bowels of humanity, fo that moft of them perifhed by the fword, cold, or famine* *!"

From

---

* O'Halloran's *Int. to the Hift. and Ant. of Ireland,* p. 382.

From passages in this Elegy, *we may infer, that, to the misfortunes of its author alone, the desertion of his mistress was owing; but I have not been able to discover the name of this fair inconstant.*

After the translation was made from the copy first obtained of this pathetic little poem, a friend transmitted to me the following stanzas, as a part of the original Elegy.—*They appeared well entitled to preservation, and are here given to the public, who may admit or reject them at pleasure.*

Nać ḋaṁṛa ḋéjrjs an ṛgéal aṛ meaṛa ṛaoj an ġṗéjn
aṗ majojn aguṛ mé ṫṛṛ mojge
Jḟ gun ṛeaṗb gać én alaḃṛa leṛ ṛéjn
aṗ ćuṁajg no aṗ ċaeḃ mojnte
Do ṗjineaḋ mo ćṗeać, ⁊ ṛúṗṅigeaḋ mo ṅeaḋ
⁊ oṛajgeaḋ mé gan en ṅeać
ṛma ṫú ṛjn aṫeać aṛuać anḋéjg aṫeaṛ
aṗṛn ṛeaṗc mo beannać ṛéjn leaṫ.

TRANSLATION.

Ah! what woes are mine to bear,
    Life's fair morn with clouds o'ercasting!
Doom'd the victim of despair!
    Youth's gay bloom, pale sorrow blasting!

Sad

Sad the bird that sings alone,
    Flies to wilds, unseen to languish,
Pours, unheard, the ceaseless moan,
    And wastes, on desart, air its anguish!

Mine, O hapless bird! thy fate!—
    The plunder'd nest,—the lonely sorrow!—
The lost—lov'd—harmonious mate!—
    The wailing night,—the chearless morrow!

O thou dear hoard of treasur'd love!
    Though these fond arms should ne'er possess thee,
Still—still my heart its faith shall prove,
    And its last sighs shall breathe to bless thee!

I am told there are several beautiful elegiac Songs still extant, composed by Edmond Ryan, *or* Edmond of the Hill, *(as he is called, from his roving life,) but the following is the only one of them that I have ever met with. The air to which it is sung* " dies in every note," *and the Poem, though usually stiled a* Song, *I have here classed under the title of* Elegy, *because it seemed more properly to belong to that species of composition.*

III.

ELEGY.

BRIGHT her locks of beauty grew,
   Curling fair, and fweetly flowing;
And her eyes of fmiling blue,
   Oh how foft! how heav'nly glowing!

Ah! poor plunder'd heart of pain!
   When wilt thou have end of mourning?—
This long, long year, I look in vain
   To fee my only hope returning.

Oh! would thy promife faithful prove,
   And to my fond, fond bofom give thee;
Lightly then my fteps would move,
   Joyful fhould my arms receive thee!

Then, once more, at early morn,
   Hand in hand we should be straying,
Where the dew-drop decks the thorn,
   With its pearls the woods arraying.

Cold and scornful as thou art,
   Love's fond vows and faith belying,
Shame for thee now rends my heart,
   My pale cheek with blushes dying!

Why art thou false to me and Love?
   (While health and joy with thee are vanish'd)
Is it because forlorn I rove,
   Without a crime, unjustly banish'd?

Safe thy charms with me should rest,
   Hither did thy pity send thee,
Pure the love that fills my breast,
   From itself it would defend thee.

'Tis thy Edmond calls thee love,
   Come, O come and heal his anguish!
Driv'n from his home, behold him rove,
   Condemn'd in exile here to languish!

O thou dear cause of all my pains!
　With thy charms each heart subduing,
Come,—on Munster's lovely plains,
　Hear again fond passion suing.

Music, mirth, and sports are here,
　Chearful friends the hours beguiling;
Oh wouldst thou, my love! appear,
　To joy my bosom reconciling!

Sweet would seem the holly's shade,
　Bright the clust'ring berries glowing;
And, in scented bloom array'd,
　Apple-blossoms round us blowing.

Cresses waving in the stream,
　Flowers its gentle banks perfuming;
Sweet the verdant paths would seem,
　All in rich luxuriance blooming.

O bright in every grace of youth!
　Gentle charmer!—lovely wonder!
Break not fond vows and tender truth!
　O rend not ties so dear asunder!

For thee all dangers would I brave,
　　Life with joy, with pride expofing;
Breaſt for thee the ſtormy wave,
　　Winds and tides in vain oppoſing.

O might I call thee now my own!
　　No added rapture joy could borrow:
'Twould be, like heav'n, when life is flown,
　　To chear the foul and heal its ſorrow.

See thy falſehood, cruel maid!
　　See my cheek no longer glowing;
Strength departed, health decay'd;
　　Life in tears of ſorrow flowing!

Why do I thus my anguiſh tell?—
　　Why pride in woe, and boaſt of ruin?—
O loſt treaſure!—fare thee well!—
　　Lov'd to madneſs——to undoing.

Yet, O hear me fondly ſwear!
　　Though thy heart to me is frozen,
Thou alone, of thouſands fair,
　　Thou alone ſhould'ſt be my choſen.

Every scene with thee would please!
Every care and fear would fly me!
Wintery storms, and raging seas,
Would lose their gloom, if thou wert nigh me!

Speak in time, while yet I live;
Leave not faithful love to languish!
O soft breath to pity give,
Ere my heart quite break with anguish.

Pale, distracted, wild I rove,
No soothing voice my woes allaying;
Sad and devious, through each grove,
My lone steps are weary straying.

O sickness, past all med'cine's art!
O sorrow, every grief exceeding!
O wound that, in my breaking heart,
Cureless, deep, to death art bleeding!

Such, O Love! thy cruel power,
Fond excess and fatal ruin!
Such—O Beauty's fairest flower!
Such thy charms, and my undoing!

How the swan adorns that neck,
  There her down and whiteness growing;
How its snow those tresses deck,
  Bright in fair luxuriance flowing.

Mine, of right, are all those charms!
  Cease with coldness then to grieve me!
Take—O take me to thy arms,
  Or those of death will soon receive me.

ADVERTISEMENT.

THE following funeral Elegy was composed by Cormac Common, " *who* (*says* Mr. Walker) " *was born in* May, 1703, *at* Woodstock, *near* Ballin-
" dangan, *in the county of* Mayo. *His parents were poor, and honeft ; re-*
" *markable for nothing but the innocence, and fimplicity of their lives.*

" *Before he had completed the firft year of his life, the fmall-pox deprived*
" *him of his fight. This circumftamce, together with the indigence of his*
" *parents, prevented him from receiving any of the advantages of education ;*
" *but, though he could not read himfelf, he could converfe with thofe who*
" *had read ; therefore, if he wants learning, he is not without knowledge.*

" *Shewing an early fondnefs for mufic, a neighbouring gentleman determined*
" *to have him taught to play on the harp : a profeffor of that inftrument*
" *was accordingly provided, and* Cormac *received a few leffons which he*
" *practifed* con amore ; *but his patron dying fuddenly, the harp dropped*
" *from his hand, and was never after taken up.—It is probable he could not*
" *afford to ftring it.*

" *But poetry was the mufe of whom he was moft enamoured. This made*
" *him liften eagerly to the Irifh fongs, and metrical tales, which he heard*
" *fung and recited around the* " *crackling faggots*" *of his father, and his*
" *neighbours. Thefe, by frequent recitation, became ftrongly impreffed upon*
" *his memory. His mind being thus ftored, and having no other avocation, he*
" *commenced a* Man of Talk, *or a* Tale Teller. " *He left no calling, for the*
" *idle trade,*" *as our Englifh* Montaigne *obferves of* Pope.

" *He*

"He was now employed in relating legendary tales, and reciting genealogies, at rural wakes, or in the hospitable halls of country squires. Endowed with a sweet voice, and a good ear, his narrations were generally graced with the charms of melody; (I say were generally graced, because at his age, 'nature sinks in years,' and we speak of the man, with respect to his powers, as if actually a tenant of the grave.) He did not, like the Tale Teller mentioned by Sir William Temple, chaunt his tales in an uninterrupted even-tone; the monotony of his modulation was frequently broken by cadences, introduced with taste, at the close of each stanza. In rehearsing any of Oisin's poems (says Mr. Ousley) he chaunts them pretty much in the manner of Cathedral Service.

"But it was in singing some of our native airs that Cormac displayed the powers of his voice; on this occasion his auditors were always enraptured. I have been assured that no singer ever did Carolan's airs, or Oisin's celebrated Hunting Song, more justice than Cormac.

"Cormac's musical powers were not confined to his voice; he composed a few airs, one of which is extremely sweet. It is to be feared that those musical effusions will die with their author.

"But it was in poetry Cormac delighted to exercise his genius; he has composed several songs and elegies that have met with applause. As his muse was generally awakened by the call of gratitude, his poetical productions are mostly panegyrical, or elegiac [a]; they extol the living, or lament the dead. Sometimes he indulged in satire, but not often, though richly endued with that dangerous gift.

"Cormac

---

[a] I have never been so fortunate as to meet with any of Cormac's compositions, except the following elegy.

"Cormac *was twice married, but is now a widower. By both his wives he had several children;* he now resides *at* Sorrell-town, *near* Dunmore, *in the county of* Galway, *with one of his daughters, who is happily married. Though his utterance is materially injured by dental losses, and though his voice is impaired by age, yet he continues to practise his profession: so seldom are we sensible of our imperfections. It is probable that where he was once admired, he is now only endured. One of his grandsons leads him about to the houses of the neighbouring gentry, who give him money, diet, and sometimes clothes. His apparel is commonly decent, and comfortable, but he is not rich, nor does he seem solicitous about wealth: his person is large and muscular, and his moral character is unstained.*"

IV.

E L E G Y

ON THE DEATH OF

JOHN BURKE CARRENTRYLE, Esq.*

YES, Erin, for her Burke, a wreath shall twine,
And Britain own the honors of his name!
O hence with tasteless joy!—with mirth and wine!
All thoughts, but those of woe, I now disclaim!

Ye sons of science!—see your friend depart!
Ye sons of song!—your patron is no more!
Ye widow'd virtues! (cherish'd in his heart,
And wedded to his soul) your loss deplore!

F f   Grief

---

* "This gentleman (says Mr. WALKER) was pre-eminent in his day, as a sportsman, and in his private character there were many amiable traits."—*Hist. Mem. of the Irish Bards*, App. p. 58.

Grief sheds its gloom on every noble breast,
  And streaming tears his worth,—his death proclaim,
Gen'rous and brave! with every virtue blest!
  Flow'r of the tribes of honorable fame!

Alas! to the cold grave he now is borne!
  No more to wake the huntsman to the chase;
No more, with early sports, to rouze the morn,
  Or lead the sprightly courser to the race.

The learn'd, and eloquent in honor's cause!
  Of soul enlighten'd, and of fame unstain'd!
The friend of justice,—to expound our laws,
  Or yield the palm, by song or science gain'd!

O death!—since thou hast laid our glory low;
  Since our lov'd Burke, alas! is now no more;
What bliss can now each rising morn bestow;
  The race, the chase, and every joy is o'er!

O grave!—thy debt, thy cruel debt is paid!
  No more on earth shall his fair virtues bloom!
Death! thou hast hewn the branch of grateful shade,
  And laid its fragrant honors in the tomb!

Sublime

Sublime his soul!—yet gentle was his heart;
   His rural sports, his gay convivial hour
Avow'd each elegant, each social art;
   Each manly grace, and each attractive power.

Friend of the friendless, patron of distress;
   Ah, none, like him, the poor man's cause would plead!
With sweet persuasion to ensure success,
   Or soothe his sorrows, or supply his need!

O tomb that shroudest his belov'd remains!
   O death, that didst our dearest hope destroy!
Thy dreary confine all our bliss contains,
   And thy cold gates are clos'd upon our joy!

Who, now, will to the race the courser train?
   Who gain, for Connaught, the disputed prize?
From rival provinces the palm obtain?—
   Alas! with him our fame, our triumph dies!

Our light is quench'd, our glory pass'd away,
   Our Burke snatch'd from us, never to return,
Whose name bright honor's fairest gifts array,
   And science hangs her wreath upon his urn.

Eternal pleasures fill'd his social hall,
    And sweetest music charm'd, with magic sound;
Science and song obey'd his friendly call,
    And varied joys still danc'd their endless round!

But now, alas! nor sport, nor muse is there!
    No echoes now the sprightly notes await;
But wailing sounds of sorrow and despair,
    That mourn the stroke of unrelenting fate!

He is for ever gone!—weep, wretched eyes!
    Flow, flow my tears!—my heart with anguish bleed!
In the cold grave the stately hunter lies,
    Chief in the manage of the bounding steed!

O bitter woe!—O sorrow uncontroul'd!
    O death remorseless that has seal'd his doom!
Thy plains, O Munster! all our glory hold,
    And fame lies buried with him, in the tomb!

Thy rival, thou (Sir Edward [a]) wilt not mourn:
    His death, to thee, shall now the plate resign;
His laurel, else, thou never should'st have worn,
    Nor had the prize of manly sports been thine.

---

[a] Sir Edward O'Brien, father to the present Sir Lucius.

See Munster pour her horsemen from their plains,
  To the lov'd dead the last sad rites to pay;
Nor Thomond one inhabitant contains,
  To guard her treasures on this fatal day!

Respectful sorrow guides their solemn pace,
  (Their steeds [b] in mourning, slow procession led:)
'Till in the tomb their much-lov'd Burke they place,
  And o'er his earth their copious anguish shed.

The seventeen hundred six and fortieth year
  Of him who died a sinful world to save,
Death came, our Burke from our fond arms to tear,
  And lay, with him, our pleasures in the grave!

How oft his loss pale memory shall regret!
  How oft our tears shall flow, our sighs ascend!
The social band, where mirth convivial met,
  Now meet to mourn for their departed friend!

No more the melody of hounds he leads!
  No more morn echoes to their chearful cries!
A gloomy stillness through the land succeeds,
  For low in earth the soul of pleasure lies!

---

[b] In the original,—they came leading their steeds,—or more literally, the horsemen came, but not mounted on their steeds.

To the dear spot my frequent steps I'll bend,
  Which all my joy,—which all my woe contains;
My tears shall, each returning month, descend,
  To bathe the earth that holds his lov'd remains!

ADVERTISEMENT.

THE following is the Elegy mentioned in Mr. WALKER's *Life of* Carolan, *compofed on the death of that Bard, by his friend* M'Cabe [a].

M'Cabe *was rather of a humorous, than a fentimental turn; he was a wit, but not a poet. It was therefore his grief, and not his mufe, that infpired him, on the prefent occafion.*

The circumftances which gave rife to this Elegy, are ftriking, and extremely affecting. M'Cabe *had been an unufual length of time without feeing his friend, and went to pay him a vifit. As he approached near the end of his journey, in paffing by a church-yard, he was met by a peafant, of whom he enquired for* Carolan. *The peafant pointed to his grave, and wept.*

M'Cabe, *fhocked and aftonifhed, was for fome time unable to fpeak; his frame fhook, his knees trembled, he had juft power to totter to the grave of his friend, and then funk to the ground. A flood of tears,*

at

---

[a] Vide *Hift. Mem. of the Irifh Bards,* Append. p. 97.

at laſt, come to his relief; and, ſtill further to diſburden his mind, he vented its anguiſh in the following lines. In the original, they are ſimple and unadorned, but pathetic to a great degree; and this is a ſpecies of beauty, in compoſition, extremely difficult to transfuſe into any other language. I do not pretend, in this, to have entirely ſucceeded, but I hope the effort will not be unacceptable;—much of the ſimplicity is unavoidably loſt;—the pathos which remains, may, perhaps, in ſome meaſure, atone for it.

V.

ELEGY

ON THE DEATH OF

CAROLAN.

I CAME, with friendship's face, to glad my heart,
But sad, and sorrowful my steps depart!
In my friend's stead—a spot of earth was shown,
And on his grave my woe-struck eyes were thrown!
No more to their distracted sight remain'd,
But the cold clay that all they lov'd contain'd:
And there his last and narrow bed was made,
And the drear tomb-stone for its covering laid!

Alas!—for this my aged heart is wrung!
Grief choaks my voice, and trembles on my tongue.
Lonely and desolate, I mourn the dead,
The friend with whom my every comfort fled!

There is no anguish can with this compare!
No pains, diseases, suffering, or despair,
Like that I feel, while such a loss I mourn,
My heart's companion from its fondness torn!
Oh insupportable, distracting grief!
Woe, that through life, can never hope relief!
Sweet-singing [a] harp!—thy melody is o'er!
Sweet friendship's voice!—I hear thy sound no more!
My bliss,—my wealth of [b] poetry is fled,
And every joy, with him I lov'd, is dead!
Alas! what wonder, (while my heart drops blood
Upon the woes that drain its vital flood,)
If maddening grief no longer can be borne,
And frenzy fill the breast, with anguish torn!

[a] [b] Both of these expressions are exactly literal—mo ceol cruit mhilis!—mo saidhbhreas dain!

SONGS.

THOUGHTS

ON

IRISH SONG.

IT is scarcely possible that any language can be more adapted to Lyric poetry than the Irish. The poetry of many of our Songs is indeed already Musick, without the aid of a tune; so great is the smoothness, and harmony of its cadences. Nor is this to be wondered at, when we consider the advantage the Irish has, in this particular, beyond every other language, of flowing off, in vowels, upon the ear.

I will just instance the two following lines:

Sa ċṙl álïñ ꝺeaẏ, na bṙáṁjṫjḃ cceaṗc,
Iṡ bṗċaꝺ jaꝺ, aṡ ꝁlaẏ ꝺo ṙíṫle!

Here

Here, out of fifty-four letters, but twenty-two are pronounced as consonants, (the rest being rendered quiescent by their aspirates) whereas, in English, and I believe in most other languages, the Italian excepted, at least two-thirds of poetry as well as prose, is necessarily composed of consonants: The Irish being singular in the happy art of cutting off, by aspirates, every sound that could injure the melody of its cadence; at the same time that it preserves its radicals, and, of course, secures etymology.

But it is not in sound alone that this language is so peculiarly adapted to the species of composition now under consideration; it is also possessed of a refined delicacy of descriptive power, and an exquisitely tender simplicity of expression; two or three little artless words, or perhaps only a single epithet, will sometimes convey such an image of sentiment, or of suffering, to the mind, that one lays down the book, to look at the *picture*. But the beauty of many of these passages is considerably impaired by translation; indeed, so sensible was I of this, that it influenced me to give up, in despair, many a sweet stanza to which I found myself quite unequal. I wished, among others, to have translated the following lines of a favourite song; but it presented ideas, of which my pen could draw no resemblance that pleased me:

Aceaṅ ꝺuḃ ꝺjleaſ ꝺjleaſ ꝺjleaſ!
Cꞃiꝑ ꝺo ecaṅ ꝺjleaſ coꞃaṁ aṅall!
Abeſjn meala, aḃꞅil balaḋ na Thyme aꞅꞃ,
Iſ ꝺꞃiṅe ʒaṅ eꞃojꝺe ṅae ꞇjuḃꞃaḋ ḋnꞇ ʒꞃaḋ!

I NEED

I need not give any comment upon thefe lines; the Englifh reader would not underftand it, and the Irifh reader could not want it, for it is impoffible to perufe them without being fenfible of their beauty.

THERE are many Irifh fongs, now in common ufe, that contain, in fcattered paffages, the moft exquifite thoughts, though on the whole too unequal for tranflation. This, I fuppofe, is chiefly occafioned by the ignorance, or inattention of thofe who learn them, and from whom alone they are to be procured. They are remembered and fung by the village maid, perhaps merely for the fake of the tunes that accompany them; of courfe, if recollection fails, it is made up with invention; any words, in this cafe, will ferve, if they anfwer to the air of the Song; and thus, often, not words alone, but entire lines, are fubftituted, fo totally unlike the reft of the compofition, that it is eafy to fee whence the difference proceeds. Sometimes too, if a line or a ftanza be wanting to a filly fong, the firft of any other one that occurs, is preffed into the fervice; and by this means, among a heap of lyric nonfenfe, one often finds a thought that would do honor to the fineft compofition.

IN thefe incongruous poems, where a line feems to plead for its refcue, it would be a pity to refufe it. Among many others, the following is an image rich in beauty: A forfaken maid compares her heart to a burning coal, bruifed black; thus retaining the heat that confumed, while it lofes the light that had cheered it.

it. In another Song, a Lover, tenderly reproaching his Miſtreſs, aſks her, Why ſhe keeps the morning ſo long within doors? and bids her come out, and bring him the day. The ſecond of the two following ſtanzas ſtruck me, as being ſo particularly beautiful, that I was tempted to tranſlate them both for its ſake.

Iſ blác ɼeal na ɼmép ɼ
Iɼ blác ueaɼ na ɼubcɼaeb ɼ
ɼɼ planua byheapp meɼn majc
lc hamaɼic aɼɼl.

Iɼ mo cviɼle ɼɼ mo pɼn ɼ
aɼɼ blac na nuball cɼmɼia ɼ
Iɼ ɼamiɼiau an ɼan ɼhuɼicc ɼ
cɼoɼɼ nuolnɼ ɼ caɼɼɼ.

TRANSLATION.

As the ſweet blackberry's modeſt bloom
    Fair flowering, greets the ſight;
Or ſtrawberries, in their rich perfume,
    Fragrance and bloom unite:
So this fair plant of tender youth,
    In outward charms can vie,
And, from within, the ſoul of truth
    Soft beaming, fills her eye.

Pulse of my heart!—dear source of care,
 Stol'n sighs, and love-breath'd vows!
Sweeter than when, through scented air,
 Gay bloom the apple boughs!
With thee no days can winter seem,
 Nor frost, nor blast can chill;
Thou the soft breeze, the cheering beam
 That keeps it summer still!

THE air of these stanzas is exquisitely charming. But the beauties of the musick of this country are, at present, almost as little known as those of its poetry. And yet there is no other musick in the world so calculated to make its way directly to the heart: it is the voice of Nature and Sentiment, and every fibre of the feeling breast is in unison with it.

BUT I beg pardon for this digression;—Musick is not the subject now under consideration.

I REGRET much that I have not been able to diversify this collection with some pieces of a sprightlier strain; but I have sought in vain for songs of wit and humour, that were worthy of the public eye.

IT has been often observed that a strain of tender pensiveness is discernible throughout, in most of the musick of this nation: a circumstance which has been variously accounted for; and the fame remarks, and the fame reafons hold good in regard to its poetry.

"We fee (fays Mr. WALKER) that mufic maintained its
"ground in this country, even after the invafion of the Eng-
"lifh, but its ftyle fuffered a change; for the fprightly Phry-
"gian gave place to the grave Doric, or foft Lydian meafure.
"Such was the nice fenfibility of the Bards, fuch was their
"tender affection for their country, that the fubjection to
"which the kingdom was reduced, affected them with the
"heavieft fadnefs. Sinking beneath this weight of fympathetic
"forrow, they became a prey to melancholy: hence the plain-
"tivenefs of their mufic; for the ideas that arife in the mind
"are always congenial to, and receive a tincture from, the in-
"fluencing paffion. Another caufe might have concurred with
"the one juft mentioned, in promoting a change in the ftyle of
"our mufic: the Bards, often driven, together with their
"patrons, by the fword of oppreffion, from the bufy haunts
"of men, were obliged to lie concealed in marfhes, in gloomy
"forefts, amongft rugged mountains, and in glynns and vallies
"refounding with the noife of falling waters, or filled with
"portentous echoes. Such fcenes as thefe, by throwing a
"fettled gloom over the fancy, muft have confiderably encreafed
"their melancholy; fo that when they attempted to fing, it
"is not to be wondered at that their voices, thus weakened
"by ftruggling againft heavy mental depreffion, fhould rife
"rather by minor thirds, which confift but of four femitones,
"than

"than by major thirds, which confift of five. Now, almoft all the airs of this period are found to be fet in the minor third, and to be of the fage and folemn nature of the mufic which Milton requires in his IL PENSEROSO[a]."

To illuftrate his pofition, Mr. WALKER introduces the following anecdote:

"About the year 1730, one Maguire, a vintner, refided near Charing-Crofs, London. His houfe was much frequented, and his uncommon fkill in playing on the harp, was an additional incentive: even the Duke of Newcaftle, and feveral of the miniftry, fometimes condefcended to vifit it. He was one night called upon to play fome Irifh tunes; he did fo; they were plaintive and folemn. His guefts demanded the reafon, and he told them, that the native compofers were too deep'y diftreffed at the fituation of their country, and her gallant fons, to be able to compofe otherwife. But, added he, take off the reftraints under which they labour, and you will not have reafon to complain of the plaintivenefs of their notes.

"OFFENCE was taken at thefe warm effufions; his houfe became gradually neglected, and he died, foon after, of a broken heart. An Irifh harper, who was a cotemporary of Maguire, and, like him, felt for the fufferings of his country, had this diftich engraven on his harp:

---

[a] *Hift. Mem. of the Irifh Bards*, p. 12.

" Cur Lyra funeſtas edit percuſſa ſonores ?
" Sicut amiſſum ſors Diadema gemit!

" But perhaps the melancholy ſpirit which breathes through
" the Iriſh muſic and poetry may be attributed to another
" cauſe ; a cauſe which operated anterior and ſubſequent to the
" invaſion of the Engliſh: We mean the remarkable ſuſcepti-
" bility of the Iriſh of the paſſion of love ; a paſſion, which the
" munificent eſtabliſhments of the bards left them at liberty
" freely to indulge. While the mind is enduring the torments
" of hope, fear, or deſpair, its effuſions cannot be gay. The
" greater number of the productions of thoſe amorous poets,
" Tibullus, Catullus, Petrarch, and Hammond, are elegiac.
" The anonymous traveller, whom we have already had occaſion
" to mention, after ſpeaking of the amorous diſpoſition of the
" Iriſh, purſues the ſubject, in his account of their poetry.
' The ſubject of theſe (their ſongs) is always love, and they ſeem
' to underſtand poetry to be deſigned for no other purpoſe than
' to ſtir up that paſſion in the mind [a].''

I have never read the Travels here cited, but it ſhould ſeem that their author intended not to extend his remarks beyond that ſpecies of poetry which may be claſſed under the title of ſongs. So far his obſervations are perfectly juſt; but the heroic poetry of our countrymen was deſigned for the nobleſt purpoſes ;—love indeed was ſtill its object,—but it was the ſublime love of country that thoſe compoſitions inſpired.

BESIDES

[a] *Hiſt. Mem. of the Iriſh Bards,* p. 125.

Besides the reasons and remarks I have quoted, and which are, of themselves, amply sufficient to account for the almost total absence of humorous poetry in our language, there are still further reasons, which appear to me to deserve attention, and which I therefore beg leave to lay before the reader.

I am not sufficiently conversant in the state of the antient music of this country, to say what that might once have been, or what degree of change it might have suffered; but it does not appear to me that the antient poetry of Ireland was *ever* composed in a very lively strain. I by no means would assert that this is *certainly* the case; for, as yet, I am but young in researches: I only conceive a probability of its being so, from my never having met with an instance to the contrary.

Love and War were the two favourite objects of passion and pursuit, with our antient countrymen, and of course, became the constant inspirers of their muse.—In love, they appear to have been always too much in earnest to trifle with their attachments; —and " the strife of swords"—" the field of death"—presented no subject to sport with. To them, also, both art and nature came arrayed in simple dignity; and afforded not that variety of circumstance, and appearance, so calculated to call forth fancy, and diversify ideas.

This seems to me to be one cause, why scarcely any thing but plaintive tenderness, or epic majesty, is to be found in the ofitions of our Bards; another reafon ftill occurs, which I will give to the reader's indulgence.

The true poet is ever an enthufiaft in his art, and enthufiafm is feldom witty. The French abound in works of wit and humour;—the Englifh are more in earneft, and therefore fall fhort of the vivacity of the Gallic mufe, but infinitely excel her in all that tends to conftitute the vital fpirit of poetry. In Ireland, this fafcinating art was ftill more univerfally in practice, and ftill more enthufiaftically admired. The mufe was here the goddefs of unbounded idolatry, and her worfhip was the bufinefs of life. Our Irifh Bards, "in the fine frenzy of exalted thought," were loft to that play of fancy, which only fports with freedom when it is not interrupted by the heart, or awed to filence by the fublime conceptions of the foul.

FANCY is, in general, the vehicle of wit; imagination that of genius. The happieft thoughts may flow in the moft harmonious, and highly adapted meafure, without one fpark of poetic fire. At leaft one half of thofe who bear the title of *Englifh Poets*, are merely men of wit and rhyme; and I believe it will be acknowledged that thofe amongft them who poffeffed the fublimeft genius, defcended but feldom to fport with it. Young, Rowe, Thomfon, Gray, &c. are inftances of this. It is by no means fuppofed neceffary for a poet to be always penfive, philofophical or fublime; he may fport with Fancy,—he may laugh with Humour, he may be gay in every company,—except that of

the

the Mufe: in her awful prefence, her true adorer is too much poffeffed by his paffion to be gay; he may be approved,—happy, —eloquent,—but hardly witty.

PERHAPS there are few fubjects that afford a more copious field for obfervation than that of Irifh fong, but the limits of my work confine me to a narrow compafs, and will not allow thefe few remarks to affume the title of ESSAY. The fubject of fong, in general, has been already fo well, and copioufly treated of by the pens of Aikin, and Ritfon, that it has nothing in ftore for me; but that of Irifh fong feemed to demand fome notice, and had never before received it.

ADVERTISEMENT.

THE two first of the following Songs are the compositions of Turlough O'Carolan, *a man much and deservedly celebrated for his poetical talents, as well as for the incomparable sweetness of all his musical pieces.*

As his life has been already given to the public by Mr. WALKER, *in his* Historical Memoirs of the Irish Bards, *I have nothing left to say upon the subject: However, for the benefit of such of my readers as have not yet had the pleasure of perusing that learned and elegant work, I will insert a few extracts from it, to gratify immediate curiosity; and the public will doubtless be better pleased to see them in* Mr. WALKER's *words than in mine.*

" Carolan *was born in the year* 1670, *in the village of* Nobber, *in the
" county of* Westmeath, *on the lands of* Carolanstown, *which were wrested
" from his ancestors by the family of the* Nugents, *on their arrival in this
" kingdom, in the reign of* Henry the Second. *His father was a poor far-
" mer, the humble proprietor of a few acres, which yielded him a scanty sub-
" sistence; of his mother I have not been able to collect any particulars.*"

" *He must have been deprived of sight at a very early period of his life, for
" he remembered no impression of colours. Thus was* ' knowledge at one en-
' trance quite shut out,' *before he had taken even a cursory view of the crea-
" tion. From this misfortune, however, he felt no uneasiness; he used merrily
" to say,* ' my eyes are transplanted into my ears.'

" *His*

"His musical genius was soon discovered, and his friends determined to cultivate it; about the age of twelve, a proper master was engaged to instruct him in the practice of the Harp; but though fond of that instrument, he never struck it with a master's hand. Genius and diligence are seldom united; and it is practice alone that can perfect us in any art. Yet his harp was rarely unstrung: but, in general, he only used it to assist him in composition; his fingers wandered among the strings, in quest of the sweets of melody."

"At what period of his life Carolan commenced itinerant musician, is not known, nor is it confidently told whether, like Arnauld Daniel, ' Il n'eut abord d'autre Apollon que le Besoin;' or whether his fondness for musick induced him to betake himself to that profession. Dr. Campbell indeed seems to attribute his choice to an early disappointment in love [a]; but we will leave these points unsettled, and follow our Bard in his peregrinations."

"Wherever he goes, the gates of the nobility and gentry are thrown open to him. Like the Demodocus of Homer, he is received with respect, and a distinguished place assigned him at the table. Near him is seated his harper, ready to accompany his voice, and supply his want of skill in practical music." ' Carolan (says Mr. Ritson [b]) seems, from the description we have of him, ' to be a genuine representative of the ancient Bards.'

"It was during his peregrinations that Carolan composed all those airs that are still the delight of his countrymen. He thought the tribute of a Song due to every house where he was entertained, and he never failed to pay it;

choosing

[a] Phil. Survey of South of Ireland.

[b] Hist. Essay on National Song.

" choosing for his subject, either the head of the family, or one of the loveliest of
" its branches."

The Biographer of our Bard, after informing us of many curious and interesting particulars, for which (fearing to exceed the limits of my work) I must refer my readers to the book from which these extracts are taken, proceeds to acquaint us, that in the year 1733 he lost a beloved, and tenderly lamented wife; and he subjoins a beautiful Monody, composed by the mourning Bard on the occasion: he also adds, that Carolan did not long survive her.—" He died
" in the month of March, 1738, in the sixty-eighth year of his age, and was
" interred in the parish church of Kilronan, in the diocese of Ardagh;
" but ' not a stone tells where he lies!' His grave indeed is still known to
" his few surviving friends, and the neighbouring hinds; and his skull is
" distinguished from the other skulls, which are promiscuously scattered about
" the church-yard, by a perforation in the forehead, through which a small
" piece of ribband is drawn.

" Though Carolan died universally lamented, he would have died unsung,
" had not the humble muse of M'Cabe poured a few elegiac strains
" over his cold remains. This faithful friend composed a short Elegy on
" his death, which is evidently the effusion of unfeigned grief: unadorned
" with meretricious ornaments, it is the picture of a mind torn with anguish[c]."

Mr. WALKER here subjoins a character of our Bard, from the elegant pen of Mr. O'Conor.

[c] The Elegy here mentioned, will be found among the modern Poems in this collection.

" Very few have I ever known who had a more vigorous mind, but a mind
" undisciplined, through the defect, or rather the absence of cultivation. Ab-
" solutely the child of Nature, he was governed by the indulgencies, and at
" times, by the caprices of that mother. His imagination, ever on the wing,
" was excentric in its poetic flight; yet, as far as that faculty can be employed
" in the harmonic art, it was steady and collected. In the variety of his musi-
" cal numbers, he knew how to make a selection, and was seldom content with
" mediocrity. So happy, so elevated was he, in some of his compositions, that
" he excited the wonder, and obtained the approbation, of a great master, who
" never saw him; I mean Geminiani."

" He outstripped his predecessors in the three species of composition used
" among the Irish; but he never omitted giving due praise to several of his
" countrymen, who excelled before him in his art. The Italian compositions he
" preferred to all others: Vivaldi charmed him; and with Corelli he was
" enraptured. He spoke elegantly in his maternal language, but had advanced
" in years before he learned English; he delivered himself but indifferently in
" that language, and yet he did not like to be corrected in his solecisms. It need
" not be concealed that he indulged in the use of spirituous liquors: this habit,
" he thought, or affected to think, added strength to the flights of his genius;
" but, in justice, it must be observed that he seldom was surprized by in-
" toxication.

" Constitutionally pious, he never omitted daily prayer, and fondly imagined
" himself inspired, when he composed some pieces of church musick. This idea
" contributed to his devotion, and thanksgiving; and, in this respect, his enthu-
" siasm was harmless, and perhaps useful. Gay by nature, and cheerful from
" habit, he was a pleasing member of society; and his talents, and his morality,
" procured him esteem and friends every where."

Besides

Besides the two following Songs, *there are more of the compositions of* Carolan *possessed of considerable merit; but as it was not in my power to give them all a place in my collection, I have selected, for translation, two that appeared to be the best amongst them; which, together with some other songs of modern date, I give, to shew of what the native genius and language of this country, even now, are capable; labouring, as they do, under every disadvantage.*

I.

SONG.

For GRACEY NUGENT[a].

By CAROLAN.

OF Gracey's charms enraptur'd will I sing!
Fragrant and fair, as blossoms of the spring;
To her sweet manners, and accomplish'd mind,
Each rival Fair the palm of Love resign'd.

How blest her sweet society to share!
To mark the ringlets of her flowing hair[b];

Her

---

[a] "The fair subject of this Song was sister to the late John Nugent, Esq; of Castle-Nugent, Culambre. She lived with her sister, Mrs. Conmee, near Belanagar, in the county of Roscommon, at the time she inspired our Bard." *Hist. Mem. of Irish Bards. Append.* p. 78.

[b] Hair is a favourite object with all the Irish Poets, and endless is the variety of their description:—"Soft misty curls."—"Thick branching tresses of bright redundance."

Her gentle accents,—her complacent mien!—
Supreme in charms, she looks—she reigns a Queen!

That

" dance."—" Locks of fair waving beauty."—" Tresses flowing on the wind like the
" bright waving flame of an inverted torch." They even affect to inspire it with
expression:—as " Locks of *gentle* lustre."—" Tresses of *tender* beauty."—" The Maid
" with the *mildly* flowing hair," &c. &c.

A friend to whom I shewed this Song, observed, that I had omitted a very lively
thought in the conclusion, which they had seen in Mr. WALKER's Memoirs. As
that version has been much read and admired, it may perhaps be necessary, to vindi-
cate my fidelity, as a translator, that I should here give a *literal* translation of the
Song, to shew that the thoughts have suffered very little, either of encrease or dimi-
nution from the poetry.

" I will sing with rapture of the Blossom of Whitenefs! Gracey, the young and
" beautiful woman, who bore away the palm of excellence in sweet manners and ac-
" complishments, from all the Fair-ones of the provinces."

" Whoever enjoys her constant society, no apprehension of any ill can assail him.—
" The Queen of soft and winning mind and manners, with her fair branching tresses
" flowing in ringlets."

" Her side like alabaster, and her neck like the swan, and her countenance like the
" Sun in summer. How blest is it for him who is promised, as riches, to be united
" to her, the branch of fair curling tendrils."

" Sweet and pleasant is your lovely conversation!—bright and sparkling your blue
" eyes!—and every day do I hear all tongues declare your praises, and how grace-
" fully your bright tresses wave down your neck!"

" I say to the Maid of youthful mildnefs, that her voice and her converse are
" sweeter than the songs of the birds! There is no delight or charm that imagina-
" tion can conceive but what is found ever attendant on Gracey."

" Her

That alabaster form—that graceful neck,
How do the Cygnet's down and whitenefs deck!—
How does that afpect fhame the cheer of day,
When fummer funs their brighteft beams difplay.

Bleft is the youth whom fav'ring fates ordain
The treafure of her love, and charms to gain!
The fragrant branch, with curling tendrils bound,
With breathing odours—blooming beauty crown'd.

Sweet is the cheer her fprightly wit fupplies!
Bright is the fparkling azure of her eyes!
Soft o'er her neck her lovely treffes flow!
Warm in her praife the tongues of rapture glow!

Her's is the voice—tun'd by harmonious Love,
Soft as the Songs that warble through the grove!
Oh! fweeter joys her converfe can impart!
Sweet to the *fenfe*, and grateful to the *heart!*

Gay

" Her teeth arranged in beautiful order, and her locks flowing in foft waving curls!
" But though it delights me to fing of thy charms, I muft quit my theme!—With a
" fincere heart I fill to thy health!"

'The reader will eafily perceive that in this literal tranflation, I have not fought for elegance of expreffion, my only object being to put it in his power to judge how clofely my verfion has adhered to my original.

Gay pleasures dance where'er her foot-steps bend;
And smiles and rapture round the fair attend:
Wit forms her speech, and Wisdom fills her mind,
And *sight* and *soul* in her their object find.

Her pearly teeth, in beauteous order plac'd;
Her neck with bright, and curling tresses grac'd:—
But ah, so fair!—in wit and charms supreme,
Unequal Song must quit its darling theme.

Here break I off;—let sparkling goblets flow,
And my full heart its cordial wishes show:
To her dear health this friendly draught I pour,
Long be her life, and blest its every hour!—

II.

S O N G.

For MABLE KELLY,

By CAROLAN.

THE youth whom fav'ring Heaven's decree
To join his fate, my Fair! with thee;
And fee that lovely head of thine
With fondnefs on his arm recline:

No thought but joy can fill his mind,
Nor any care can entrance find,
Nor ficknefs hurt, nor terror fhake,—
And Death will fpare him, for thy fake!

For the bright flowing of thy hair,
That decks a face fo heavenly fair;
And a fair form, to match that face,
The rival of the Cygnet's grace.

When with calm dignity she moves,
Where the clear stream her hue improves;
Where she her snowy bosom laves,
And floats, majestic, on the waves.

Grace gave thy form, in beauty gay,
And rang'd thy teeth in bright array;
All tongues with joy thy praises tell,
And love delights with thee to dwell.

To thee harmonious powers belong,
That add to verse the charms of song;
Soft melody to numbers join,
And make the Poet half divine.

As when the softly blushing rose
Close by some neighbouring lilly grows;
Such is the glow thy cheeks diffuse,
And such their bright and blended hues!

The timid lustre of thine eye[a]
With Nature's purest tints can vie;

---

[a] It is generally believed that Carolan, (as his Biographer tells us) "remembered no impression of colours."—But I cannot acquiesce in this opinion: I think it must have been formed without sufficient grounds, for how was it possi-

With the sweet blue-bell's azure gem,
That droops upon its modest stem!

The Poets of Ierne's plains
To thee devote their choicest strains;
And oft their harps for thee are strung,
And oft thy matchless charms are sung:

Thy voice, that binds the list'ning soul,—
That can the wildest rage controul;
Bid the fierce Crane its powers obey,
And charm him from his finney prey.

Nor doubt I of its wond'rous art;
Nor hear with unimpassion'd heart;
Thy health, thy beauties,—ever dear!
Oft crown my glass with sweetest cheer!

Since the fam'd Fair of ancient days,
Whom Bards and Worlds conspir'd to praise,
Not one like thee has since appear'd,
Like thee, to every heart endear'd.

How

ble that his description could be thus glowing, without he retained the clearest recollection, and the most animated ideas, of every beauty that sight can convey to the mind?

How blest the Bard, O lovely Maid!
To find thee in thy charms array'd!—
Thy pearly teeth,—thy flowing hair,—
Thy neck, beyond the Cygnet, fair!——

As when the simple birds, at night,
Fly round the torch's fatal light,—
Wild, and with extacy elate,
Unconscious of approaching fate.

So the soft splendours of thy face,
And thy fair form's enchanting grace;
Allure to death unwary Love,
And thousands the bright ruin prove!

Ev'n he whose hapless eyes [b] no ray
Admit from Beauty's cheering day;
Yet, though he cannot *see* the light,
He feels it warm, and knows it bright.

In beauty, talents, taste refin'd,
And all the graces of the mind,

---

[b] Every Reader of taste or feeling must surely be struck with the beauty of this passage.—Can any thing be more elegant, or more pathetic, than the manner in which Carolan alludes to his want of sight!—but, indeed, his little pieces abound in all the riches of natural genius.

In *all* unmatch'd thy charms remain,
Nor meet a rival on the plain.

Thy slender foot,—thine azure eye,—
Thy smiling lip, of scarlet dye,—
Thy tapering hand, so soft and fair,—
The bright redundance of thy hair!—

O blest be the auspicious day
That gave them to thy Poet's lay!
O'er rival Bards [c] to lift his name,
Inspire his verse, and swell his fame!——

---

[c] How modestly the Poet here introduces a prophesy of his future reputation for genius!

III.
SONG.
By PATRICK LINDEN.

O FAIRER than the mountain snow,
When o'er it north's pure breezes blow!
In all its dazzling lustre drest,
But purer, softer is thy breast!

Colla[a] the Great, whose ample sway
Beheld two kingdoms homage pay,
Now gives the happy bard to see
Thy branch adorn the royal tree!

No foreign graft's inferior shoot
Has dar'd insult the mighty root!
Pure from its stem thy bloom ascends,
And from its height in fragrance bends!

---

[a] He was monarch of Ireland in the beginning of the fourth century. By the second kingdom, we must suppose the poet means the Dal-Riadas of Scotland.

Hadst thou been present, on the day
When beauty bore the prize away,
Thy charms had won the royal swain,
And Venus 'self had su'd in vain!

With soften'd fire, imperial blood
Pours through thy frame its generous flood;
Rich in thy azure veins it flows,
Bright in thy blushing cheek it glows!

That blood whence noble SAVAGE sprung,
And he whose deeds the bards have sung,
Great CONALL-CEARNACH [b], conquering name!
The champion of heroic fame!

Fair offspring of the royal race!
Mild fragrance! fascinating grace!
Whose touch with magic can inspire
The tender harp's melodious wire!

See how the swan presumptuous strives,
Where glowing Majesty revives,
With proud contention, to bespeak
The soft dominion of that cheek!

Beneath

Beneath it, sure, with subtle heed,
Some rose by stealth its leaf convey'd;
To shed its bright and beauteous dye,
And still the varying bloom supply.

The tresses of thy silken hair
As curling mists are soft and fair,
Bright waving o'er thy graceful neck,
Its pure and tender snow to deck!

But O! to speak the rapture found!
In thy dear voice's magic found!
Its powers could death itself controul,
And call back the expiring soul!

The tide that fill'd the veins of Kings,
From whom thy noble lineage springs;
The royal blood of Colla, see
Renew'd, O charming maid! in thee.

Nor in thy bosom slacks its pace,
Nor fades it in thy lovely face;
But there with soft enchantment glows,
And like the blossom's tint it shows.

How does thy needle's art pourtray
Each pictur'd form, in bright array!
With Nature's felf maintaining ftrife,
It gives its own creation life!

O perfect, all-accomplifh'd maid!
In beauty's every charm array'd:
Thee ever fhall my numbers hail,
Fair lilly of the royal vale!

IV.

SONG.

THE MAID OF THE VALLEY.

HAVE you not seen the charmer of the vale?
  Nor heard her praise, in Love's fond accents drest?—
Nor how that Love has turn'd my youth so pale!—
  Nor how those graces rob my soul of rest!—

That softest cheek, where dimp'ling cherubs play!
  That bashful eye, whose beams dissolve the heart!—
Ah, gaze no more, fond wretch!—no longer stay!—
  'Tis death!—but ah, 'tis worse than death to part!

My blessings round the happy mansion wait,
  That guards that form, in tender beauty drest!
Those lips, of truth and smiles the rosy seat!
  Those matchless charms, by every bard confest!

That slender brow!—that hand so dazzling fair,
No silk its hue or softness can express!
No feather'd songsters can their down compare
With half the beauty those dear hands possess!

Love in thy every feature couch'd a dart!
O'er thy fair face, and bosom's white he play'd;
Love in thy golden tresses chain'd my heart,
And heaven's own smile thy 'witching face array'd!

Not *Deirdre*'s charms that on each bosom stole [a],
And led the champions of our isle away;
Nor she whose eyes threw fetters o'er the soul,
The fam'd Blanaide [b] like thee the heart could sway!

Of

---

[a] See notes to the poem of *Conloch*.

[b] As the story to which this passage alludes is striking to a great degree, and related in a few words, I will quote it at large for the reader.

"Feircheirtne was OLLAMH FILEA to Conrigh, a celebrated chieftain, who lived
"in splendour on the banks of the Fionnglaise, in the county of Kerry. This
"warrior was married to Blanaide, a lady of transcendant beauty, who had been the
"meed of his prowess in single combat with Congculionne, a knight of the red
"branch. But the lady was secretly attached to the knight; and in an accidental
"interview which she had with him, offered to follow his fortunes, if he would, at
"a certain time, and on receiving a certain signal (both of which she mentioned)
"storm the castle, and put her husband, and his attendants, to the sword. Congcu-
"lionne promised to follow her directions, and did so, inundating the castle with the
"blood of its inhabitants. Feircheirtne, however, escaped the slaughter, and pur-
"sued, at a distance, Blanaide and her paramour, to the court of Concovar Mac-
"Nessa,

Of beauty's garden, oh thou fairest flower!
    Accept my vows, and *truth* for *treasure* take!
Oh deign to share with me Love's blissful power,
    Nor constant faith, for fleeting wealth, forsake!

My muse her harp shall at thy bidding bring,
    And roll th' heroic tide of verse along;
And Finian Chiefs, and arms shall wake the string,
    And Love and War divide the lofty song!

"Nessa, determined to sacrifice his perfidious mistress to the manes of his patron.

"When the Bard arrived at Emania, he found Concovar, and his court, together with the amorous fugitives, walking on the top of a rock, called *Rinchin Beara*, enjoying the extensive prospect which it commanded. Blanaide, happening to detach herself from the rest of the company, stood, wrapped in deep meditation, on that part of the cliff which overhung a deep precipice. The Bard, stepping up to her, began an adulatory conversation; then suddenly springing forward, he seized her in his arms, and throwing himself, with her, headlong down the precipice, both were dashed to pieces." *Hist. Mem. of the Irish Bards*, p. 32. See also KEATING.

IRISH ORIGINALS

OF THE

HEROIC POEMS.

ADVERTISEMENT.

THESE originals are copied, with the utmost exactness, from the different collections whence they were taken: the Translator, therefore, is not answerable for any supposed incorrectness in orthography, &c. which may possibly be discovered in many parts of them, as it was not thought expedient to make the smallest alteration whatever, not even so much as the addition of a point, or an accent.

THE IRISH ORIGINALS
OF THE
HEROIC POEMS.

I.

Teacht Conlaoich go hÉirinn.

Táinig tríat an borbláoc
an curajò cróda Conlaoch
an ṡna mḟrċa gánṙċa gṙjnn
ó óṙn ṡgaċaiġ go hÉjṙinn
fáilte ḋujt alaojch linn
amaccójm áluinn ajṙmġṙinn
is cosṁail le do ċeas nán nóúil
go rabnis real an reacráin
Anojs ó tainigir anojr
o crích ojrtear an ḋoṁain
do ḋeoṙbaḋ do ġajġge Éṙinn
aṙ ṡeaḋ tjmċeara aneirin
Cojṁeaḋ an ráon ara romaib
léṙ ċnċ móṙlaoċajb analbнn
no cógram do liós óṙ leas
aneirjc ċjóra an oroicetjo

Olas é sin á cciósa ne sealad
is nar trilleaḋ le aonneaċ é ge hiomḋa
coisgte me tusa do cáċ
o niog go lá an luán bráit
Nior sguir an laoċ da lámaċ
Coṅlaoċh sraoċda sorránach
no gur ceanglaḋ céad dar slraig
a ngéibionn is suát pén aisris
An sin canas Conċubḃa ne cáċ
ciod ġeaḃmóis do ḋul na ḋáil
do ḃainseaḋ easra no sgéal
is na ttiocsaḋ sa ḋiomḋa raiḋe
Eirgios Conall nar lag lám
do ḃuain sgéala don macaṁ
se ḋeorḃaim le srain an laoicc
gur ceanglaḋ Conall le Coṅlóich
Sgéala uain ar ceann na Con
do raio asrorsg Ulaḋ
go duṅ dealgan grianaċ grinn
sean nḋun ṡhiálmar ḋeitcinn
sáilte o gaċ ón roime an ccoin
is mall ċangóis dar ccaḃair
ata Conall mar stead amḃroid
is céad dar slóig na coimideas
IS deacair ḋuinn gan ḃeiṫ amḃron
deis na ḃsear do raċaḋ accorgur
is deacair ḋuinn dul ċum caṫa
leis an laoċ ler ceanglaḋ Conall
Na smuain gan dul na ḋáil
alóiċ na narm naiṫġéar
alaim is treise gan teiḃeaḋ ne neaċ
suaiġail hoide 7 é ccuiḃreach

An

An tan ċualaiḋ Cuċulainn na laun
eiṫin aguf cuiḃṗeaċ Ċomill
an cunaiḋ ṫo buḋ ṫpeíne lám
ṫeíṫ aġ buain fġéala ḋon macám
Ṫṗoiḋ ma bo heíṫin ḋiṫ
no fġéala ċabaipṫ ṫaiṫ map ċapaiḋ
beip ṫo poġa aċiaḃnḋe boġ
ful ma heaġal ḋiṫ ṫo ċomṗac
Ní ċuġof liom óm ċupach
fġéala ċabaipṫ ḋaon ċupaiḋ
Ìf ḋa ṫuġaṁ ṫo neaċ ḟa neim
Ìf ṫoḋ ġealġnṁiḟ feiṁ ḋó noffṁin
Ain fin ṫpoipṫo ṗe ċéile
Ìf ba ṫeape comṗaic ḋob aíḋméile
an maċ oin ġo ḃṗuaip aġoin
ṗe fiḟf na epóṁiġe comiloiṁ
Anċiḟ éġlaoiċċ aiṫpiḟ ṫo fġéal
Ó aṫá ṫo ċṗéuċṫa ġo háḋḃéil
Ìf ġeáṗn ġo ṫioċfaim ḋ ṫo leaṗ
Ìf na ceil feafḋa ṫimṫeaf
Léiġ ḋiṁ ṫiṫim ap ṁfaiġṫe
ḋṗiṫ liom oip Ìf ṫṁ m'aṫaip
ḋ ṫeḟ ġo ḃfeiciḋ fin fáil
meiḋ m'ċhulaing Ṁin ṫeaġmáil
Is mé Coṁlaoich mac na Con
oiġṗe ḋíleaf ḋṗna ḋealġan
Ìf me an ṗún aḋ fhúġḃaif amḃṗoiṁ
anḋuṁ fġaṫaiġ Ìf ṫṁ aġ fóġluim.
Aṁiṫ ṫo ḃfeáṗin ġo mbeiṫ ṫo maṫaip
aḋ laṫaip an am na coifaipne
no ġo ṫaipnġeaḋ fi ḋeápa
faḋ ċpéafa aguf ṫṁ ġonṫa

Mo mallaſ aɼp mo ṁaċaɼp
ōɼ ɼí ċúp mɼʃe ʃa ṡeaɼɼaɼb
aʒaoɼa a Cuċrlɼnn
aɼʒ ɼéuċaɼn le ꝺo ċleaɼaɼb
Mo ṁallaſ ꝺoꝺ ṁaṫaɼp
ōɼ ɼunꞇe ꝺo bɼ̇ anɼomaꝺ ꝺo ċealʒaɼb
Iſ ʒupab é meúꝺ ꝺo bɼ̇ ꝺona hule ɼunꞇe
ꝺo beɼp ꝺon beɼꞇ ꝺeaɼʒaꝺ
IS me Conlaoċ iſ ɼɼōp len aɼċɼnſ
naɼ ꞇeɼbe pɼáṁ ō béal ꞇpoꝺa
naċ ꞇuʒ ſʒéala ꝺo neaċ ɼán nʒɼéɼn
muna mbeɼꞇ ſpéaɼa na coɼn nʒleɼce
A Cuċuɼlɼnn na napm nʒlɼc
iſ maɼpʒ ōīꞇ naɼ aɼꞇɼn mé
an ꞇɼáꞇ ꝺo ċaɼċɼnn an ꞇɼleaʒ ʒo ſɼaɼ ɼan
anꝺɼaɼʒ abun, iſ ahuploɼnn
Da mbéɼnɼe 7 mo Ċonlaoċ cáom
aɼʒ ɼnɼɼꞇ cleaɼ d́ aonꞇaob
ɼɼn eɼpeann o ꞇɼnn ʒo ꞇɼnn
ꝺo ɼéabaṁaoɼſ apaōn eaꝺɼpɼn.
Maɼ ċɼ́m aɼɼm an laōɼʒ
ſʒɼáṫ aʒuſ lann Ċonlaojé
iſ maɼ ſɼn ꝺo bɼnɼe aʒ caōɼ
maɼ ɼbeaɼ ʒan ṁac ʒan ṁnaōɼ.
IS mé an ꞇaṫaɼp ꝺo ṁaɼɼb anmac
iſ naɼ ċaɼċeaꝺ mé cɼoō na ɼɼbɼaꞇ
iſ mé an cnáɼm naċ ɼɼl ɼe ɼopuſ
an ꝺá lúɼm ꝺo bɼ̇ ɼe lɼáꞇ ꝺonɼſ.
IS mé an báɼc ō ċuɼ̇n ʒo ꞇɼnn
iſ mé an lonʒ ɼaɼ nꝺul ꝺa ſꞇɼɼɼn
iſ me an ꞇubaʟ amōaɼɼ an ċɼaɼn
iſ beaʒ ꝺo ɼaoɼlɼeaꝺ ꝺé ꝺo ċɼꞇɼn.

Tpɼuʒ

Truaġ ſin a aoinḟeaṛ Noiſe
do ṫoiẏg don ċriċe Ulaḋ
do ċoṁṛac ṛe coinneuaiẓne
uch! uch! ca truaiġe tuṛaſ
Truaġ naċ neach oile aṛ doṁan
atá aṛ ṫollaḋ do ṫaoiṛſe
ẓo marḃninn atéṛaic
céd aṛ ċédaiḃ do ḋóinip
Truaġ ſin a Ċonluoiċ ċalma
aḋamna ṛiġ ẓan ḟonloſ
nach émo báſ do ḋearḃaḋ
ſul do ṫreáẓouṛ do ċórṁcoṛṛ
Maiſ don teaġlach ón ċrḟaoḃruaiṡ
'ſdo ċeann caoṁſluaiġ na ccuṛaḋ
naċ neaċ ḋióbh do ṁarḃh ṁóinmac
in tſéoṛſlat ca mó pudaṛ
Maiſ do Laoġaiṛe bhuáḋach
naċ byſaṛuſ é dot ṫromġun
maiſ don cuṛaiḋ do Ċonall
naṛ ṁarḃ tſ accoṁ ṫrom coṁṛic
Maiſ do cuṁſẓṛaiḋ meand macha
naċ tug ḋaṁ ſaémn cuṁa
maiſ d'Ḟorbhaiḋe ċaoṁ ċruṫach
maiſ do Ḋhubhṫach daol ulaḋ
Maiſ do Ċoṛmac ċonlinẓeaſ
naċ laiſ do roinn haṛmſa
naċ é do ṛuáiṛ muṛ bhall ẓona
in ſẓiáṫ ċoṛcṛa, no in lainnſa

Truaġ

Truág nać ȧan Muṁajn ṁajġnjṫ
no ȷlaȷġnjbh na lann bhȧcóbhṗaċh
no acċṗȧċin na ṁoṗblaoċh
ṫo ċujṫ mo Conlaoċh cóṁȧa
Truág nać ȧan jnnjaċ ojṗȧajṗe
ṫoṗċujṫ jn cuṁġjṫ eaṫha
ṫȧhjoȧ aṗaġaṫ gan ṫjoġajlt
o ṗjoġṫajṫ camna maċha
Tṗṫaġ naċh accṗjȧċajb Loċlaṅ
ṫo ċṁċ accoṁȧṗom ṫṗoṫa
no accṗjuċajb na gṗȧjge
no jṗann ejġjn ṫon ṫoṁan
Ṫa ṁaṗbṫaoj ċṅ a ṫeagmajl
ȧa neaȧṗajṅ nṫ ȧa njȧbejṗnn
no jccṁjċh Saxan na ȧaṫnṗlṫġ
nj bjaṫ claṫċlṫṫ aṗ ṁjnntjnn
Truág nać jgcnjoċa cṗujċneaċ
na bṗjan ȧa ȧujlteaċ ṫṫṁṫa
ṫo ċujtjȧ a ojġ lṗċṁajṗ
no jgcnjċh ȧulċajṗ na Soṗċa
O ṫajṁȧj anojȧ um beaṫajṫh
jȧ ṗoṁajċ ṫṗheaṗajb Alban
naċ leṫ ṫo ṫṗṫċṫaṫ hṫajllȧj
'ȧaȧ majċ ṫṫajṗljb na bȧhṗancaċ
Uch! jȧ meaȧa mujṗ ċaṗla
mo nuṫ jȧ ṫaṁȧa aṫouṗȧ
a Chonlṫjċ na ȧleaġ gcoṗeṗa
me ȧejn ṫ nṫṫṗtaṫ ċṗola
Aȷo bejċ ȧa buajṫ gan ṗojṁeaṗṫ
aṗ ṫojṫeaȧ ṫṁċ ȧan ċṗjċȧj
gan coṁṗac ċojṫċhe aṗ nȧġe
Truág naṗ ṁṁṅ ṫṁtȧj jȧȧe

Ṫo

Do ṡaṫ rṁam céo cumaiḋ
mo ḃeiṫ ḋubḃaċ iṅ ḃjónġnaḋ
ṫaréiṡ coṁraic ré méaṁaċ
mo ċréċta anoiṡ iṡ iomḋa
Ní ḃjonġnaḋ mo ḃeiṫ ṫuirṡeaċ
ṡgan meic uirneaċ ṫo laċair
aġ ṡiu me ḋéiṡ na rioġḟear
ġan mac ṫíleaṡ ġan ḃraċair.
Ġan Conṫaoċ ca niṡ iṡ ḋainme
ġan Nóiṡi ġan Aiṅnle armṁaḋ
ḃeiṫ ġan Arḋan iṡ ionnṡa
noċa liomṡa naċ lánṫruaġ
       T - r - u - a - g - h   ṡi - n.

───────────────────

II.

Laoiḋ Ṡlaġnuiṡ ṁoir

Aiċléiriġ ċanraṡ na Sailm
oḋ liom réin ní mait an ċall
Naċ eiṡḋionn tú ṫallan beaġ ṡġéil
air an ḃréin naċ ḃracaiṡ ariaṁ
Ḋar mo ċúḃaiṡ aḋeiġmeic ṡhinn
ġe ḃinn leaṫ ṫeaṡ ar an ḃréin
rié na ṡalm ar ṡeaḋ mo ḃéoil
ṡeaḋ ṡin iṡ céol ḋaṁ réin
Ṡla ṫóir aġ iomarḃáiḋ ṫo ṡalm
le ṡúana ġaoiḋeal na narm noċt
oċ! aiċléiriġ iṡ lán olc liom
nar ṡearuṡ ṫo ċeaṅ re ṫo ċorp

Ġaḃam

Ḃaḃam do ċumaince oġláoiċ ṁóin
ṡuiġe do ḃéoil is ḃinn liom ṫéin
an callaṅ toġaiṡ aiṙ ċhionn.

Is noṁaiṫ liom ceaṡ aiṙ an ḃṙéin
Lá óiṡn aġ ṡiaḋaċ na leaṙġ
naċ ṫaṗla ṡealġ aiṙ aṙ nġaṙ
ġo ḃṙacamaṙ ṁóṙan ḃáṙc
aġ ceaṡ ṡan cṙúiġ caiṡ leaṙ
Ciġṁáoiḋ anoiṡ aġuṡ anṡaṙ
cṙuiṁġiḋ an ṡhiaṅ aṡ ġaċ aiṙḋ
ṡeaċt ccaṫa aniorġoil ġo ṗṙaḃ
Ciġṁaḃiḋ ṡo ṁac inġine caiḋġ .
Aṡ é ġlóṙ do ċhan ṙinn
Sioṅ ṡéiṅiḋe ṡlaiċ an cṡlóiġ
ġe ḃe ṙaċaḋ ḋiáṙṙaiḋ ṡġéal
ġo ḃṙuiġeaḋ ṡéin aḃlác ṡa ḃṡaiḋ
Aṅ ṡin do ṙáiḋ Conán máol
ṁac Móṙne ṡa claḃn ġnioṁ
aṡáṙ ṁeic Cuḃaill na ccaṫ
cia ḃiaḋ ann aṡ ṡlaiċt, no ṙiġ
Aḋuḃaiṙt leiṡ Conán aṙiṡ
aḋiġċhinn ciaṙaċaḋ ann
aṡ ṡeaṙġuṡ ṡioṙġliċ do ṁac
o ṡé ċleaċt ḋol na ccionn
Oṙt mo ṁallaṡ a Choṅaiṙn ṁáoil
do ṙáiḋ ṡeaṙġuṡ ṡa caoiṅ cruṫ
ṙaċaḋṡa ḋiáṙṙaḋ na ṡġéal
a ġṙáḋ na ḃṡean 'ṡiṡ a do ġuṫ
Ġiṡaiṡioṡ ṡeaṙġuṡ aṙṁaċ óġ
aṅ ṡa ṙóḋ aġcoinne na ḃṡeaṙ
iṡ ṡiáṡṙaiġioṡ do ġuṫ ṁóṙ
cia ḃiaḋ na ṡloiġ ċaṡuiġ caiṡ leaṙ?

Aċa

Atá Mágnus oruinn mar thrjáṫ
mac an Mheirḋjġ na sġjaṫ nḋearg
ajrḋrjġ locḻann ceañ na ccrjoċ
gjolla ꝼa mór rjoċh jꝼ ꝼearg

O. Créad d'ēlꝼajꝼ an bujḋean borb
ꝼa rjġ locḻann na long mbréac
mar ḋjarrajġ cumojr ar ann
jꝼ romajṫ attaḃjjġ tajr lear

Do ṡhreagajr ꝼjn Mágnus go borb
ajrḋrjġ locḻann na longmbréac
do béura mē abean ó ꝼhjonn
dajmḋeojn ajr truin, agus bran

ḃheúrajḋ an ꝼhján comrac crꝼajḋ
doc ꝼlúaġ ꝼul adtjrbrajḋ bran
jꝼ cujrꝼjḋ ꝼjonn caṫ anoḻrꝼ
ꝼul ꝼa ttugajḋ uajḋ abean

Dar do lájmꝼe a ċheargnꝼ rhéjl
aꝼ an bhꝼéjn ge mór do ċeann
do béarad ljom bran
no comrac djan ꝼear da cjonn

Aꝼ do lájm ge mór do ḋojġ
aꝼ do rlóġ ge mór do ṁrjn
an ljón atajng tꝼ tajr lear
nj béura tu bran tajr tujnn

Tjlleaꝼ ꝼearġuꝼ mo braṫajr rējn
ꝼa ꝼamalta le grējn aċruṫ
jñrjġeaꝼ rē na ꝼġéala ṫall
abꝼjáġurjꝼe ꝼhjnn nar ċrill guṫ

Ajrḋrjġ Locḻann rro ꝼa ṫrajġ
cad ē an ꝼaṫ ta ḋrjnn aċejrt
nj ġéabajḋ gan braḻaḋ lann
no to bean roo cꝼ ro na brejṫ

Ní cirbrað mise mo bean
d'fhear go-racað me agcrí
'sni cirbrað mebran d'ais
go ndeaca an buf rm béal
Do ráið mac Cubaill re Goll
is mór an glon dúṁ beit a tos
gan coṁras oibreisigeac teann
do cabairt do ris Loclan na narm nos
Dá an luimisn orsa arhinn
ó to chí tí mar tóim anos
ris tonnbarcac na ccomlann tean
sgarfa me aceann re na corp.
Do ráið Oscar go mbris
conszioðra ris ísí torc
is clann an dú comairleac deús
bioð mo minstir yesn da ccors
Do ráið mac Inisðeach anáis
ris siounnloclann dáil gan ġó
conszioðra é d'on byesn
no da bẏéadairn ni bur mó
Earlain na huise ge teann
to ráið Diarmid donn gan on
conszeaðra é ton byesn
no tntseað yesn air aron
Aisling do connairc aresn
ar ra yaolan ra léor aceart
ris cire na byear ngorm
gur sgaras aceann re na corp
beiris beannas, beiris buið
do ráið mac Cubaill na ngruiðið ndeas
Slagnur mac micriðs na sluas
conszre mise ge mía arhears

Τιγιο

Tigio ann ſin an ſhján
teannaio optha anapm áig
ſleag ⁊ gſalajnn gaċ ſjn mojn
'ſoo ċuáoap pompa go tpúig
Anojoche ſjn oujnn go lá
mop gnaċ ljnn abejċ gan ċeol
ſleaó, ⁊ ſjón cpóch jſ céjn
ſe bj agajnn ſeſjn ſán ól
Slaſ ſjn oujnn guſ an oapa lá
go bſacamap na ſlojg pe pupt
mejpge mg Loċlann anájg
oá tógbajl ſan tpájg pe ap nuſ
Iomóa cotann iomóa tpſaċ
iomóa ſgjaċ, ⁊ lujpeach oeapg
iomóa tōiſeach jſ mac pjog
nj pajb láoch óſob gan apm.
Dob iomóa clojójom go noopnclaó ojn
oob iomóa ſpól oa ċup pe cpann
accaċ ſvlteach ſhjnn na bſleaó
oob iomóa ſleag oſ ap ccjonn.
Dob iomóa ann clogao cpuajó
oob iomóa tuaċ aguſ ga
ann ſa ċompac oo bj ann
oob iomóa pjg aguſ ſlajċ
Noſap geal gpeſne pe cpann
bpatach ſhjnn ſa léop atpeaſ
lán oo ċloċajb tjne anojn
oá liom ſeſjn ſa mop ameaſ
Noſap óġnne ſulang topajo
bpataċ guſll mojn mejc Moſpne
jſ mjnje aſuájp an ſpól chopaċ
tſſ, jſ oejpeaó ſjopmajſeach

Ag cromad aicinn ʃan cceaṫ
do ṗinnc gaċ ꝼlaıṫ map do ġeall
ꝼjána Éıpeann na ccoṁlann ccpꝼaıd
bꝛıꝼjd aıp ꝼhluáġ ınıꝼe Ġall.
Chaıṗla mac cubaıll na ccuách
le pıġ Loċlann na puáġ naıṡ
pe ċéıle aıp tentın naꝼluáġ
och! aċléıꝛıġ, ıꝼ tpꝼaġ an duıʃl.
Do ꝛinneadıp impeaꝼaın ċeann
go mad coꝼaṁaıl ꝛe dá opd
coṁpac ꝛuılteaċ an da pıġ
ꝼa gontaċ ambꝛıġ ꝼa ccolg
Ceangaltap pıġ Loċlann ꝼan tpeaꝼ
ꝛe mac Cubaıll na ccleaꝼ mbopb
eıꝛıon aꝼ gep ṁóp an gníóṁ
do ċeangaıl ꝼıonn é ꝛe na ċolg
JS ann ʃın do ꝛaıd Conán maol
gıolla do bí ꝛıáṁ ꝛe holc
cꝛuıgbıd daṁ Máġnuꝼ na lann
go ꝼgapꝼad acfann ꝛe na ċopp
Ní bꝼuıl páıꝛt daṁꝼa, no ġaol
ꝛıot aċonaın maoıl gan ċéıll
o ċáꝛla mé ꝼo ġꝛáꝼaıḃ ꝼhınn
ıꝼ ꝼeapp lıom ann, no ꝼú do ṁeın
O ċáꝛla tú ꝼo mo ġꝛáꝼuıḃ ꝛéın
'ꝼnach deaꝛna mé ꝼáp aꝛ ꝼhlaıṫ
ꝛuáıꝛgéolad tꝛé ón bꝛéın
alaṁh tꝛéın na ṁóp ccaṫ
Ġaḃ do poġa a Ṡláġnuꝼ ṁın
map paċaıꝛ ꝼlán ıd ċıp ꝛéın
cuṁonn, caḃıꝛeaꝼ aguꝼ gꝛád
no do ꝼlán aḃeıꝼ ꝼán bꝛéın?

Fꝛeıtınıꝼe

sgeitimse sin go bráż
an ġein mairreas dáil mo ċorp
aon buille ataġaiḋse a ṡinn
airreach liom andearmus ort
An cablaċ sin tainiġ a ttráiż
no slúaġ le ccuiri gaċ gléo
ċugain as ger mór astairm
ba lia da mairb, no da mbeó
Ag sin ḃuitsi turus ṡinn
aċlesriġ na mbeann mbláż
no ġairća na ggéolan sa ccill
oċ! ba binre liom an lá.
Ag sin sgéala go brion
aċlesriġ na mborb treas
do ṁac riġ Loċlann na slóġ
is tú hainmneaḋ an treas.
Dair da láimse aċlesriġ ċáid
da mbeićea ar an tráiġ o ḋeas
ag eas laoġaire na sreab séim
s an bréin ba mór do meas
Ge taoimse meata gan tlaċt
ag sin ḋáoib go beas mo sgéil
me gan ċraoisiġ gan ċolg
ag eisteas re dord bar cclsar.

A - ċ - l - e - i - r - i - g - h.   sinṫ

III.

Laoiḋ na Sealga.

Oisín. A Ṗáḋruig an ccuala tu an tsealg?
aṁsc Chalpruinn na ḃfaisim ṙaiṁh
do roinneaḋ an ċonar le Fjonn
ṡgan én neaċ ann d'ḟianaiḃ
Ní ċualas aṁsc an Ríg
Oisín eile na ngnioṁ ngarg
inniṡ dúinn is na can go
cionnas a roinneaḋ leó an tsealg?
Ní ċana mósṙne an ṫian go
arṡáṁ leo nióṙ luaiḋeaḋ bréug
aċt le ṙiṙinne is le neart sláṁ
tigmóṙ slán as gaċ móiḋm
Níor ṙuig cleiṙeaċ aciil
ge gur ḃinn niḃ aċanaiḋ ṗraism
dob ṡiṙinnig no an ṫian
sin nar loc angliaḋ gang
Níor ṙuig coṁmais ón neaċ accrisc
a ráḋuig cóiṁ is binne glór
dob ṡiṙinnig no Fjonn anaiṡ
sean ar ḃaiṡm do ḃronnaḋ ór
Da mairẹaḋ mac Moṙna tnear
no Goll cróḋa nar ċar sęuḋ
no mac I Duiḃne na mban
laoċ do ċuiṙeaḋ cat air ċęuḋ
Da mairẹaḋ mac garaiḋ na lán
sear nar ġann ag cur an úir
Oscar no mac Roṅain Ṡrinn
do crónan san cill níor ṙaiṁ

Da

(279)

Dá maireaḋ Feargus fíle fionn
fear do niaḋ raṁ ar an bṫeiṁ
no Daire ṡinneaḋ gan loṡ
angus do ċluig ni beiṫ mo ṡpéis
Dá maireaḋ aoḋ beag mac ḟinn
na ṡólan grinn nar ṡar neaċ
no Conan maol bi gan ġruaig
adṡaig me ṡóḋ ġruaim le ṡeal
Aḃac beag do ḃi aig ṡionn
ċuireaḋ gaċ cionn na toirrċim ṡuain
ba ḃinne liom rogair a ḃeil
no aḃṡril do ċléir aroig, ṡto ṫraiḋ

p. Leig as aḃeiṫ da niom
anic an riġ dob ṡheáṁr cliṡd
geill don té niod gaċ ṡeart
crom do ċeann is ṡeac do ġlún
buail hus is ṡil do ḋér
cried don té tá os do cionn
gid gurab iongnaḋ leatsa aluaḋ
aṡé do rug braiḋ air ṡionn
Uċ (ar Oiṡin) mo ṡgeal tṡuag
ni ḃinn liom rain do ġloir
guilṡiod ṡrasa suiṡ ṡa do ḋia
as cionn an ṡión gan aḃeiṫ beo
IS mór an ceannaċ liom ṡ do ḋia
beiṫ meaṡg do ċliar mar atáim
gan ḃiaḋ gan eadaċ gan ṡpórt
gan bronnaḋ oir air ḋairm
Gan gair gaḋar no ṡtoc
gan coimead puirt na cuán
a ḃṡuaras ttcraṡ is do ḋiṫ biḋ
maiṡim do riġ niṁe aluach

p. Leig

(280)

P. Leig bhomarbaḋ as
Oisin moir na sreas sréan
sionn na bslaic sa bshril da ċöib
iṅ comṁópaḋ sin ne rig na neull
Aise oja érm neaṁ agus calaṁ
ase co beir nearc na laoċh
ase oo ċruċaiġ an maġ bán
ase oo beir bláċ na ccaop
Aise beir gealaċ agus grsan
ase beir sjrġ ar ljnn
ase oo ċruċaiġ córća is bláċ
njor bjonann cráċ agus eusa sjnn

O. Ní ar ċruċuġaḋ cošča no bláċ
ċug mo rig séin arusl
as ar ċasgairc coppa laoch
acosnaṁ erioċ sa cur aċlṁiḋ
An suisġė air rsabra ar resig
ar nosaḋ meirg acers slois
d ṁjrċ sječoll air snaṁ
d coṁeaḋ ċaṡė ṁaṁrsir gleöiḋ
Apaċrng ea rasb co ḋja
an lá cainig an djós ersaṅ car leap
se mnaoi rig Loċlann na long
ler éiċ aṅomaḋ sonn sa cress
No an lá cainig caisle ṁac creṁ
sbear ar an bseir oo ċsr ár
iṅ le oo rig oo éiċ an sear
as ne laiṁ Ofcair ameasg ċasė
No an lá sa caṁc Maġnas mör
sear ba bonb glor snar ėjm
is oúċċa oa maṁeaḋ oo ḋja
go cenoeobaḋ se le siana sjnn

Ailleann

Ailleann mac a nóinthir móir
ṡear ṅe nóḃéide teaṁair na ṡloġ tréan
nj láṁ ar lairn do ġaḃ do ḋjá
ḋol da clóiḋ aṡ ṡionn ṡéjn
Aṡ jomḋa cleaṡ ġnjoṁ iṡ ġleó
maoiḋtiġ ṅe ṡjana ṡájl
nj ċualaṡ ġo nḋéanaḋ éaṡ
Ríġ na néull ġun ḋearġ alúm

p. Sġriṡim dar njomarbaḋ ar ġaċ tóiḃ
a ṡeanoir maojl ata ġan ċéjll
ata dja ḋ neaṁ na njoṁ
jṡ ta an fhjan uile jḃṡéjn

o. Apadruiġ naċ tríaġ naċ ccoṅġjoḋ dja
luṡ na bṡján aċḃur ar fhjonn
7 dja ṡéjn da mḃjaḋ anajṡe
ġo troisṡeaḋ an ṡlajṫ da ċjonn
Nj minjc adṡrlajuiġ ríġ na bṡján
éin neaċ arṡaṁ anajṡe no nġuájṡ
ġan ṡjaṡġajlt le hairġjod no ṡe hór
no troṡaċ ṡlúiġ ġo mḃeirteaḋ braiḋ
Apadruiġ da mḃeiṅṡ, ġan ċéjll
ṡearṡajn le do ċléjr uile accjnn
nj ḃeiṫ baċall no leaḃar ḃán
no cloġ na tráċ aṅ do ċjll

p. Aṡ binn leam aḃeiṫ tiṡ ar an ḃṡéjn
a ṁeiṡ an ríġ aṡ újtne tealḃ
naċ crṁajn leat mar ġeallraṡ óṡinn
cionnaṡ aṡṁóṅaḋ leó an tṡealġ.

o. Apadruiġ ġiḋ úḋḃar caḃj
ḃain aḃeiṫ rjom anéuṡa úrḋ
aiṫreoṡaḋ ġe tóirn ṡa ḃrón.
cjonnaṡ do rjnneaḋ leó an tṡealġ

Lá dá raibeamáoiṡ Fiana Finn
a naluiṁin ṡliṁ na ṡleaġ séro
ag iṁiṙt ḟiċċill 'ṡaiġ ól
cloiṡoion ċeoil is ag bronnaḋ séro
Aḟ gur éiriġe Fionn an rlaiṫ
air an braṫ oṡ Alṁiṁin ṡin
go bracaiḋ ċuiġe ann ṡa róo
an eiliḋ óg air aleiṁ luiṫċ
Ṡhoir ċuiġe ṡéeolan 7 bran
do leiġ ṡead oppa araon
gan ṡhioṡ do cáċ ṡo an ól
gur lean ṡa róo an eiliḋ maol.
Ní raib leiṡ aṡ mac an luin
aḋá ċoin aguṡ é ṡein
air loṙg na heiliḋe go ḋián
go ṡliab gruiṁ na ṁón péiḋ
Air ndol don eiliḋ ṡa tṡliab
ṡionn na diaiġ ṡa ḋá ċoin
mór briḋoṡ dú ṡoir, no ṡiar
car gab an ṡaiḋ ṡa cċnoc.
Do ġab ṡionn ṡoir ṡa tṡliab
ṡa ḋá ċoin ṡiár ar líṫ
'ṡa paoriṙg nár boċ le dia
mar ċug aṡriar ánoú ceíl
Chualaiḋ ṡionn 'ṡniór ċian uaḋ
gul ar bruaċ an loċa ṡhéiṁ
aṡ ann do bí an macaoṁ mná
dob ṡheárr cáil da bracaiḋ ṡé
Do bí agruaiḋ mar an Róṡ
aguṡ abeól ar ḋaṫ na cċaér
do bí acneiṡ mar an mbláṫ
ṡa leaca báin mar an ácl.

Air

Air ḃaċ an oiṡr do ḃí aroic
mar ṗeulc air aroṡġ do ḃí
'ṡa ṗaoṗraiġ da ḃṡaiċṡea aṫpeaċ
do ḃéaṗċa do ṡéaṗc don ṁnaoi.
Ḋruideaṡ fionn aġ iáṗṅaiṡò ṡġeúl
air innaoi ṡeiṅh na cċṫaċ nóiṗ
oḋiaṡṅaiġ mo ṅiġ don ġnṁṫ nġil
an ḃṡacaiṁ cr mo ċoiṗ ṡa coiṗ?
Ann do ṡeilġ ni ṁhril mo ṡḃeiṡ
iṡ ni ṁhaca mé do ḋá ċoiṗ
a Ṗi na ṡeiṗe ġan cáṗ
iṡ meaṡa liom ṡáċ mo ġṡil
Au é do ċéile do ṡuaiṗ ḃáṡ
a iṅġean ċlaiṡċ, nó do ṁac
nó caò é an ṡáċ ṡa ḃṡil do ċói
aiṅoiṗ ċṙiṁ iṡ áilne oṗeach
Ṅó caò aṡ aḃṡil do ḃṗóṅ
a aiṅṇiṗ óġ na mboṡ ṁiṗ
nó an ṡéiòiṗ ċṡuṅcaċċ (f ṡionn)
iṡ ouḃaċ liom do ḃeiċ mar ċhiṁ
fáil oiṗ do ḃi ṡo mo ġlaiċ
do ṗáiṡò iṅġean óġ na ḃṡolc ṡéiṁi
ċṅiċiṅ com laiṁ ṡan cṡṗeaḃ
aġ ṡiṅ máoḃaṅ ba ḃeiċ iḃṗéiṅ
Ġeaṡa naṗ ċhṡlaiṅġ laoch.
cṅiṗiṅ do ċioṅṅ a Ṗi na ḃṗhiáṅ
mar ċuġaiṗ mṡhaiṅṅe ċuġam caiṗ aiṗ
ċṅic ṅe heaṡ na ṡṅeaḃ ṅoiṡáṅ
Níoṗ ċhulaiṅġ fionn cuṗ na nġeaṡ
cṡáċ ċṅiṗ òe aṅaiṡò ṡo na ċṅeṡ ġléẏi
ċuaiṗ ġo ḃṗuaċ an loċa ṡṅáṁ
f ċhuṗaiṡleaṁ ṁina na mḃaṡṡ ṗéiṡò

Do

Do chuartaigh an loch ye crīg
mōr fhaig ann clūid no ceaṗn
no go ttug an ṫaiṁne cōiṁ ar aiṡ
do ṫrī o miogūin na ngruaid ndearg
Trāṫ fuair an ṫaiṁne cōiṁ ar aiṡ
nī ṙaiṁic leiṡ aṫabairt go bruaċ
an tráṫ ṙinneaḋ feanoir criȯn liaṫ
do riġ na bffian cia gur ṫrīaġ
Do ḃioḋmairne ffiana ffinn
analuiṁin ṡim na fluaġ ṙein
ag imirt air eanlaiḋ iṡ ag ōl
acloiṡdion ceoil ṡa bronnaḋ fead
Eirġius cōilte ameaṡg ċaiċ
iṡ dfiafraiġ oṡ aird do gaċ fear
an bfacabair mac Chubaill ṡeiġil
a ḃuiḋean fein na fleaġ fean?
No eiriġe Conan mac Morna
nī ċuala ariaṁ ceol doḃ ṡōiḃne
ma tā fionn air iarraiḋ
go raiḃ ambliaḋna aċōilte
Mac Chubaill ma ṫeaṡdaiġ uait
a Chōilte ċruaiḋ na ccoṡ ccōl
ġabairm oram do laiṁh
oṡ cionn ċaiċh aḃeir mo riġ
Do bimair an ṡrian ṡa brōn
ṡa cionn ar floiġ aḃeir dā noiṡe
no gur mioḋ oruinn cion gaiṙe
iṡ dūinne bāḋḃar aḃeir ciōi.
Gluaiṡteor linn o aluiṁin amach
buiḋean ċalma na ccaṫ ċruaiḋ
a lorg aḋū chon aguṡ fhinn
triūr grinn do beiṙeaḋ buaiḋ

(285)

bhí mise agus Cóilte ar tús
fa n-ṡian uile go dluṫ a n-ḋáil
go sliaḃ guilinn o tuaiṫ
mar tugamar buaiḋ a cáċ
Amarc beag dá tugamar uáiṁ
andiaiġ na ruag cia tí an ṡiún
a bruaċ an loċa fa brón
aċ seanóir mór agus é críon
Do ċuaḋmar uile na ḋáil
is ċuirseaḋ se grásn a gaċ sear
cnáṁa loma do bí críon
ag an ṡear a ceileaḋ gnói 7 gean
Ḋeasamuirne gurab easbaiḋ bíḋ
tug a an laoċ abeiṫ gan ċruṫ
no gur an sársaire do bí se
ċainig acéin le sruṫ
Dsiarnaiġmuirne don ṡear críon
an bsacaiḋ se laoċ go ngoil
iad roiṁe amaċ ar séol
eiliḋ óg is ḋá ċoin
Níor raiḋ sionn a bsagail na sgéal
gurab é sein ris na brian
gur leiġ le Cóilte arsn
an sear lír do bí dian
An uair suaramar dearbaḋ na sgéal
gurab é sionn sein do bí ann
do leigeamar trí gárta gruḋ
soo ċuirsioḋs bruc as gaċ gleann.
Deirġe Conan maol go borb
is nosas aċoilg go diún
do mallaiġ se sionn go beas
is do mallaiġ so seaċ an ṡiún

Di

Dá mbeiṫ ṡíoṡ agam ġur tr ṡionn
báiniṡiun an ṡean ċionn ṡin ṫiot
oṡ tr nar ṁaoiḋ anoiṡ no nṡáiṁ
mo ġal arṡáiṁ no mo ġuṡoiṁ
Aṡe maoinloèt ḋ to ċruṫ
ġan an ṡhian nle beiṫ mar ṫáin
ġo nteargaiṁ mo ṡleaġ ṡmo lann
ġo tiṡeaḋ niom to leaċta, ṡto lá
On lá marḃaḋ Crḃall na cclíar
rè mac 9Iorna na ṡgiaċ nḃin
ni ṡhuilmaoiṡne o ṡin aṡ T noṡt
ṡa byhril beḋ ḋini ni ḋa nteḋin

Oṡg. Aṡ mṡi mbeiṫ an cruṫ abṡril ṡioṁ
ṡġur puḋar nṁ è beiṫ mar tá
a Chonain ṁaoil ata gan ċèill
briṡṡiun to ḃèal go cnáiṁ
Erġioṡ Oṡgar ṡear ṡa teann
ṡġur tot ċaint nṡ ṡa mḃ
aċonain ṁaoil ata gan ċèill
naċ ruġ bèin anaġaiḋ gleoiḋ.

Con. Aṡ beaġ mo ṡpèiṡ aṁ to ġlór
aṁic Oiṡin ba mḃr baoiṡ
ṡnaċ raiḃ to ṁaiṫ abṡionn ṡèin
aṡ acoġnaḋ aṁèin go ṡmḃṡ
IS ṡinne ṡèin to niaḋ an ġuṡoiṁ
iṡ ni hiaḋ clanna baoiṡġne boġ
beiḋ to mac Oiṡin to ḋèoiġ
aġ iomċar leaḃar ban iṡ clog
Oiṡair ṡeir to to ġlór
ni caint to ḋearḃaṡ aṡ ġuṡoiṁ
ṡeuċmaoiṡ aṡ coṁair ċáich
neart ar láiṁ 'ṡar mbriṡ

Thuġ

Thug Oscar an sidead prap
do léim Conan ameasg cáich
ruagras ermaisce aran byhéin
is suiras dó féin as féin báis
Ro eirge an Fhian go gaig
acosg Oscair na narm núig
eidir mo macsa 7 Conán maol
gur ceanglad siod agus puint
Fiasraigeas Caoilte an treas feas
do mac Cumaill nar cleas cám
cia haca do tuitta dé
do mill do ghné mar atá?
Ingean ghuilinn (do ráid fionn)
geasa um ceann do chir si
dul sa bprsac an locha snámh
d'fágail an fháinne do tit síos
Nar fhillmaoidne slán on ccnoc
do ráid Conan nar bolc méin
go mbcsaid guilinn é gan moill
mur ccuirid fionn ah achruc féin
Chruinnigeamairne anois sa nár
cuireamar sonn sgiat saoi go deos
go sliab Guilinn o tuaidh
go tugamar fionn air guaillib fear
Air sead os naoidce agus ocht lá
bámar gan spás ag tocailt na hrám
go tainic cugainn amach
Guilionn aireib as an raim
Cuac ceapnac is é lan
do bi sláim guilinn cóir
do mac Cumaill nar mait gné
gur toibir si an tosgar air

Ar ól díġe dó as an ccorn̄
is é na luiġe d' ṡhíor go ran̄
caiṅic aċruċ ṡein ṡa ńṡam
d' ris na briṡan ṡna neaċ ṡeang
Do léiġeamar cri ġarca ġrod
sco ċuirsios brṅc as gaċ gleann
sa parornġ naċ rial son mibiad
an ccuala sosṁe riaṁ an csealġ
a - b - h - a - d - r - u - i - g.

IV.

Laoiḋ an Ṁhoiġre bhoirb. sonn anos.

Sġéal beag aġum air Fhionn
ni sġél naċ ccuirsio arṅm é
air ṁac Cubaill ba maic goil
ba cuṁain sin re mo ráe
Do báṁairne beaġan slóiġ
air earsráḋ nic bobair na ṁoill
cig cuġain ṡa séol ar leap
an cupaċ beag is bean ann
Caoġad láoċ dṡinn mun Ri
ba maic air nġniom 'sar nġarc
sin dar nóeis as mairġ ad chi
do ġabaṁabis d' ġaċ crich neart
Eirġeamóio uile go dian
as fionn na briṡan aġus Goll
d'saisoin an cuṁaċ ṡa háo céim
na réiṁ ag sġailceaḋ na ttonn

Níor ṡan an curaċ gan ċeaf.
gur ġaḃ calaḋ fan bport buḋ gnáṫ
'fmar do ṫainiġ air an eaf
ad éirġe af macaoṁ mná
Dob ionann ḋealraḋ ói 'fdon ġréin
dob ṡéarr améin nós adealḃ
an iníġean foin táinic iccéin
do ḃamar féin roimpe ann
Ráinic fi poball ḟinn
'fdo ḃeannaiġ fí go gríin dó
do ṡreagair mac Cuṁaill nar ċim
go huṁal ḃinn í gan tóġ
Suiġeaf aḃriaġnuife Ġhuill
ar laiṁ ḋaif ḟinn mic Cuḃyll
gaċ aon ói dar aḋearc
air aċéile níor ċuiṁneaċ
fiarraiġeaf fion fa deang dreaċ
ca hairm don iníġin álain uir
ca treaḃ af attangaif aḃean
innif fgél go maiṫ dúinn?
If mé iníġean ríġ fo ṫuinn
iinéofad go crvinn mo ḋáil
níor ṡáġaf talaṁ fa níaḋań grian
nar farraf féin do ṡlaiṫ fáil
briġ mo riuḃail ann gaċ ród
a iníġean óg af maiṫ dealḃ
an táoḃ fo táinġaif iccéin
taḃair ḋaṁ féin ṡiof go dearḃ
Alo ċoimriġe ort óf tu fionn
do ṁiḋ rinn an macaoṁ mná
A ṡeaḃaf huirriġe 'fdo ḃráḋ
gaḃ mo ċoimriġe go tráċ tráṫ

P p   Do

Do ṗáiḋ mo ṗíġ ba maiṫ ṙioṫ
ṫaḃair ṙḣios cia ṫói ⁊ do ṫḣí
ġaḃairṁe do ċoimrīġe aḃean
⁊ ġaċ ṙear ᴅa ḃṙuil iceiṫ
Aṫa riom ne ṙioċh do ṁuir
laoċ aṙ maiṫ ġoil ⁊ mo loṅg
mac ṗíġ na Sorċha iṙ ġéṙ arm
ᴅó ba hainm an 9loiṫne borb
Ġeaṙa do ċuiṙeaṙ na ċionn
rio ġo mbeiriun aṙ ḟhion do ṙal
naċ béiniṙi aiġe do iinaoi
ġéṙ maiṫ aġriṙom aġuṙ aġh
Do ṗáiḋ Oṙġaṙ do ġlór ṁiṙ
ṙeaṙ ċoiṙġṫe ṙin ġaċ lói
rio ġo bṙóiṙeiṙ ṙionn do ġeiṙ
ir riaċṙa ṫuṙa riṙ do ṁinaoi
Eiṙġior Oṙġaṙ aġuṙ Ġoll
borb acċoṙġaṙ lonn na ċċaċ
na ṙeaṙari ġaṙ don ṫṙlóġ
ċioiṙ an ṙeaṙ móṙ 'ṙan bean
Aᴅ ċimóiṙ ċuġairn ⁊ ṙᴅéuᴅ
laoċ ṙa iṁéuᴅ oṙ ġaċ ṙeaṙ
aṙioḃal na ṙairiġe ġo ᴅian
ṙa injomhal ċéᴅna ⁊ ġaḃ an bean
Cloġaᴅ ṫeann ṫeiṙiniġe ṙo aċeann
aġ an ṙhean naṙ ċim 'ṙᴅo bí ṫṙen
an ṙġiaċ iomlan bí aiṙ aḋeiṙ"
ṫhoim lán aċċleaṙ aiṙ an celé
Dhu ṁanéiṙ ġaiṙġe ġo mbṙaᴅ
na ṙeaṙaṁ irġablairi aṙġéiṫ
aṙ reaṙṫ ⁊ ġaiṙġe, aṙ ġoil
irí ṙhaċa ṙeaṙ maṙ ṙin aṙé

Au

An cloiḋioṁ ṫrom toirteaṁuil nar ḟaṅ
bi tall ar taoḃ an ḟiġir ṁóir
'ṡaiġ iṁpir cleaṡ óṡ acionn
aġ teaṡ do iccionn an tṡlóiġ
bḣi néull ṡlata, iṡ roṡġ rioġḋa
ṡo an ḟiġir ṡaiṁ ṡa caoiṁ cruṫ
maiṫ aṡnṡaḋ, ṡa ġeal aḋéuḋ
ba lṡaiṫe aṡtéuḋ no ġaċ ṡruṫ
9iar do ċaṡiuiġ an ṡtéuḋ iṫṡir
ṡa ṡear nar ṁiṡn leiṡ an bṡéin
ni ṡacaṡ ṡaṁail an ḟiġir
teaṡ ġo noiġe ṡin iccéin
ón tuinn mar ċaṡiuiġ iṫṡir
ḋ'ṡiaṡraiġ mo Riġ ba maiṫ cliuḋ
an aiċiṅġeann tuṡa abean
an é ṡṡò an ṡear aḋein tṡ?
Aiċiuiġim aiṁeic Cubaill ġriuu
aṡ ruḋṡ riom é ḋon ḟéin
taiṅġiḋ miṡe ḋo breiṫ riṡ
cia móir ḋo ċreiṡe ṡiṅ ṡéil
Tiġ an laoċ ṡo ṡa maiṫ claṡ
re ṡioċ, ṡre neart ar ccionn
iṡ ḋ'ṡṡṡaḋaiġ uáiṁ an bean
ḋo bḣi nġar ḋo ġṡaluiun ṡiṅ
Ṫuġ mac 9ḃrna urċar ḋṡan
ġo crúḋa na ḋṡaiġ ḋa ṡleiġ
nior ḟan an turċar ḋo bḣi ḋṡan
ḋa ṡġeiṫ ġo nḋéarna ḋá blaḋ
Do ċaiṫ Oṡṡar ba mór ṡearġ
aċraoiṡeaċ ḋearġ ḋa láiṁ ċlé
re ṡ iiiaṅḃ ṡe Sṫéuḋ an ḟiġir
mór an béuḋ ḋo roiṅe léi

Fán do ṫuit an sceó sa leing
iompóiḋeas ré seing, 'sne síoċ
is d'ṡóżair żér boṛb an cóṁ
coṁrac air an ċóżaḋ láoċ
Ré muiṫ ḋiomsa séin as d'ṡioṁ
cáoża laoċ nar ṫim na ḃáil
cia ḋ ṫeann anżaisże sa ṫrosd
do żeall accoiż ré na láiṁ
Do ċeangair trí ṁóriḃair go mbráiḋ
san iorgril ċrráiḋ srl do sżuir
cia ḋ ḋóċar ceangal na ccris ccćól
ḋ żaċ ón oiob sin do ċur
Flann mac Móŗna crráiḋ an cás
ruair bás żér ṁóŗ an ṫéus
ní raib láoċ da ṫaing as
gan aċneas lán do ċréus
Fár mbeiṫ an caoża laoċ garḃ
aż żaḃair anarm dó go leor
do beiṫmóis żan caḃair o neaċ
da bráżaḋ uáiṁ an searṫ cóir
Do beirreaḋ ḋá béim go mear
go oian ar żaċ sear oiob sin
do beiṫmaois uile san uáiż
da bráżaḋ ráinn coṁrac sin
Do ċuaiḋ Goll an aiżniḋ ṁin
do learḋaḋ an fir ba żar ohó
cia be ad ċisseaḋ sad ann sin
do ba żarḃ ażoil sa nżléo
ḃáḋan acclosóṁṫe żan toss
aż snaoiḋeaḋ coŗr aguis sżiaṫ
acoṁṁairé coṁrac aż ḋis
ní fbaisssioḋ arís rem rae

Do

Do torċraḋ ye goll na narm nuaiġ
mac ríġ na Sorcha gen éis cruaiḋ
ay maġ talaṁ ytaiṁc an bean
nén ċrc anyear yn ya ccyan
Aḋlaicceay nyun ag an Eay
an laoċ yay ċeann treiye iy guyon
curċar aiy ya bnuġaiḋ gaċ méoiy
yainnċ óiy anonúiy mo Riġ
Déiy triciy an yhiy móiy
A boyḋ an ċuaiy, tryaġ an ċéiy
Do bi iniġean Riġ yo ċuiny
bliaḋaiy aig fyonn yan byéiy
Leiċ bliaḋaiy do Ġhoḷḷ na narm nuaiġ
laoċ Donn nay ċláiċ iccath
na luiġe yo ḋeaġxhioy nyun
Da leiġeay aig fyonn na byleaġ
Alaċaiy yéiy ya ḋearġ ḋyeach
niony ēur neoċ tryaġ no tréṅ
anoy ó ċáiṁcaiġ mo ċruth
ay miċhe ḋaṁ ygur dom ygél.

S-g-e-u-l   b-e-a-g   a-g-u-m. &c.

THE
IRISH ORIGINALS
OF THE
ODES.

THE
IRISH ORIGINALS
OF THE
ODES.

I.

Rofg Ofguip mjc Ohjn pe huf cata Zabpa.

Ejpjg a Ofguip yhéjl ayhjp an cofgpip cpuajd
le do bpatajg ájg bejp neapc aguf buajd
Ainiejc Ohjn na mbéimjon gabajd cpejfe gaca comlojn
na feuc do méud cyhoplpnn ajp cach no go tojpujp
gab bpofdad bn byjljd go hofgup mac ganajd
na Rjgte ata atagajd cpaojejd aguf tanajg
Jonfajg ajp mac Chopmuic gab ceanfala acompac
no go byagtap ejpic le do fleag djrbpujc
bfad bpajneojn go drajbfeac o ceanuajl do cpopfeach
fpeagajp jad go tajbfeac da leadpad, fda nojpleach
Ainic pjg gan tajpe do nj gujom jf fogla
bud deapbta do fgéala go meanmnach angabpa
Afcop flat go ngajpge cloin go luat amejpge
fa cogad jf ujpde fgap apajch pe cajpbpe
bj mup tpiun a ttujle gjon gup tpom jn tejpe
tabajp fojcead gola o gach Rj go pojle

                                                                    +)a

Na gabh ofaḋ uaċa cofgair arīghthe
a Ofguir éiniġ ſrḃċa tarſa aguſ tríopċa
Aġnríſ iſ cáoiṁe cnoċū éiniġ aoċfſ accaċha
leán le ſeirg mo ġoċha aṁeirg iſ ḋearg ḋaċa
Ḋéana maiṙċa troma bī air conſaḋ goile
cinn air do luċċ ſala ſgan ſionn ao ġoire
Ceannuſ ḋona ſīanaiḃ ḋo leanaſ tōgſgéala
coſain aġ aguſ áireaṁ taḃair ġairċa atteaṁnaiġ
Ġiḋ aſbſaḋaċ anoiſeaſ buḋ bſaḋaċ do ċunaſ
ḋo ċaċha ḋa namrſ cuir ſlaċha ḋa ccumuſ
A Ofguir ċruċach áluinn bī go ſuḃaċ ſīrḃinn
aċapa ḋáṁ éireann láiṁ air ḋo ġnfſ ṁīnḋuiṁ
A Ofguir naċ ḋtuġ eiteaċ go coſgur nach oḃċach
cuir tormán ḋo ḃraċach ḋa nairgain go ḋoċnach
ſráoċ ġéire ḋo lainne o ċréime ḋo buille
ḋo lſaċ bſ gaċ duine ḋoḋ lſaḋſā ſan ccruiṫċ
Taḃair ſnaſa tréana gaḃ tneiſe angaḃna
aċūio ſīana banḃa oir aġ iaiririḋ taḃra
Aġnríſ iſ áirḋe molaḋ aniir ċalma na ccupaiġ
aġlóir éireann uile taḃair lén air ſhéir Ulaḋ
Ayhlaiġ na ſlſaġ ſoċaiḋe maiġ ḋo luaḋ air Ėaċraiḋe
beir leaċ ḋo ſgiaċ conċnaiḋe aġhir na tréiġ aṫhraiḋe
Ḋo ſleaġa go nḋōġrairg le haġḃuiḋ ḋo ḃéirinionn
ḋo ċloiḋiṁe go nḋoiġrinn ḋo ċlaoiḋeaḋ bſcar néireaṁ
Ḋo ġéplanna ḋa mbſalaḋ ċéan tana ḋa bſīanaiḃ
ḋo ġairſge na ſſaraċh ſneaſdaiſl īaḋ aguſ éiniġ. &c.

Qq

II.

Rofg Ghojll mac Mopna.

Apo aigneach Goll. ear cogaið fjnn
laoć leabajp lonn. foghajl naċ tjm
Goll cpuċaċ caoṁ. Saop ejneach ṡað
ṡaopṡnaojðaċ aċaob. mapajge na ṡliag
Mac Mopna meap. ṡa cpoða agal.
a ċljr ṡa ṡean. ṡeap ṡejneaṁinċ ṡjn.
Laoċ ṡejnnjðe ṡjal. ỳ gjle glop.
nj ṡaob aċṡall. laoċ uobða mop.
Nj tajṡ oo nj. map ċejo accaċ
pejn ṡlaċa ṡaoj. ce mjn aċneaṡ.
Aṁejn nj mjon, ṡa ṡgejṁ gan gpon
ỳ ṡe ỳ glojne tṡhjop. ojte na Sgol.
Njop lag alaṁ. ṡeap ċejtgeal caoṁ.
naċ tpejgean Dajn. accogað pṡaṁ.
Of bappajb beann. japṡpaṡ opt pojṁ.
ṡa beagal ljnn. aċagpa pjot ṡhjnn.
Ge tpom aċljṡ. 'ṡmajċ Goll um njð.
gjð mop nj tpeṡċ. ṡajċ ṡluajg oo pjg.
Cajopeaṁ na noaṁ. leaopaċ na ṡlojg
tonn ṡajppge tpen. Goll meaṁnaċ mop.
buð beagal bit aṡhjnn. laoċ cjnnte ceapt.
ṡpaoċ mjllte a neapt
A tepjnn pjot. aṡhjnn an ṡhujlt tajṡ
ap goll na bpjṡ. aṁejpge nj tajṡ.
ỳ majpg taṡṁaṡ njṡ.
ṡlajċ gan ṡheall. gpajn ċeað ap goll
ajp mead ap ċeann. accaċ nj tjm.

Apðejpjm

Adeirim riot aċinn. comairl is geall.
ríṫ buan do ġoll. gan ṫráċ. gan ṡeall
ḟaigneaḋ go trom. Adeirim riot aċinn
na roiriḋs ndoiṁ. bí ar eagla ġuill
ge buan re maiṫ. acaċ ni ḋóiġ.
ioinnraiġṫeaċ áig. cionṡealaċ flóiġ.
Uaṡal aġean. a eineaċ ni mion
ruilteaċ an reair.
Duara na rgol. oirdeirceaċ re flráiġ
toirbeartaċ trén. corg caċa is buan.
fós rlat é. ar rial lomlán da reire
doinne ina ċholt. abruinne mar ċaile
iomlan aċorp.
Eire ra éióf. buḋ cóir da érir.
is meanmnaċ bíor. is dealbaċ aġnír.
An gairgiḋeaċ grinn. ni bfuil ni or goll.
ni ċeirim oir ċinn. is treire é na toinn
flairteamuil aċhór. Daiṫeamuil aénear.
ar goll na clir. ni flim a ṫreas.
Mileata mór. bronntaċ aḋáil.
conṡaḋac aṫrebin. aṡearg go briut áġ.
agur rioċ abuannaċt ar each.
Lámacaḋ laoċ. roġa na rioġ.
leoṁan ar áġ. eróda ra ġuioim
leabar aláṁ.
Cleaiṫ coṁur brán. ronar na bríain
mbrdálaċ caoin. iorġalaċ dian
Eirineaċ artair. buan rríu an rir.
buaiḋ comlann air
Leiomeaċ aġair. ronar na rod.
rolar aḋead
cuiriḋ re lean air gach trean da ṁéad.

Do gnác na ġap. oɼgan na ccon
ɼo ġɼáḋ na mban. bjon ḋájm maɼ ɼjn
flajt leaɼgaċ caojm. ɼlaṫċleaċ uɼ.
ɼeaɼ cljɼoe ɼaoɼ. ɼeaɼ bɼjɼ mɼ́ɼ.
Na ccɼaojɼeaċ ccoɼɼ. leaṫan alann.
caċaɼ ġoll. ɼjċaojɼeaċ teann.
Tɼéjġ ċɼjoċ aġujll. bj ɼjóċḋa ɼjnn
ɼe do ɼéjd gan mejng. tɼjan ɼjoḋajḋ o ɼhjoṅ
Nj ɼɼ́aɼ mo méjn. tɼéjgjmɼe mɼjoch.
ójb aɼḃeanġujɼ ɼḃéjl.
Do ɼġujɼ mo ġɼɼ́ajm. aċaɼa gan ċejlg.
a béal tana ḋeaɼg.
Aj ejneaċ aɼ lɼ́t. do ċlɼ́ɼ oɼ́ ájɼo.

áɼo ajgneaḋ ġɼjll. ɼjnjt.

III.

Muɼjɼ Mac Ḋájḃjḋ ḋuḃ Mac Ġeaɼalt cct.
ajɼ na ɼeɼjoḃaḋ ajɼ lung ag dol don Eaɼɼ́ájn.

beaṅajġ an longɼo, a ċɼjoɼt ċájḋ.
Aj n tɼjon an toṅɼo ɼan tjɼ.
bjoḋ ċajngjol 'naɼ cclejt ḋaɼ ccóɼjɼ,
ɼomajnn maɼ ɼġéjt ḋajngjn ḋjn.
Sjċjġ gajɼbɼjon gajm da ġlóɼ.
mjnjġ gaċ mujɼ ajmnjɼn ɼḃɼaɼ.
Fɼaoċ an eaɼajġ cuɼ ajɼ ccul,
ḋúnn go dul taɼ ceaṅajḃ cuan

Dojġ

Doilg me ġám' éíl do ċup.
ne mun te 'ríʃ doilg ḋam,
mun ríanboċaċ na ɼealg ɼean,
tɼeaḃ na ɼɼeaḃ ngnjaníɼoċaċ nglan
Cuɼn me go ɼeaɼcaɼn ċum ɼeoɼl,
a Ḋḧ, gan eaɼbaɼḋ aɼn nɼujl.
ó'n tɼíon ġaɼḃ ɼhuaɼn nnuɼn nnóɼn,
ɼe cóɼn gloɼn go ccolṁnɼn ccɼ̟íɼn.
Maɼċ mo coɼnaċ aɼóḃɼeaċ ɼ̟ɼ,
taɼóḃɼeaċ a toɼnaḋ 'ɼa taoḃ,
long ġéagaċ boṅógaċ bɼ̟an,
ɼtuaḋ ċéaḋaċ ċɼoṅógaċ ċaoṁ.
Long gan tluɼ a ttaċaɼn aɼm,
gan ɼċát a ɼcaċaṁ na ɼtoɼm.
ɼeoltúɼn tɼe ċláɼn na cceaṅ ngaɼḃ
maɼn buḋ ɼúl maɼb gaċ gleaṅ goɼnn.
Tɼe ġnjanbaċ gaċ tɼṁe tɼuġ,
aɼn ɼɼaɼnlan ḋa ġaɼṁe an ġaċt
lɼnġeaḋ taɼn ċablaċ na ccɼɼɼoċ,
aɼmaċ a ɼɼoc ɼɼ a ɼɼaɼcc
Sluoɼ̟ ɼaḋɼ̟ɼ ɼoɼleɼnneaċ tɼéan
ɼoɼnɼnnneaċ maɼn ḋɼagón ḋɼɼɼn,
bɼeaclong na ɼeolbɼataċ ɼaoɼn,
taoḃ cɼeatlom oɼɼɼlataċ ɼ̟ɼn.
bɼɼɼġ ḋealbaċ naċɼaċ ngɼɼoḃaċ
ġaɼnġ beaṅbaċlaċ ċɼocɼaċ na ccolg,
ɼlɼoɼ ɼnaɼċaom ɼɼ ɼaoḃɼaċ ɼeaɼng,
na ɼɼɼnaɼ ċaoɼn nḋeaɼg nḃaoġlaċ nboɼnb.
Tɼoḃlaɼg ɼɼṁ aɼɼɼġ na ɼnaṅ
taɼn lɼṁ ɼɼ gaċ nɼɼo buɼ leam
gan baoġal taɼn bolgaɼb na ttoṅ.
a noṅ ɼeac boɼnḋaɼb na mḃeaṅ.

An tabhran ceangail.

Beannaiġ an longṡo anonn tar ṡáile aig ḋul
bacalaċ trumpaċ trumpaċ lan-éliġde,
an ċreatulaċ ṡġúrṡaċ príntaċ lan trioṡmiċ
marbṫaċ bronntaċ ċubarṫaċ úiteaṡaċ.

Aiṫéim air ṡoṡa criṡort neaċ d'ṡulaiġ an páiṡ,
nár bríṡteár ton brióin na (ton) triṡ na bṡuilm ġo bráṫ.
brillaḋ maiṫ ġaoiṫe is tabice is triteaḋ 'na deaġaiḋ
o ċiuṁṡaiḃ dṡin braoi ġo taoḃ na crunne ton 'ṡpáin.

_____

THE

IRISH ORIGINALS

OF THE

ELEGIES.

THE
IRISH ORIGINALS
OF THE
ELEGIES.

I.

O ɓfapūjn ccc.

Féaċ oṗam a jnɣean Eoɣajn, me ḃ'n ḃaɣ aṗ najèḃeoḋajó
cj nſò jſ oojòɣanca onḃſj a ṗojneaica ſóṗ ſṽlḃjn
Na baoj man ċāċ a'm' èṽnɣe, ſéaċ van' ṡḃjne oṗnnɣe,
nj ɣuṗab jnċḣeāċca aṗ novṗeaċ, a ḃe ċejnḃaica eṗajḃċċaċ.
Aſ ſaoa an cṗéjnṡe aċājn ſoñ. ɣan ajṗe aɣ aonṁnaoj oṗam,
a injan ſlóṅɣ baſcana bṗeaɣ, ſòjn meaſḃajòṡj jſ méjɣean.
Nana ḃſòjnċeaṗ njoo òṗejé òṽn ɣaċ anḃuajn va ḃſṽl oṗnñ,
oul ſa eṗja'ò jſ eṗjoċ vomċeaſ, njn ſṗjoċ o ljajɣ mo lejɣeaſ.
Coṗajve òjc lejɣjoſ mo lṽc, oo eṗéjɣeaſ ɣaċ óɣ oṗòṽjṗe,
oṗc ɣéṗ ḃſojṗéavnjan ṗe cāċ a ſḃolc ſḃojɣɣaɣaċ ſḃjoñblaċ.
Dhaojḃſ, ſóſ a ḃṗjaċaṗ njān, oo ṗavaſ cojl aſ cṗomɣṗā'ò,
cojneao mo eṗojòċ ne a eojſ, cuɣ me ḋejſ, le cſoɣṗojſ.
Rṽn naṗ noċoaman vo ṽeāċ, a èṽl ſḃolcṗanjaṗ ſḃājnɣċaċ
a loſ a noċaṗna òṽc, ſójneſjon ṗjḃ (cṗaċ) mo eṗeaḃlṽo
ſ, naṗ an éjɣeancaſj ſo, a ſcuaɣ ɣnéɣealcaſj ɣṗjunɣlan.

                                                        Cṽn

(305)

Cuir aris, re tromgrad té, do da laim a ceiñne a céile
a craob chionga ain agnait gean, na rronra trút a'm' timceall.
Re póig ir milre na mil rin cugam an art uaignig,
a ciab chiongcholtac eangcruin, an béal bioñ rhoclac balrim
Tabair arir lead bair bain rarcad doéd ain mo deasluim
rúg raor do glainmeor am glaic, dom aimdeoin a chial ordairc.
Da rore coimpéid re gloine tóg iad gan chior aondrine,
a cŕl réid tiugelaodac triom. ar réac go chiocnamad orom.
Do beit mar roin bud badac, ir beit roilbir rogradac,
ronn toirmeirce ar ndoig, roibrirte rnáit ar raogoil.
O bur do geabam go grad, ro amain a mianaim orad
tu réin ag an tag bud crád, na réac do. rcéin ad rcátán.
Sul meallaid rerin ain aon, na réac ain an rrbolt rriongclaon.
luga rceal drine no dir. a gloine mar néim nuaidgrir.
Mar roin ror cian ro clor, rceal neamgnac ain Narchrur,
an rear bud rcamda rcéim, riotaide na rrhead rrbolteréid
Ain ngabáil do (oia do bail,) la éigin re taob tobair
do deare 'ran rrut nar rcard rneab, a trut a dealb 'ra déanam.
Tug grad riocmar rolaid go buoteroideac banamail.
Da gurúr chimnioloa réin, gur crír dimbriioga doirein
A rcút réin do mill an Mac, do baoi ror da ioimrlad.
go tug bar do mar deirtear, ga mo cár d'a cemningtear.
Na mealtar ribr mar rin, ort réin, go rirgric roilig
a chiongcholtac ir réim roet do rcéin iongantac eatroét
Do dú éré comban re laog, roilig iad, a bar bareaol
'ran deare ŕr mearbrorcac mall,'ran crl gaib-leareac geúgeam
roilig ror an béal mar rub 'ran da gruad mar gréin rámrad
bain na graob bhigte rreneta, ra taob ride roimonta.
Choidee arir na réac orta glaca míne méarcorma,
troid geal malla tiát ar brin, rála reangmalla reangrin.
Muna ti dot ailneact réin, do buairead a gil gurúiréid
do cúc ni robuana ruib, - - - - - - gac art orair.

R r   Da

Da meallta ne fillead na ṡrḋ ṡin Éirion a cṡab claoḋṡn,
mo nuar ni ṡoiṁeallta ṡiḃ a ṡtuaḋ ṡoineanta ṡrilḃin.
- - - - ḋaoiḃ a ḋreac nár goid mo croiḋe o a ceartlár.
o'n ġoid ġén ġeairrḟaoġlaċ me neamḃaoġal onc an oiṡġréid.
Aċt an tuaċ go léir ruiḃ iṡ da mḃeiḋ aonoṁne ad aġaiḋ,
ni ḋric nac compánaċ cill, a cruit ċiompánaċ téroḃin.
Tuġaiḋ uaiḃ aiġeaċ mo croiḋe, a ġnúiṡ romaiṡeaċ ainglioḋe,
a ré ċḃṡornár ġoirm mar ġloin, iṡ orm ne ṡioiṡriaḋ ṡeacaiḋ.

II.

Sileaċ aon ċḃean gur oil do ṡéin me, 'nuair luiġin dom mion,
ṡteid a ḋa ċrian ṡios oiom 'nuair a ṡmuinim air do comrad liom.
ṡneaċta ṡioraiḋe 'gur é da ṡior-cur ṡaoi ṡiaḃ ui ċḃloin
'go ṡṡuil mo ġnáoṡa mar bláit nan ailniḋe air an ooioiḋnean
don.
Sil me ċḃéin nac a ceaṡacc ṡṡré orm raċṡad ġriaḋ mo croiḋe
'ṡnaċ ṡaġṡeaċ ṡé na ḋéiġ me mar ġeall air miaoin;—
ṡaraoir ġén nac ṡṡuilim ṡéin aġuṡ an ṡear a craiġ mo croiḋe,
an ġleańtan ṡleiḃe 'ṡuṡ me ṡṡad o aeḋ-neaċ, iṡ a oriċt beiċ
na luiḋe.
Ta ṡéirin le mo céad ṡeare an mo ṁóea ṡioṡ,—
'ṡṡearaiḃ Éirion ni léiṡṡioiṡ mo ḃron ṡaraoir;—
'nuair a ṡmuiniṁṡe air a curṡaiḋe 'ṡair a ċṡṡ ḃread don,
bin a ġén ġol bṡ-ioṡal iṡ aġ oṡnail go trom.
Go ṡṡad me ṡéirin la an aonaiġ ḋm ḃuacair don,
iṡ compad ṡeiniḋe no ḋeiġṡin ḃ plur na ṡṡear;—
ṡaraoir ġén nac ṡṡuilim ṡéin aġuṡ an ṡaġart air ṡail,
no go nóḃlamaoṡ air ccṡrṡaiḋe ṡul ṡa otéid ṡe anon.

pé

Pé nap boic leiṡ é, molfaḋ miṡe ġnáṫ mo ċroiḋe;
Iṡ pé nap boic leiṡ é, fuiḋṫe mé le na ṫaoiḃ;—
pé nap boic leiṡ é, mile aiṫrine ṫri lar a ċroiḋe,
'Ṡa ṗéaiṫ an ṫṡolaiṡ am béal a poḃail, iṡ ṫu bṛeoiḋ mo ċroiḋe.
'Sa ḃia ṁiliṡ ċreaḋ ḋ ḋionḟaṡ, ma iniġin ṫu uaim?
Nil eolaṡ ċum ṫo ṫiġe agum, ċum ṫo ṫinṗ na ṫo ċluiṫ:
Tá mo ḃáiṫi ṡaoi leaṫrom aguṡ mo máimi ṡaoi ḃrón;—
Tá mo ġaolṫa go mór a ṡṡeinġ liom, aguṡ mo ġráḋ ḃṛaṫ uaim.
Tá fuiriṫ air mo ṡṫille 'ruion ċoḋail me néal,
Aċ a fuiṡṛeam oṛṫṡa, ċéaḋ ġṛáḋ; má ḃṡhaḋ an oiċe a péir;
Ṡaoi ṫo ċurṡaiḋeṡe ṫo ḋiulṫa me an ṫoṁan uile go léir;—
'Ṡa ċṛaeḃin ċuḃarṫa ċaḋ aṡ a ḣaḃaṛṡaṡa ṫo leaḃar am bṛeiṡ?

III.

Ambreaṫain iṡ méiṛim ṡhaeṫaṛaiḋ an ṫáṛoġhlaiṫ ċlú
bhaṫhuṡ gan éiṡeaċt, iṡ ġéaṛ ṫhu aṫṗáṫht ar ċeṫl
Aṫhaṛaiḋ na héiṡṡe ṫo ṛiaṛaṫh ḋáimh go hṫir
mon bainṫreaḃhaċh an ṡhéiṡle ġur eaġ ṫu a Sheain ṫé ḃurċ
Aṡ ṫubhhaċh ṫo ṫheiġhṫe aṫáiṫ Tiaġheaṛnaiḋh lan ṫo ċhṛmhaiṫh
a phlúr na ṫṫṛeabh buṫh ġaolmhar ċáil aguṡ ċlú;
buṫh ṡṡġaċh ṡial an ṫáṛoġhlaiṫh Seaan ṫé ḃurċ
'ṡo Ḋún-mór ó ṫhṛiall ṡe ṫa an ṡiaṫh ṡa Ṛáṡ ain ġṫil
An ṡialṡheaṛ ṡáimh iṡ ṡéaṛ ṫo ṫhuiṡeaṫh ġaċh ċṛú
aṛṡaṛ ġaċh ṫáimh buṫh ġṇáċh leiṡ eineaċh iṡ ċlú
ṡiáiġh ċhṛiṡhe ṡáil, 'ṅa Ṛáṡ aṫ iniġhṫh ain ċeṫl
O ṫhṛiall an báṡ ain Sheain mhac ċhoiṛnieil brṛċ

Aleac ata ar ghear-chlýrd ajr ghéjg ujr chumarajg bhrèadh
ann aló bhý réjmeamhujl. rpójrt, chlub.rjújg agur Rájr
jr leat abhejth pléjdeamujl cejmeamhujl mar ar rollar do chách
'rgur ajr do thajrgjdh go láeteamhajl tá pléjrur chonnar ar lár
Cja do chujrrear clujthmhjde na Rár ar rjubhal?
cja bhéarrar buajd an churrajg go connacht no bárr gach clr
cja bhéarrar chugajnn le cumar an pláta ón mumhajn
o déag uájnn cojnneal nacujdeachta Seáan de burc
Ardchlajth mhójr bhejr ceannar a cclr ra rpórt
jr ann do lán halla buth gnath ajtear jr majdheacht-céojl
njel ann ájt aca ach gájr rgreadajgh rmrýc jr brójn
remo chriadh deacrach an rtájdniarcach abejth na lujghe an-
      dunnror
9]o géar chrmha an té rd chujr an bár ar ccrl
o léjg rjr go céjn clrdh go clár na Muman
mrr ach gur éag uajnn an rear réjmeamrl Seaan de burc
nj béarrach Sjr Eudbard cojm-réjg rd an pláta 4 rjubal
Ta cead ag gach marcach ó clár na mrmán
teacht le na neacrajd gan géarnan rrjnn
ta ajrgjod gan allar le rágajl a ttuajrn
njel rear abacad nuajr nac majrean agajn Seaan de brrc
Seact ccead déag gan bréjg jr da rhjchjod 4 trr
go ceart a Sé, do rejr an dáta nuath
o teact mjc Dé d4 ráeraid o cájn an ubajll
go teaf an lae rrájr éag ér Sheaájn de brrc
Ar dubhac an Green club ag caojnead o báraigead ér
agur read na tjne cójdhche an rhárach chjnn
ta an rragajd rjrrgljc ro ljóg mo crad ran drn
agur rjn crmmjogad mjóra do mjmré ajr Shéaan de brrc.

IV. Eamonn

IV.

Eamonn a cnuic.

Sa chúl áluinn deas, na bfhainnighib ccéart,
Is bréad jad, fas glas do fúile!
Ísgo bfhuil mo chroidhe da flad, mar áinjéyjó gad,
Le bljagain móir chada fúil leat.
Da bfhuigins o chéart beit mur cejle leat,
Is eadrom deas do fjubalfuinn!
" Ísgo réisrain gac sgairt ais éalod le 'm seapc"
air coilltig sgabta an dirsceta!
Sgo deiniin sein abean, ce mór é do meas,
Is nairn liom tu dom djultad!
Ce dráig tu me gan fláinte agam?
Sgan fac no coir air mo fjrbalta.
Ir dana mo lám, 'sno fhairteas mo ghrad,
Atéagar! ma bjonn tu fjubal liom,
Eamonn a cnuic ata agad ann,
Sas daer anois ann a dóthaid
Sa ghrad sa cumann! sa ghrad gac noimne!
An trjallfa seal don mumain liom?
Mur abfhagmaóir go deiniin ceol 7 imirt,
Is uairle na bfhear a sgrad.
Cópa cuilinn, sama 7 bjolar,
blaca 7 blas na nublaib.
Planda don doilleabar sinn 7 torainn,
Is fásac go mulla glínne.
Sa báb cneasda chom! do pairt liom na sgóil,
Ísgo snáimfinn atóidj ad déigs,
Ísgo miséarr liom do géan, afearr sa run na bfhear!
No náirus na móm mar éagfuinn!

och!

cṫ! iṡ ṫáaċ laṡ aḃjoim, ṡmo ṡlaince uaim do ṡuiḋeiii,
le ṡráḋ ceapc ton muiój do ṫṗéiṡ me.
ṡo ocbáil liom da móiḋeam: aċ ṡlan leac amóim!
o ḋṡúṡaiṡ me ain ḃiṫ na céille.
Sdo beaprmu aleaḃap ṡan breiṡ ònc le ṡḃuḃoun,
ṡo ndéanrnu cu do ċoṡaḋ ain cead ḃean.
ṡo paċaum leac anouu cain crénmuin na tconu,
" ṡo tcreiṡpnu an doman ṡo léin opc*."
man andéap cu an am ṡo néloḋ cu liom
iṡ créic miṡe ṡann ṡan éiṡpaċc,
map énṡeic anṡleann, ṡan éipim ṡan meaḃajp
ṡói ṡeaṡa na ccpann um aenap.
Scainṡi laṡ, iṡ im époiḋe cu an cneaḋ
ṡaṡ deinin naċ ṡap ḋam ṡaeṡiom!
le biomaṗcaiḋ ṡeapc do pírṡ na mban,
ṡa pioḃ map eola ain ṡenloċ.
adliójte daice ċṡopċa caṡda,
ṡlúcimac ṡuaṡda cṗúeḃaċ!
ṡmup byḃuiṡe me o ceapc ḃeić map céile leac,
iṡ téiṡiu ṡup ṡap aċṡuṡ ḋam

* This, and another line, marked with inverted commas, were wanting in the copy when it was firſt obtained ; but as the ſenſe was perfect without them, it was tranſlated, and ſent to preſs.—Since that, theſe lines were ſupplied from recollection, and are here given to the Iriſh reader.

V. Ṫuṡ

V.

Thug me an cuairt ⁊ baineac liom, m'afcar fme air eif mo
    frbail,
air uaiġ mo caraid fdo mearaiġ fin radarc mo ful
ni bruair me agum ⁊ me falcad na ndeor go hur,
ac cruad leac daingean air leabaid na creab rocumaṅ.
Ni trean mo labairt fe mearom nac crf nairc,
acn boct fgaite me ⁊ coilleaf mo cfl baire,
niel pion, nil peanaid, niel galra co trom craice,
le heug na ccarad, no fgarad na ccompanac.
Mo leun! mo deacair! mo miilead! mo bron, f'mo crad!
mo ceol crfic milif! mo binneaf! mo fafobrior dain!
cia hoifgead air dfine beit air builead, no brein mar taim!
no deora fola do filead do deiġ gac la.

THE IRISH ORIGINALS OF THE SONGS.

THE
IRISH ORIGINALS
OF THE
SONGS.

I.

Is mian liom tras ar blát na sinne
Guirers an ainnir ir srgaid
sgunab í nug bárr aceail sa tvigrs
air mnaib bráad glice na corigead
Cia be biad na haice daoidce so ló]
ní baogal do áctirse caoidce no brón
aige an niognin trémi is aoibne méin
rí cíl na crraebh sna brhuinnig
Ataob muir ael sa rsob mrr gér
sa gnaoi mrr grémi agrainpaid
naċ caraid don ce da geallad mar srre
bheir aicise geug na ccamolaoi
as suaire sas sairni do náire glnamnil
as alunn deas do rvilglar
se clainm gaċ lú aig cuċ da aienir
gur sainneaċ cas do ċrltair

Sir

Sírd mar adeirim leis anóigṁnaoi féin
ḃfuil aglór níos binne nó ceol na néan
níl rians nó greann dá sṁrainġ ceaṅ
naċ bfuiġṫear go cinnte ag Ṡracey
Alrḃ na sérd ar oluiṡṫeas déad
aċt na ccraeḃ sna bfáinniġ
giḋ ionṁuin liom féin ér
sdadaim don sgéal. aċ dólsain
gan bréig to sláinte.

II.

Ce be abṡuil se andún to-
alúm abeiṫ saoi na cionn
measuim naċ eagal báṡ do
go bráṫ nó ann aḃéo beiṫ cinn
Aċṫ oeas na mbaċall sáinneaċ sionn
aċom nir cala gile snáṁ air acrinn
gnáċ ⁊ sgéis don ġarraid; Máible féin ní Cheallaid
déad as deise ar leagad anárus cinn
Suiel céol dar binne árṡeolad an duine
naċ ar ḃéol dó cuisge arúd an sgaċ céim
ta gruaid mar Rós an oṡiele. as bran na ċóṁarsa an
        lile.
arois as inine ġlaise blát nó an ċnáeḃ

Se

Sé ḋeiṙ ġaċ ollaṁ molaḋ ċláṙ ḟíol néill
ġo ccuiṙtea na coṙṙa ċollaḋ le ṡúṙġuṫ béil
níel aṁṙuṡ liom ann. aṙéiṁ laḃṙaċ ḃinn
aċ ḃítaṙ liun ġo ġṙinn ḋo ṡláinte ṡéin
Oḋéaġaḋaṙ na mna máṅla
aiṙ aṫṙáċtaiṙiṡ an ḋoṁan ġo léiṙ
meaṡiṁ naċ ṡuil na ṁáic ann
aċ Máiḃle le ciṙ ṡġaċ céim
An ṡaċt ġaċ duine acċáiliġeaċt ṡa cċéill
aṡ áġiṙṙ ḋon ṡhile aṙáġail ón ḋéiṡ
cṙí na ccṙaeḃ iṡ ṡinne, líṙ na ṫéaḋ aṡ binne
ṡnuaḋ na ġeiṡe ġile ḃṙáiġe ṡa ṫaeḃ.
Níel aen ḋa ḃṙeiċ naċ ioṅġantaċ acleaṡ
naċ néiṙḋiṙṡ aġeiṫ amḃaṙṙ na ccṙaeḃ
ṡa ṫé naċ léiṙ ḋo an ċoinneal
lán ḋo ṡṙeiṡ aleiṁiḃh
ṡi aṡ ṡeaṙṙ méiṙ iṡ twiġṡi ḋo náiẏiṙn ġaeḋeal
Si aṡ ḋeiṡe coṡṡa ḃoṡṡa lámh ⁊ ḃéal
péiṙe ṙoṡġ iṡ ṡṙilt aṡáṡ ġo ṡéiṙ
ta an ḃáiṙe ṡo liun
aṡáṙuġaḋh luċt ġṙinn
ṡa ṙáḋ ġo ḃṡuaiṙ me aċ ṡhoill. aṡ áġiṙaṙ liom é.

III. Inġean

III.

Ingean tais na mbáncíoch is áilne no laétse bruacc
do ṗrіоnіѕhuil colla dá eríoc aɼ̱uſ tríd aѕhrēama muaſ
don tráoі да ttaşmað ndán do beіṫ ndáіl na mbarn ndḃécc
.i. cuaіnt
do móіṫɣíð leatſa an táilleaɣan ſaр ѕáſ ɣrím an ḃuda uáſ
ta cóір ar laſað dáрoѕhuіl na Sábрſeaċ déanta іo
şрſajḃ
⁊ on lóch meaр Conall céaрnaċ énір áрéata neіpрınn uáір
ſ̱an brón дod ɣól nior táірe a blaіṫ cóім na méuрlaş luáċ
do рjoѕhuil Cholla рioѕрaід іonna ó ɣacdeal ɣlaſ do ɣluáiſ
ta dać na hєala cclóдіón ne béo ɣріſ na ccóр aѕрáрn
іna leaca ɣloіn na hóіs іnşіne іſ рóſ lіonta brάon aѕáſ
ɣać рlanдa teaſ да cóрnдlóіtє ѕoрſɣóilte ſóntaſ tláіṫ
ſ̱ać рubрað teaſ да béol cáoim dtєobaрtað ſіn dóіne
ón mbáſ
ta deaрşhuіl céaрt ſіól Rőіɣ ⁊ móрéolla an ріɣ tuɣ bárр
ɣan ſeaрɣað airraд ɣać nórlaіɣ don рórіiórla móіṫɣіl blaіṫ
aſ tealbać oіbрioɣað améoр mín aр ſіól ſіόſ le ſráоnрð
lárn
ſ̱ać míр ді vіlє aр lí na lіlє ó brőjşċіb ɣo láр.

IV. bean

IV.

bean dub an gleanna.

Ab̓acaḋ tu? no an cc̓ala tu an ftuipe deḃ aille gnaoi?
ingleanta duḃa fme in uaignoſ, gan fuaimnioſ do la no
  oiḋċe,
beilin caoin aſnaipoifg do ḃuain me fdo ċraḋaiġ mo ċroiḋe,
mo ḃean̄aċt ṡein go buan lei ga di an ccuan fo ḃe ait imbiḋ
Ata fe fgniobta piniōnta do ċom feang fdo mala ċael
fdo beilin tamuiḋ faoi fin na faoilyin do neafaċ bneag,
do ċroḃ af gile faf mine, ioḋa an fioda fnu clum na neán,
faf buapea ċraioḋte bimfe nuain afmaoinim an fganuin lei.
Nuain aḋeancaf i do ċeiḋ me, le gén feape da gnaoi foa
  fnó.
amiona ċioċa glegal, aḋeiḋḋeaf, fa diaoi fholt oin,
ba gile aopeac na Deiptrne ċuin laċċpa na Miḋe an feoḋ,
fna blanad mjn na cclaenpofg le an traċċad na mílte
  tréon.
Apluif na mḃan, na treig me a ḃeeṫlac le faint da fdóin,
gan ċiu gan meaf gan ḃeafa aċ blaeḋeapaċt if bnuiḋean
  if gleo,
if ciuin do finifin dreaċta bneaga gaoiḋeilge ḋuit oiḋċe an
  ṡomain,
fdo fgnuidofuin foain na feine go leinċeain fna mileaḋ móin.

MÄON:

AN

IRISH TALE.

ADVERTISEMENT.

THE story of the following Tale *is to be found in the ancient history of* Ireland, *and is related by* KEATING, O'HALLORAN, WARNER, *&c.*

TO

Mr. and Mrs. TRANT,

THIS

TALE

Is respectfully addressed,

By their obliged,

And most obedient Servant,

Charlotte Brooke.

INTRODUCTION.

Accomplish'd Pair! these simple lays,
  With favour's eye peruse;
And take from me, in artless phrase,
  The message of the Muse.

A Muse, who ne'er, on Pindus' mount,
  Trod inspiration's ground;
Nor drank sweet frenzy from the fount,
  Where raptures breathe around.

But a bright Power, whom Nature forms,
  And Nature's scenes inspire;
Who mounts the winds, and rides the storms,
  And glows with Heaven's own fire!

Who train'd, of old, our sires to fame,
  And led them to the field;
Taught them to glow with Freedom's flame,
  And Freedom's arms to wield.

With the wild WAR-SONG fir'd the soul,
  And sped the daring blow!—
Or, bow'd to Pity's soft controul,
  Wept o'er a dying foe.

Or search'd all Nature's treasures round,
  To deck a favourite fair;
Or tun'd to love a tender sound,
  And sang a faithful pair.

This power, while late my couch I press'd,
  To mental sight appear'd;
To my charm'd soul sweet words addres'd,
  By waking Fancy heard.

Shrin'd in the form of reverend age,
  The friendly vision came;
Rob'd as of old, a Bardic Sage,
  And took * Craftiné's name.

" O thou, (he cry'd) whose timid mind
" Its purpose would delay!
" Half shrinking from it,—yet inclin'd,—
" Half daring, to essay.

" Let not the frown of critic wrath,
" Or smile of critic scorn,
" Affright thee from the splendid path,
" Fame and the Muse adorn.

" The

---

* Cᴘᴀɪʀᴛɪɴᴇ, a celebrated Irish Bard who flourished in A. M. 3648. *Vide* Kᴇᴀᴛɪɴɢ.

" The critic storm, that proudly rends
" The oaks of Learning's Hill,
" Will pafs thy fhrub, that lowly bends,
" Nor deign its growth to kill.

" Shine, while thou can'ft, pale trembling beam,
" Ere fun's eclipfe thy ray;
" Thy little ftar awhile may gleam,
" 'Till Phœbus brings the day.

" For oft the Mufe, a gentle gueft,
" Dwells in a female form;
" And patriot fire, a female breaft,
" May fure unqueftion'd warm.

" No more thy glorious tafk refufe,
" Nor fhrink from fancy'd harms,
" But, to the eye of Britain's Mufe,
" Prefent a fifter's charms.

" Thee hath the fweet enchantrefs taught
" The accents of her tongue;
" Pour'd on thine ear her lofty thought,
" Celeftial as fhe fung.

" Now let her fee thy grateful heart
" With fond ambition burn,
" Proud if thou can'ft, at leaft in part,
" Her benefits return.

" Long, her neglected harp unstrung,
  " With glooms encircl'd round;
" Long o'er its silent form she hung,
  " Nor gave her soul to sound.

" Rous'd from her trance, again to reign,
  " And re-assert her fame,
" She comes, and deigns thy humble strain
  " The herald of her claim.

" Swells not thy soul with noble pride,
  " This honor to embrace,
" Which partial fates for thee decide,
  " With such distinguish'd grace?—

" Coward!—from the bright path assign'd,
  " Thy feet had turn'd away,
" From the bright prize thine eye declin'd,
  " Too weak for Glory's ray:

" Did not a steadier soul exhort,
  " A steadier counsel guide,
" With zeal thy timid mind support,
  " And its vain terrors chide.

" I know the Pair by Genius lov'd,
  " By every Muse inspir'd,
" Who thy unpractis'd strains approv'd,
  " And thy ambition fir'd!

" To

" To *them* the Mufe [b] of ancient days
" Avows the tribute due;
" To *them* her grateful thanks fhe pays,
" And—coward!—not to you.

" What fhould fhe do her love to fhew?—
" From all her ample ftore,
" What favours can her hand beftow
" That were not theirs before?

" Yes, fhe can add thofe generous joys,
" That fympathy of hearts,
" Which kindred fentiment employs,
" And worth to worth imparts.

" Go then to thy accomplifh'd friends;
" The Mufe commands thee go;
" Bear them the grateful gift fhe fends,
" 'Tis all fhe can beftow.

" Bear them the pride of ancient days;
" Truth, fcience, virtue, fame;
" The lover's faith, the poet's praife,
" The patriotic flame!

U u " All

[b] The mention of *the Mufe*, in this place, may appear rather too claflical, but the ancient Irifh had their Mufe, as well as the Greeks and Romans, and her name was be-gubu.

" All in the royal Pair confefs'd,
" Whofe TALE the Bard purfues;
" Like them, united, grac'd and blefs'd
" By Virtue, and the Mufe.

T A L E.

BOW'D to dark Cobthach's fierce command,
　When ſtruggling Erin groan'd ;
And, cruſh'd beneath his bloody hand,
　Her ſlaughter'd ſons bemoan'd ;

Of all whoſe honeſt pity dar'd
　One tear humane to ſhed ;
My life alone the ſavage ſpar'd,
　Nor touch'd the ſacred head.

Protected by the Muſe's pow'r,
　And the Bard's hallow'd name,
I ſcap'd the death-devoted hour,
　The hour of blood and ſhame !

When Nature pleaded, Pity wept,
  And Confcience cry'd in vain;
When all the powers of vengeance flept
  Upon a monarch flain.

Shock'd Hiftory, from the dreadful day,
  Recoil'd with horror pale,
And, fhrinking from the dire difplay,
  Left half untold the tale!

But I, fad witnefs of the fcene!
  Can well its woes atteft;
When the dark blade, with murder keen,
  Spar'd not a brother's breaft [b].

When Nature, prefcient as my foul,
  With earthquakes rock'd the ground;
Air bade its deepeft thunders roll,
  And lightnings flafh'd around!

While,

[b] Cobthach, a prince of an envious and afpiring temper, repining at the greatnefs of his brother, Laoghaire Lork, then monarch of Ireland, determined to wade through murder to the throne. To effect this purpofe, he pretended illnefs, and was conftantly and affectionately vifited by his unfufpecting brother; but finding that he ftill came attended, and, therefore, gave no opportunity for the meditated blow, he requefted a private interview with him; it was granted, and the following day appointed for the purpofe; Laoghaire came, but found his brother apparently dead; and bending over him, in the bitternefs of his forrow, was ftabbed, by the perfidious and ungrateful Cobthach, to the heart. See KEATING, WARNER, &c.

While, on each blasting beam, thin forms,
   (The sons of death) were rear'd;
And, louder than the mingling storms,
   The shrieks of ghosts were heard!

Till, Oh! dark, chearless, slow and late,
   The burden'd morn arose;
When forth, to meet impending fate,
   Alone the monarch goes.

In vain some guard do I conjure;
   No heed will he bestow:
I follow to the fatal door,—
   I hear the deadly blow!—

Hold, villain, hold!—but short'ning breath
   Arrests my feeble cries;
And seals awhile, in transient death,
   My light-detesting eyes.

Yet soon, to further horrors doom'd,
   I rais'd my sickening head;
And Life her languid pow'rs resum'd,—
   To see Life's comfort fled.

The groans of Death around me rife,
   Scarce yet distinctly heard!
While Fate, to my unclosing eyes,
   In bloody pomp appear'd!—

As when the Spirit of the Deep
  His dreadful course maintains;
While his loos'd winds o'er Ocean sweep,
  And gloomy horror reigns!

Satiate with groans, and fierce with blood,
  The dark malignant power
Rides, in grim triumph, o'er the flood,
  And rules the deathful hour!

So the dire Cobthach, drunk with gore,
  And glorying to destroy;
Aloft victorious horrors bore,
  And smil'd with hideous joy.

Close by the murder'd Monarch's side,
  The earth brave Ollioll [c] press'd;
A dagger, bath'd in life's warm tide,
  Yet quivering in his breast.

Clasp'd round the dying Prince's neck,
  His little Maon [d] lay;
While the third dagger rose to strike
  Its unresisting prey.

Rous'd

[c] Ollioll Aine, son to Laoghaire Lorc, who was thus murdered by his brother Cobthach.

[d] Maon, son to Ollioll Aine.

Rous'd at that fight; to madnefs ftung,
　　I rufh'd amid the foe;
And, o'er the trembling victim flung,
　　I met the deftin'd blow.

O happy wound! clofe to my breaft,
　　(Tho' ftreaming from the knife)
My precious charge, thus fav'd, I prefs'd,
　　And guarded him with life.

Shock'd at the facrilegious ftroke,
　　The arm of death recoil'd;
While from the croud the paffions broke
　　That in their bofoms boil'd.

The royal blood, that round them ftream'd,
　　They could with calmnefs view;
But, for the Bard, their frenzy deem'd
　　The fierceft vengeance due!

A thoufand fwords to guard me rofe,
　　Amid the conflict's roar;
While fafe, from his furrounding foes,
　　My trembling charge I bore.

Long while he feem'd, with life alone,
　　To fcape that fatal day;
For Reafon, from his little throne,
　　In terror fled away.

While thus bereft of fenfe he grew,
  No fears the court invade,
And fafe in the Ufurper's view,
  The beauteous maniac play'd.

Reafon, at length, a fecond dawn,
  With cheering luftre, fhed;
And, from the Tyrant's pow'r withdrawn,
  To Munfter's King we fled.

There, long conceal'd from every foe,
  Beneath the royal care,
I faw my lovely fcion grow,
  And fhoot its branch in air.

Oh, while I view'd his blooming face,
  And watch'd his opening mind;
While, in a form of matchlefs grace,
  I faw each virtue fhrin'd;

With more than a parental pride,
  My throbbing heart o'erflow'd;
And each fond thought, to hope ally'd,
  With fweet prediction glow'd!

One daughter, bright in beauty's dawn,
  The royal cares beguil'd;
All fportive as the gladfome fawn,
  And as the moon-beam mild.

                                    Like

Like the firſt infants of the ſpring,
  Sweet opening to the view;
Fann'd by the breeze's tender wing,
  And freſh with morning dew.

Such were fair Moriat's growing charms,
  So bright her dawning ſky;
And beauty, young, with early harms,
  Was cradled in her eye.

By ties of ſweet attraction drawn,
  And pair'd by infant love,
Oft, lightly ſporting o'er the lawn,
  The royal children rove;

Together chaſe the gilded fly,
  Or pluck the blooming flower;
Or boughs, with buſy hands, ſupply,
  To weave the little bower.

But now, as years and ſtature grow,
  Maturer ſports ariſe;
Now Mäon bends the ſtrongeſt bow,
  And Moriat gives the prize.

Light dance the happy hours along,
  To love's enchanting lay;
And pleaſure tunes Her ſweeteſt ſong!
  And every ſcene is gay.

But foon each beauteous vifion flies
   That blifsful fancy forms;
As the foft fmile of azure fkies
   Is chac'd by chiding ftorms.

Again fate lours, and dangers frown—
   The bloody Cobthach hears—
Once more the dagger threats to drown
   In Mäon's blood his fears.

And muft we fly?—muft Mäon's heart
   Its Moriat then forego?—
Muft he with every comfort part,
   To fhun his cruel foe?—

He muft; there are no other means
   Of life or fafety nigh;
Our only hope on Gallia leans,
   And thither muft he fly.

What tears!—what anguifh!—what defpair!—
   At length he bade adieu;
Ah when again his faithful fair,—
   His native land to view?—

" Yes, foon again! (he proudly cries;)
   " In vengeance too array'd!
" On this right arm my hope relies,
   " And Gallia's friendly aid."

But

But Mäon knew not yet, how near,
    How tenderly ally'd,
To his own blood;—how very dear
    The victims that had dy'd.

First, his weak health, and tender years,
    Bade the dire truth conceal,
Which after, (though from different fears,)
    We did not dare reveal.

For when,' as strength and knowledge grew,
    He heard the tale unfold;
But half its horrors giv'n to view,
    And half his wrongs untold:

When, but as kindred to his fire,
    The Monarch's death he heard;
Then, in his soul's quick mounting fire,
    His royal race appear'd.

Indignant passions fill'd his eye,
    And from his accents broke;
While the pale lip, and bursting sigh,
    His burden'd soul bespoke.

In vain, his fury to assuage,
    I every art bestow'd;
Still, with the rash resolves of rage,
    His restless bosom glow'd.

In such a cause, his arm alone
  Of ample *force* he deems;
And, to pluck murder from its throne,
  A flight adventure seems.

His youth, his rashness I bewail'd,—
  I trembled to behold;
And fear, and pitying love prevail'd
  To leave dire truths untold.

To Gallia now fate call'd—still, still
  His birth we dar'd not shew;
We dreaded lest some fatal ill
  Should from the knowledge flow.

Youth's headlong passions mov'd our fears
  The secret to secure,
Till practis'd thought, and manlier years,
  His mind and arm mature.

When, from his weeping Moriat torn,
  He bade the last adieu;
When from her sight—her palace borne,
  He ceas'd its walls to view;

Then fresh distractions fill'd his breast,
  The fears of anxious love;
Ah!—by some happier youth addrest,—
  Should Moriat faithless prove!

He ſtopp'd—his frame with anguiſh ſhook;
  With groans his boſom roſe;
The wildneſs of his air and look
  My ſoul with terror froze.

" Dear guardian of my orphan ſtate!
  (At length he faultering cry'd,)
" Thee too—thee too his cruel fate
  " From Mäon muſt divide!

" To tend thy lovelier pupil's youth,
  " Do thou behind remain;
" Remind her of her Mäon's truth,
  " His conſtancy, his pain.

" Thou who haſt form'd my Moriat's heart,
  " With ſweet and happy ſkill;
" Obedient to thy gentle art,
  " And faſhion'd to thy will:

" O ſtill that heart, thoſe wiſhes guide
  " Beneath ſoft Love's controul;
" Whate'er in abſence may betide,
  " To ſhake me from her ſoul.

" Should ever, from that beauteous breaſt,
  " Its fond impreſſion ſtray;
" Should aught e'er chafe the tender gueſt,
  " With thoughtleſs mirth away;

" Then

" Then let thy sweet and melting hand
" On the soft harp complain,
" More skilful than the magic wand,
" Awake the powerful strain.

" To call, like spirits from their sphere,
" Each trembling passion round,
" Its spellful potency to hear,
" And sigh to ev'ry sound!

" The mournful sweetness soon will bring
" To mind her Maon's woe;
" And mem'ry, o'er the tender string,
" In faithful tears will flow.

" Alas, thine eye rejects my prayer!
" O yet, let pity sway!
" Or see vain life no more my care,
" Or now consent to stay!"

Distracted,—shock'd at his command;
  In vain all arts I try'd,
His cruel purpose to withstand,
  And with him still abide:

In vain all arguments addrest,
  In vain did I implore;
He wept—he strain'd me to his breast,—
  But left me on the shore.

Sad,

Sad, devious, carelefs of their courfe,
    My lonely fteps return'd,
While forrow drain'd its weeping fource,
    And age's anguifh mourn'd.

Bereft of him for whom alone
    Life deign'd to keep a care,
For him I heav'd the ceafelefs groan,
    And breath'd the ceafelefs pray'r.

I only liv'd at his requeft,
    His bidding to obey;
And chear his Moriat's faithful breaft,
    To wafting grief a prey.

From her fair eye to wipe the tear,
    Her guardian and her guide:
Dear to my heart! but doubly dear,
    As Mäon's deftin'd bride.

O, abfence! tedious thy delay,
    And fad thy hours appear;
While numbering fighs recount each day
    That fills the long, long year.

Yet not devoid of hope we griev'd,
    For oft glad tidings came;
Oft our reviving fouls receiv'd
    The news of Mäon's fame.

The prince of Gallia's fertile land,
  To Erin's throne ally'd,
Grac'd his young kinsman with command,
  And plac'd him near his side.

Together o'er the martial field
  They chafe the routed foe;
Together war's fierce terrors wield,
  And strike the glorious blow!

At length, to him the sole command
  Of Gallia's armies fell,
For now, his train'd and valiant hand
  Well knew her foes to quell.

The terror of the Gallic arms
  To east,—to west he spread,
And, safe return'd from fierce alarms,
  His conquering powers he led.

All tongues his prowess now attest;
  Exulting Moriat hears;
The sounds bring rapture to her breast,
  And musick to her ears.

" Now, now, (she cry'd) what hinders now
  " The work his virtue plan'd?
" What hinders to perform his vow,
  " And free his captive land?"

" Ah

" Ah Moriat! bright in every charm
" That Nature's power could give!
" Ah, haste thy tender breast to arm,
" Hear the dire news—and live!

" Prepare thy Mäon to disown;
" Thy thoughts from love divide;
" The daughter of the Gallic throne
" Is destin'd for his bride."

Ah sounds of death!—she faints, she falls!
Down sinks the beauteous head.—
At length our care to life recalls,
But peace, alas! is fled.

" Where now is Virtue?—where is Love?
" O Faith! O Pity!—where?
" Can Mäon cruel,—perjur'd prove,
" And false as fondly swear?

" Ah no, ah no!—it cannot be!—
" Too well that heart I know!—
" Alas!—now, now the cause I see
" Whence all my sorrows flow!

" Fly, fly Craftinè!—to thy Lord
" My soul's entreaty bear!
" And O! may Heaven calm seas afford,
" And swiftest winds prepare!

" Tell

" Tell him, it is my true requeſt,
" It is my firm command,
" That Love, a fond imprudent gueſt,
" No more reſtrain his hand.

" Tell him, he freely may eſpouſe
" My happy rival's charms;
" Tell him, I give him back his vows,
" I yield him to her arms.

" So may the ſtrength of Gallia's throne
" Attend a filial prayer,
" And force our tyrant to atone
" For all the wrongs we bear.

" Alas! I fear it will not be!—
" Too faithful is his heart!
" From vows ſo dear,—from Love and me
" He never will depart.

" Even now, perhaps, his ſoftening ſoul
" The fond ideas move,
" And yield it to the ſweet controul
" Of—ah, too mighty Love!

" Friends, kindred, country, honor, fame,
" And vengeance are forgot;
" And, with a fond, ill-omen'd flame,
" His ſighing ſoul is fraught.

" O haſte

" O hafte thee then, ere yet too late,
" To fhield thy pupil's fame;
" To fnatch it from impending fate,
" And from impending fhame!

" Tell him his country claims him now.—
" To her his heart he owes;
" And fhall a love-breath'd wifh, or vow,
" That glorious claim oppofe?—

" Tell him to act the patriot part
" That Erin's woes demand;
" Tell him, would he fecure my heart,
" He muft refign my hand.—

" Hafte, hafte thee hence!—tell him—yet ftay!—
" O Heaven! my heart infpire!
" O what—what further fhall I fay,
" His foul with fame to fire?—

" Soft—foft—'tis mine!—O happy hour!
" It cannot fail to move!
" O bleft be Erin's guardian pow'r!
" And bleft be patriot love!"

While thus the fweet Enthufiaft fpeaks,
   She feems o'er earth to rife;
Sublime emotions flufh her cheeks,
   And fill her radiant eyes!

In her foft hand the ftyle fhe takes [1],
And the beech tablet holds;
And there the foul of glory wakes,
And all her heart unfolds.

" 'Tis done!—now hafte thee hence, (fhe cry'd)
" With this to Gallia fly;—
" And O! let all thy power be try'd,
" To gain him to comply!

" O fire his foul with glory's flame!
" O fend me from his heart!
" Before his country, and his fame,
" Let blufhing love depart!—

" For me,—on duty I rely,
" My firm fupport to prove;
" And Erin fhall the room fupply
" Of Mäon and of love."

" Bleft be thy foul! O peerlefs maid!
" Bright fun of virtue's heaven!
" For O! to thee, her light, her aid,
" And all her powers are given!"

I went:

---

[1] " Before the ufe of paper or parchment, the matter on which the Irifh wrote
" their letters was on tables cut out of a beech tree, and fmoothed by a plane, which
" they infcribed with an iron pencil, called a *ftyle*; the letters themfelves were
" anciently termed *Feadha* (woods) from the matter on which they were written,
" as well as becaufe they were the names of trees; and this was the practice of other
" nations before paper and parchment were difcovered." WARNER's *Hift. Irel.*
Int. p. 65.

I went:—I bounded o'er the wave,
 To Gallia's verdant shore;
The winds a swift conveyance gave,
 And soon to harbour bore.

And soon, at Gallia's splendid court,
 I lowly bent the knee,
While fondest hopes my heart transport,
 Again my Prince to see.

My hopes were just.—Sublime he came,
 Array'd in glory's charms!
I panted to unfold my name,—
 To rush into his arms!—

It must not be;—a close disguise
 My face and form conceals;
No token, to my Mäon's eyes,
 As yet, his Bard reveals.

Patient, as Moriat bade, I wait,
 Collecting all my power,
'Till, to the busy forms of state,
 Succeeds the festive hour.

The feast is o'er:—the light'ned board
 With sparkling shells is crown'd;
And numbers next their aid afford,
 And give new soul to sound.

Then,

Then, then my harp I trembling take,
   And touch its lofty string,
While Moriat's lines its powers awake,
   And, as she bade I sing.

———

Mäon ! bright and deathless name !
Heir of Glory !—son of fame !
Hear, O hear the Muse's strain !
Hear the mourning Bard complain !—
Hear him, while his anguish flows
O'er thy bleeding country's woes.
Hear, by him, her Genius speak !
Hear her, aid and pity seek !

" Mäon, (she cries) behold my ruin'd land !
   " The prostrate wall,—the blood-stain'd field :—
" Behold my slaughter'd sons, and captive sires,
" Thy vengeance imprecate, thy aid demand !
      " (From reeking swords and raging fires
         " No arm but thine to shield.)
      " Come see what yet remains to tell
            " Of horrors that befell !
" Come see where death, in bloody pomp array'd,
      " Triumph'd o'er thy slaughter'd race !
      " Where murder shew'd his daring face,
         " And shook his deadly blade.
                              " Hark !

" Hark!—hark!—that deep-drawn figh!—
" Hark!—from the tomb my flaughter'd Princes cry!
  " Still Attention! hold thy breath!—
  " Liften to the words of death!—
  " Start not Mäon!—arm thy breaft!
  " Hear thy royal birth confeft.
  " Hear the fhade of Laoghaire tell
  " All the woes his houfe befell."

" Son of my fon! (he cries,) O Mäon! hear!—
  " Yes, yes,—our child thou art!
  " Well may the unexpected tale
    " Thus turn thy beauty pale!
  " Yet chear, my fon, thy fainting heart,
    " And filent, give thine ear.

    " Son of Ollioll's love art thou,
    " Offspring of his early vow.
  " One dreadful morn our fall beheld,
  " One dagger drank our kindred blood;
  " One mingling tide the flaughter fwell'd,
" And murder bath'd amid the royal flood.

  " Again,—again they rife to fight!—
    " The horrors of that fatal day!—
  " Encircling peril! wild affright!
    " Groans of death, and deep difmay!

" See

" See Erin's dying Princes prefs the ground!
" See gafping patriots bleed around!
" See thy grandfire's clofing eye!
" Hear his laſt expiring figh!
" Hear thy murder'd fire, in death,
" Blefs thee with his lateſt breath!—

" Tears!—ſhall tears for blood be paid?—
" Vengeance hopes for manly aid!
" There—to yon tomb direct thine eyes!—
" See the ſhade of Ollioll rife!
" Hark!—he groans!—his airy fide
   " Still ſhews the wound of death!
" Still, from his bofom, flows the crimfon tide,
" As when he firſt refign'd his guiltlefs breath!

" Mäon! (he cries,) O hear thy fire!
" See, from the tomb, his mangled form arife!
   " Vengeance!—vengeance to infpire,
      " It meets thine aching eyes!

" Speak I to an infant's ears,
" With ſhuddering blood and flowing tears?—
" Roufe thee!—roufe thy daring foul!
" Start at once for glory's goal!

                                        " Ruſh

" Rush on Murder's blood-stain'd throne!
" Tear from his brow my crown!
" Pluck, pluck the fierce barbarian down!
" And be triumphant vengeance all thy own!"

Ha!—I behold thy sparkling eyes!
Erin!—'tis done!—thy Tyrant dies!
Thy Mäon comes to free his groaning land!
To do the work his early virtue plann'd.
He comes, the heir of Laoghaire's splendid crown!
He comes, the heir of Ollioll's bright renown!
   He comes, the arm of Gallia's host;
   Valour's fierce and lovely boast!
   Gallia's grateful debt is paid;
   See, she gives her generous aid!
   Her warriors round their hero press;
They rush, his wrongs, his country to redress.

   But, ah! what star of beauty's sky
   Beams wonder on my dazzled eye?
     What form of light is here?
And wherefore falls that softly trembling tear?—
   Fair vision! do thy sorrows flow,
    To balm a stranger's woe!—

Thofe dear drops that Pity brings,
How bright, how beauteous they appear!
The radiance of each tender tear
Might gem the diadems of kings!

Ah, 'tis Gallia's royal fair!—
Her fole and lovely heir!—
O Nature! fee thy power confeft!
See that dear, that beauteous breaft
  Beat with thy myftic throb!
  Hear the big fob
Heave the foft heart, and fhake the tender frame!
O bright abode of Pity's power!
Sweet altar of her trembling flame!
Well (faireft!) in this fateful hour,
Well may thy tears thy kindred race proclaim!
Well may'ft thou weep for Erin's woes,
Since, in thy veins, the blood of Laoghaire flows!

  Monarch of the Gallic throne,
    Lift to my voice!—
An union that might make the world thy own,
    Now courts thy choice.

See the bright daughter of thy love!
Yet unmated is thy dove.
Can that foft hand a fcepter wield?—
Can that fair breaft a nation fhield?—

                              No,

No,—but with our prince ally'd,
Erin's lov'd and lovely bride,
Then, our joint empire, how might it extend!
And wide our glittering standards be unfurl'd!
To our united power the earth might bend,
And our high sceptre, then, should sway a world!

Thus, delegated, while I spoke,
  My mandate to obey;
Swift on my words the Princess broke,
  And rapt my powers away.

" Never will I consent (she cry'd)
  " To wear thy country's crown;
" Nor ever be thy Mäon's bride,
  " Tho' splendid his renown!

" Yet think not, Bard, my senseless breast
  " Quite dead to Glory's flame;
" Think not I slight a Prince, confest
  " The favourite son of fame.

" Once, Bard,—I do not blush to own,
  " Tho' Gallia's royal heir,
" I would have given the world's high throne,
  " A Cot with him to share.

" But, when I heard the tender tales
  " His gentle accents told;
" How sweet a rose the royal vales
  " Of Fearmorka [a] hold;

" I shrunk from the ungenerous thought
  " That might their loves destroy;
" And, in his dearer peace, I sought
  " To find reflected joy.

" Nor now could world's my heart persuade
  " To be thy Maon's bride,
" Or, from his blest Momonian maid,
  " His faithful vows divide.

" But who art thou, whose wishes tower
  " Wide empire, thus, to wield;
" Who, to Ambition's haughty power,
  " Would Love a victim yield?"—

" O maid of Heaven!"—I could no more,
  For tears my words arrest;
And joy the garb of sorrow wore,
  Big heaving in my breast.

With rapture mute, the close disguise
  Quick from my limbs I threw;

And

---

[a] In the west of Munster.

And ſtraight, to Mäon's wondering eyes,
Craftinè ſtood to view.

Forward, with lightning's ſpeed, he ſprung,
And caught me to his heart;
While eager round my neck he clung,
As if no more to part.

Then ſudden, ſtarting from my breaſt,
His eye my form ſurvey'd;
Its ſearching beams his doubts expreſt,
And ſtruggling ſoul diſplay'd.

" And is it then Craftinè ſpeaks?
(At length he fault'ring cry'd,)
" Is it that honour'd ſage who ſeeks
" His pupil to miſguide?

" Can then Craftinè bid me fly
" From Virtue's firm controul;
" And bid the breath of fame ſupply
" Her empire in my ſoul!

" Does the ſage guide of Mäon's youth
" Now teach the traitor's art;—
" Teach, with the ſmiles of ſeeming truth,
" To veil a venal heart?

" One

" One lovely maid of heavenly charms,
 " Bethroth'd, and won, to leave;
" And, wedded to another's arms,
 " Her generous foul deceive!

" A double traitor fhall I prove,
 " And ftain with guilt my name!—
" Loft both to honour, and to love,
 " To virtue, and to fhame!—

" No, royal Aidé, form'd to blefs!
 " Thou would'ft difdain the art;
" And charms like thine fhould fure poffefs
 " An undivided heart.

" Sweet maid! with each endowment bleft
 " That favouring Heaven could give,
" O! ever, in my grateful breaft,
 " Shall thy dear image live!

" But further, by a form fo bright,
 " Had my fond foul been won;
" Won by thy charms, thou lovely light
 " Of Virtue's facred fun!

" To thee had changing paffion ftray'd
 " From vows of earlier youth;
" Thy bright example, glorious maid!
 " Had fham'd me into truth.

" Yet think me not, tho' true to love,
" So dead to virtuous fame,
" To prize a felfifh joy above
" The patriot's hallow'd flame.

" O Erin! that I hold thee dear,
" This arm fhall foon atteft;
" For now revenge—revenge draws near,
" In death and terrors dreft!

" And, O rever'd and royal fhades!
" Ye dwellers of my foul!
" Whofe memory this fad heart pervades,
" With limitlefs controul!

" Bend from your clouds each radiant face,
" While, firm as fate's decrees,
" I fwear, the manes of my race,
" With vengeance to appeafe!

" But Moriat!—never from my breaft
" Shall thy mild virtues part!
" There ever fhalt thou reign, confeft
" The fov'reign of my heart!

" Say Bard, who thus thy foul has fway'd?
" Who could thy fenfe mifguide,
" To bid me leave my lovely maid,
" And feek another bride?"

" No

" No art, O Mäon, fway'd my breaſt,
" But Power the mandate gave;
" Deny'd my age its needful reſt,
" And fped me o'er the wave."

" What haughty power could thus aſſume
" An empire o'er my foul?—
" O'er Love and Virtue thus prefume
" To arrogate controul?"——

" A power, to whom thy humble vow
" E'er long ſhall be addreſt;
" A power to whom thy foul ſhall bow,
" And ſtoop its lofty creſt."

" Ha! tell me then,—who, who ſhall dare
" To dictate to my heart?
" To bid it from its wiſh forbear,
" And from its love depart?"—

" Earneſt, O Prince! was my command,
" And urgent was my fpeed;
" A mandate from thy Moriat's hand
" This fruitleſs voyage decreed."

" Moriat!—away—it cannot be!
" Shame on thy cruel art!—
" Hence, hence away, while yet thou'rt free,
" And with thy tale depart."——

" Unjuſtly,

" Unjuſtly, Prince, am I difgrac'd,
" And guiltlefs do I ſtand;
" Behold the characters ſhe trac'd;
" Behold her well known hand."

" Ha!—blindnefs to my tortur'd fight!
" O hope! behold thy grave!—
" O death to every fond delight
" That Love to promife gave!

" Say, Bard, while fenfe yet lives to hear,
" Whence came this cruel change?
" O what, from vows fo fond, fo dear,
" Could fuch a foul eſtrange?

" What happy rival, in her heart,
" Now holds her Mäon's place,
" Who thus, with fuch fuccefsful art,
" His image could efface?

" Miſtaken Prince! no fecond flame
" Thy Moriat's heart can prove;
" And it is only Mäon's *fame*
" Can rival Mäon's *love*.

" O haſte, (ſhe cry'd) haſte, to thy Lord,
" My foul's entreaty bear!
" And O may Heaven calm feas afford,
" And fwifteſt winds prepare!

3 A

" Tell him his country claims him now,
" To *her* his heart he owes;
" And shall a love-breath'd wish or vow
" That glorious claim oppose?

" Tell him to act the patriot part
" That Erin's woes demand;
" Tell him, would he secure my heart,
" He must resign my hand.

" For me, on duty I rely
" My firm support to prove,
" And Erin shall the room supply
" Of Mäon and of Love.

" Tell him he freely may espouse
" My happy rival's charms;
" Tell him I give him back his vows,
" I yield him to her arms.

" So may the strength of Gallia's throne,
" Attend a filial prayer,
" And force one tyrant to atone
" For all the wrongs we bear."

" Now Prince,—now judge thy Moriat's heart;
" Now blame her dear command;
" Now, if thou wilt, condemn the part
" Her patriot virtue plan'd!"

With

With rapturous wonder's fweet alarm,—
With fpeechlefs joy oppreft,
The trembling Mäon reach'd his arm,—
And funk upon my breaft.——

Diffolv'd in the applauding tear
  That heart to virtue pays,
The wondering melting croud appear,
  While on the fcene they gaze.

Low at the feet of Gallia's throne
  The lovely Aidé bow'd;
Sweet in perfuafive charms fhe fhone,
  And thus her fuit avow'd:

" Now, now a boon, my royal fire!
  " If ever I was dear,
" O grant me now one fole defire,
  " One fond petition hear.

" Let now the flower of Gallia's hoft
  " Our Mäon's arm attend,
" And fpeed him hence to Erin's coaft,
  " His country to defend.

" To tear the murderer of his race
  " From his infulted throne,
" His wrongs, with vengeance, to efface,
  " And blood with blood atone."

Propitious to the warm requeſt
Of his enchanting child,
Her ſuit the royal Father bleſt,
And with acceptance fmil'd.

Then riſing, on the Prince ſhe turn'd
Her more than angel face;
Her eye with heav'nly radiance burn'd,
And beam'd benignant grace.

" Now go;—to Erin's happy ſhore
" Direct thy courſe, (ſhe cry'd)
" Peace to thy native land reſtore,
" And o'er its realms preſide;

" And tell that ſiſter of my ſoul,
" Thy lov'd Momonian Maid,
" Like her, I ſtrain to Virtue's goal,
" On Glory's wing convey'd.

" Tell her, though oceans roll between
" Our ſhores, at diſtance plac'd,
" Yet is ſhe by my ſpirit ſeen,
" And by my heart embrac'd.

" And ſay,—when death diſſolves our frames;—
" When free to Æther's wing,
" And borne aloft on pureſt flames,
" Our ſouls exulting ſpring:

" Rivals

" Rivals no more, we then shall meet;
" In air's bright chariots move;
" And joyful join in union sweet,
" And everlasting love.——"

Thus while she spoke, tears dimm'd her sight;
   Her cheek its rose withdrew;
And quick as lightning's radiant flight,
   She vanish'd from our view:

Mäon, pale, mute, o'erwhelm'd, distress'd,
   Had sunk before the Maid,
And, to the spot her feet had press'd
   His grateful lips he laid.

A while the pitying Monarch gaz'd,
   And dropt a tender tear;
Then from the earth the youth he rais'd,
   His drooping soul to chear.—

Now, snatch'd from every trophied wall,
   Bright standards float in air,
And, to their Champion's glorious call,
   The Gallic Chiefs repair.

Fate wing'd, along the rolling wave,
   Their ships exulting flew;
And Erin soon her harbours gave
   To our enraptur'd view.

Then Retribution's dreadful hour
    Appall'd the guilty breaſt!
Stern frown'd the terror-giving power,
    In blood and vengeance dreſt.

As when fierce NEITH[n] mounts his car,
    With dreadful ſplendours bright;
And, thundering in the front of war,
    Sweeps o'er the fields of fight!

Diſmay'd before the withering God,
    The routed armies fly;
Death in his arm, fate in his nod,
    And battles in his eye!

So his bright car our Mäon grac'd,
    In martial charms array'd:
So his young arm, by vengeance brac'd,
    Shook high its deadly blade!

But the ſoft muſe, of war no more
    Will undelighted tell:
She loves the calm, the peaceful ſhore,
    Where gentler virtues dwell.

---

[n] The God of Battles of the Pagan Iriſh.

Haste we from the avenging powers
 Of Justice and of fate;
Haste we to Fearmorka's bowers,
 With Love's fond hopes elate.

Ah Moriat! how will thy soft breast
 The mighty joy sustain?
Ah gently, rapture!—see, opprest
 She sinks upon the plain.

She sinks—but Love's extended arms
 From earth her beauties raise;
And Love's soft voice awakes her charms,
 And cordial cheer conveys.

Speechless awhile, she looks,—she sighs
 Unutterable joy;
Nor memory yet a thought supplies
 The transport to destroy.

At length, her recollected breast
 Recalls the Gallic Bride,
When shuddering, back she shrinks distress'd,
 Nor seeks her soul to hide.

" Ah Mäon! go! (she trembling cries,)
 " Another claims thee now:
" Go, go where fame with love allies
 " To plight thy nobler vow."

" No, my foul's treasure! never more
" From thy dear arms to part;
" Here will I kneel, and here adore
" With a devoted heart.

" Ah, could'ſt thou think with empty fame
" Thine image to efface?—
" Or bid me, with another flame,
" This bosom to disgrace!

" Bright Aidé would with scorn have view'd
" The wretch, to honor dead;
" And shame and hatred had pursu'd
" This base and guilty head.

" Come, dearer than the world's renown!
" (And now, at length, my own!")
" Come, with thy virtues gem my crown,
" And consecrate my throne!"——

How shall the Muse the Tale pursue?—
What words her strain shall swell?—
Or paint to sympathy's fond view
What language fails to tell?

Think all that Glory can bestow!
That Virtue's soul imparts!
Conceive the nameless joys that flow
From Love's selected hearts.

Conceive

Conceive the Patriot's glowing breaſt
　Whom grateful nations crown!
With virtue, love, and empire bleſt,
　And honor's clear renown.—

Here let me end.—And now, O Maid!
　Receive the Bard's adieu;—
Invoke the favouring Muſe's aid,
　And ſtill thy taſk purſue.

'Twill give new objects to thy ken;
　Of care thy breaſt beguile;
And, on the labours of thy pen
　Thy country's eye will ſmile.

I came thy ardour to excite.—
　Once more, O Maid! adieu.—
He ſpoke, and loſt in ſplendid light
　He vaniſh'd from my view.

T H E   E N D.

www.ingramcontent.com/pod-product-compliance
Lightning Source LLC
Chambersburg PA
CBHW020108010526
44115CB00008B/737